SAMPSON TECHNICAL INSTITUTE

NORTH CAROLINA
STATE BOARD OF EDUCATION
DEPT. OF COMMUNITY COLLEGES
LIBRARIES

SAMPSON TECHNICAL INSTITUTE

NORTH CAROLINA
STATE BOARD OF EDUCATION
DEPT. OF COMMUNITY COLLEGES
LIBRARIES

HISTORIC HOUSES
RESTORED AND PRESERVED

NA
7328
P22

6-5-78

14248

HISTORIC HOUSES
RESTORED AND PRESERVED

BY MARIAN PAGE

WHITNEY LIBRARY OF DESIGN
an imprint of Watson-Guptill Publications, New York

Copyright © 1976 by Whitney Library of Design

First published 1976 in New York by Whitney Library of Design,
an imprint of Watson-Guptill Publications,
a division of Billboard Publications, Inc.,
1515 Broadway, New York, N.Y. 10036

Manufactured in U.S.A.

Library of Congress Cataloging in Publication Data
Page, Marian, 1918–
  Historic houses restored and preserved.
  Bibliography: p.
  Includes index.
  1. Architecture, Domestic—England—Conservation
and restoration. 2. Historic buildings—England
—Conservation and restoration. 3. Architecture,
Domestic—United States—Conservation and restora-
tion. 4. Historic buildings—United States—
Conservation and restoration. 5. Architecture—
United States—English influences. I. Title.
NA7328.P22   728'.028   76-18966
ISBN 0-8230-7275-4

All rights reserved. No part of this publication
may be reproduced or used in any form or by any means—graphic,
electronic, or mechanical, including photocopying, recording, taping,
or information storage and retrieval systems—without
written permission of the publisher.

First Printing, 1976

Acknowledgments

I am grateful to a number of people and organizations who helped in the preparation of this book including the many authors and editors whose published work has made my task both easier and more enjoyable. I have tried to list most of the latter in the bibliography. There are, however, certain people I am particularly indebted to for their kindness in making information and material available to me. I would especially like to thank Milton L. Grigg, FAIA, of Charlottesville, and Albert Simons, FAIA, of Charleston for their courteous assistance. I would also like to thank the many members of the staff of the National Trust for Historic Preservation who were always ready with assistance, particularly Nathaniel Neblett, AIA, and Raymond V. Shepherd, Jr., for their suggestions and help, and Terry B. Morton for writing the preface.

I would also like to express my indebtedness to Joseph T. Butler, Curator of Sleepy Hollow Restorations; J.M.A. Dinkel, Deputy Director and Keeper of the Royal Pavilion at Brighton; Frances R. Edmunds, Director of Historic Charleston Foundation; Robert H. Garbee, AIA, of Lynchburg; the Honorable Desmond Guinness of the Irish Georgian Society; John D. Milner, AIA, and Norman D. Askins of National Heritage Corporation; Dorothy Stroud, Assistant Curator of Sir John Soane's Museum; and a special thanks to Olive Smith for her generosity in letting me use the Hardwick Hall photographs of her late husband Edwin Smith, a photographer who possessed a rare sensitivity to the subtleties of architecture. I am also indebted to Jack E. Boucher for permission to quote from his booklet *Lucy The Margate Elephant*, and the Virginia Historical Society for permission to quote from the Tayloe family papers.

Among other organizations whose personnel has been particularly helpful I would like to mention the National Park Service, the Advisory Council on Historic Preservation, the Preservation Society of Newport County, the American Institute of Architects Foundation, Historic Columbia Foundation, Historic Savannah Foundation, and the Munson-Williams-Proctor Institute.

Contents

Foreword

Weeks Hall lived most of his life at The Shadows-on-the-Teche, his family home in New Iberia, La., which he described as a "placid seclusion from a changing world." Daniel Chester French remarked of his summer home in the Berkshire Hills near Stockbridge, Mass., that "I live here six months of the year—in heaven." Frederic E. Church considered his fantasy villa Olana, near Hudson, N.Y., to be the "center of the universe."

These personal words of head and heart are clues to how much an environment—especially the home—can affect and mean to one's life. They are also enticements to discover what these places have that made their owners respond with depth and enthusiasm.

Hall's treasured inheritance and the French and Church creations are characteristic of thousands of historic houses open to the public in the United States. The latter is owned by New York State and is operated as a historic house museum under its Office of Parks and Recreation; the other two are properties of the National Trust for Historic Preservation. The Shadows is one of five Trust properties included in this alluring armchair tour of 18 significant American and English landmarks.

Through detailed history, vivid description, and pertinent quotes, Marian Page revives these homes and the lives and personalities of their former owners. She shows that the past can be enjoyed from the pages of a book, and not only by viewing a house and its environment or from the actual use of some part of it. One's life is enriched and extended through the imagination as well as by experience of the spatial, tactile, and visual senses. Imaginary experiences may be even more personal than physical experiences such as feeling space relationships of rooms, holding a finely executed bowl, or discovering an unusual vista. But old buildings, like some books, are not merely physical things; both can be the framework for our fantasies.

The National Trust was organized in 1949 with a charter from Congress and has been a prime force in awakening the public to the need for preserving our rich heritage of sites, buildings, and objects. Our landmarks include representatives of all geographic areas, all phases and periods of the country's history, all architectural styles and building types from homes and architectural follies to mills, courthouses, covered bridges, churches, and barns. Landmarks are of local and state importance as well as national significance.

From its beginning the Trust was empowered to accept historic properties and administer them as public museums. Its earliest involvement was with Woodlawn Plantation, the home of Nelly Custis, Martha Washington's granddaughter and George Washington's foster daughter, and originally part of their Mount Vernon estate in Virginia. The second property in which the Trust assumed a responsibility and the first it formally owned was Casa Amesti, a 19th-century adobe in Monterey, Calif. It was accepted by the Trust in 1954 without an endowment and was immediately put to adaptive use, earning its way as a men's club. The two—one in the East and one in the West—are characteristic of two kinds of property protection. One method is restoration and museum interpretation and the other illustrates protection by nonmuseum purposes. A number of protective techniques such as easements and tax incentives that do not involve property acquisition or operation by an organization such as the National Trust now are also gaining wide use.

Owners of historic property have a responsibility to conduct original research, a never-ending task, as clues continue to be found that add pieces to the puzzle of the past. The Trust is conducting extensive and comprehensive research at Drayton Hall, near Charleston, S.C., one of its newest properties. Working simultaneously at the site is a team of three professionals—an archaeologist, an architect, and an architectural historian.

The archaeological research is being done through excavation; the architectural examination through recording of fabric by measured drawings, photographs and analysis of materials and painted surfaces; and the documentary exploration in family papers of letters, diaries, and bills by the architectural historian.

What the archaeologist unearths at Drayton Hall is often confirmed or expanded by the work of the other two disciplines. For example, an investigation was made of the physical features of the main building, its roof shape and covering material. The archaeologist found a definite drip line, which indicated no change in the roof shape over the years; this evidence was corroborated by physical features apparent to the architect. Using the diary of Drayton Hall's second owner, the architectural historian discovered that problems had been recorded with a slate roof, which traditionally had been assumed to be a lead sheet roof, and a stereoscopic photograph of the 1860s seems to confirm this. Similar examination of other aspects of the structure may provide physical and documentary evidence of changes to the structure. This new or different history that is unraveling at Drayton Hall may continue for years.

Such pictorial narratives about historic properties from Elizabethan England and Colonial America to the Romantic Era in both countries dramatize fascinating and fruitful yesterdays. Through this work Marian Page also seeks to highlight the need for a quality environment in each American's life, not just in the museum or the public urban and rural setting. She and other preservationists are teaching lessons of personal property stewardship that stress the importance of the creation and appreciation of beauty and its protection in individual lives. Each one's home should be "in heaven," the "center of the universe," and "placid seclusion from a changing world."

Terry B. Morton
Vice President / Editor
The Preservation Press
The National Trust for
Historic Preservation

Preface

The houses on the following pages represent a wide range of restoration and preservation philosophies and techniques. There are houses restored to a particular period; houses that have been partly restored to reflect an early period and partly adapted for modern use; houses that have been preserved to reflect the successive generations, tastes, and styles that have given them their special character; houses that have come down to us almost intact and are thus rare documents of their time, place, and culture; one house that has been adapted for present-day use as a residence while preserving the integrity of its architecture.

Some of these essays originally appeared in *Interiors* magazine between 1961 and 1970 as part of a series on Historic Restorations. While restoration philosophies may not have been quite as sophisticated in the 1960s as they are now, none of these houses, as far as I know, have needed any major re-restoration. Perhaps if The Shadows had been restored in 1976 instead of 1961, the furnishings would have been closer to the way its last owner left them. Philosophies change and the emphasis is more and more on preservation rather than restoration.

To restore a historic house requires scholarly and technical skills as well as sleuthing and psychological skills. It combines the subtleties of art with the hard facts of science, building codes, and money raising. It requires someone who can creep into the minds and hearts of those whose house it was, who can listen with a third ear to a person or persons who are not there but have left invisible traces of themselves. A house takes on the coloration of those who lived most fully between its walls or, as the poet Conrad Aiken put it, "The amazing house that was oneself."

An old house, moreover, is not only the story of those who lived in it, a record of their tastes and achievements, it is a primary and irreplaceable part of the story of civilization. If we didn't have Drayton Hall, or The Shadows, or Cliveden, or the Octagon, or Lyndhurst . . . we would be in danger of thinking that a house was nothing more than a standardized split-level in a modern development or a sterile corner in a concrete tower. We need comparisons. We need to know that structures of great integrity and charm that relate to their environment have existed and with a little understanding can still exist. The painter Washington Allston put it another way when he told a student that by studying the old masters "You will imbibe their spirit insensibly, otherwise you will as insensibly fall into the manner of your contemporaries." A thoughtfully preserved house is a kind of collaboration between ourselves, our ancestors, our children, and our grandchildren.

"In the enormous picture of a developing and changing civilization this matter of the preservation of buildings may seem a detail almost trivial and barely relevant," says Sir John Summerson in his perceptive essay on *The Past in the Future.* "Yet it has its importance. The future of civilization depends, I believe, largely on our observation and interpretation of the natural history of our species; and the study of species includes the study of habitat."

Elizabethan England and Colonial America

Hardwick Hall

American building in the 18th century, like England's Elizabethan Hardwick Hall in the 16th, moved away from the earlier medieval styles with an increasing awareness of classicism. Although at first glance such gaunt clapboarded houses in the northern colonies as Newport's Hunter House and such style-conscious plantation mansions of the south as Drayton Hall outside of Charleston do not bear much resemblance to each other nor to Hardwick Hall, a closer examination shows the American houses to be natural offspring—albeit a simpler breed—of that great country house. Hardwick was one of the first houses in England to turn its back on the medieval tradition of building picturesque, asymmetric, stone-gabled manor houses. Hardwick's horizontal proportions and its symmetrical facade look toward the classical period. America's 18th-century houses show a similar consciousness of the classic with their symmetrically balanced facades. It was the Elizabethans who discovered America. It was their children who settled the New England and southern colonies. Those settlers knew such great Elizabethan houses as Hardwick Hall as well as the more indigenous houses that set the pattern for the rambling medieval style of America's 17th-century architecture, which led in the 18th century to a movement away from the earlier medieval styles toward classicism.

Nor is it surprising that there were differences between the 18th-century houses of New England and those in the southern colonies. The northerners were traders and the mark of success was the merchant's townhouse, while the agrarian society of the south revolved around the great plantation houses.

Climate, communication, and religion were other factors that determined differences in building. The New Englanders were rebels. They were looking for religious freedom and had no desire to keep in touch with the mother country. They came from the middle classes of small English towns where government was resented and individual success revered. They had neither time nor desire to weigh matters of taste or dare departures of style in the arts. Their winters were frigid, their summers torrid, and their houses had to cope with these climatic extremes. Thus the design of New England's colonial houses owes something to the weather, something to Elizabethan England, and something to the Puritan ethic.

The southerners had no quarrel with the Anglican church or the King. In fashions, manners, and architecture, they kept in close touch with England. The ships that took tobacco and rice from docks on the James and the Ashley to docks in London returned with the latest fashions, furnishings, and ideas. Thus the southern planters were consistently more *au courant* than the northern merchants. The more liberal religion, more genial climate, as well as a more aristocratic way of life could not help influencing their building style. The southern plantation houses, of which Drayton Hall is a fine example, were even stylistically ahead of Philadelphia's style-conscious Cliveden although antedating it by many years. Drayton Hall, in fact, shows many features of the new Palladianism that was at its height in England when the southern plantation house was built.

Philadelphia was more than a geographical link between the north and south. In temperament, manners, and tastes, Philadelphians shared characteristics with both their northern and southern neighbors. Like the southerners, 18th-century Philadelphians kept in touch with England and the latest fashions. But the plainness and seriousness of their Quaker heritage persisted, giving Philadelphians a certain kinship with the Puritanical northerners.

And of course there were other European colonists who built houses influenced by what they had known as well as by local conditions. One such example was the Dutch, who impressed a distinctive architectural style on the Hudson River Valley that is apparent to this day. As a social and economic institution, the Dutch manors were equivalent to the holdings of the landed aristocracy of the south but their manor houses were much simpler. They had more in common with New England's clapboarded houses except that they were usually built of stone with wide, covered verandas. Hunter House in Newport and Van Cortlandt Manor house on the Hudson possess some of the charming "primitive" qualities of early colonial portraits, while Cliveden and Drayton Hall suggest the more sophisticated portraits of Benjamin West or John Singleton Copley.

Like Bess of Hardwick, 18th-century southern colonists were *nouveau riches* and the extravagance and ostentation of their houses was their way of showing that they knew how to enjoy the pleasures of the world. The Philadelphians may have known how to enjoy the pleasures of the world but their Quaker background kept them from proclaiming it. The northerners were often horrified by those pleasures. The Bostonian John Quincy, Jr., who visited Charleston in 1773, may have admired but did not approve of the luxury of:

Azure blue satin window curtains, rich blue paper with gilt, moshee borders, most elegant pictures, excessive grand and costly looking glasses. . . .

And he concluded that "the state of religion here is repugnant not only to the ordinances and institutions of Jesus Christ, but to every law of sound policy." And that art-shy New Englander John Adams wrote his Abigail:

I cannot help suspecting that the more elegance, the less virtue, in all times and countries.

Drayton Hall

Certainly the Westover of William Byrd II, the Stratford of Thomas Lee, and the Drayton Hall of John Drayton are not in the same category with the New Englanders' modest foursquare houses. But then people in all ages and all places have probably designed their houses as status symbols whether to proclaim their godliness or their worldliness, their riches or their frugality, their individuality or their proficiency in following fashion, their industry or even their indolence.

Newport's Hunter House and the Dutch-influenced Van Cortlandt Manor house have been restored to reflect an early period in their history.

20008076

Hunter House

Hardwick Hall and Drayton Hall are those rare "originals" that have kept the particular flavor of their time and culture over the centuries. That is also largely true of Cliveden. These three great houses need little if any restoration but careful and sympathetic preservation. From such houses we can learn something about how things really were. For no matter how expertly restored a house may be, the hand and thought of another age cannot be entirely obliterated.

Much as been learned in this country since Hunter House and Van Cortlandt Manor house were restored. But only recently have the ideas expressed by Ruskin in the 19th century begun to be understood:

> Do not let us deceive ourselves in this important matter; it is *impossible*, as impossible as to raise the dead, to restore anything that has ever been great or beautiful in architecture. That which I have . . . insisted upon as the life of the whole, the spirit which is given only by the hand and eye of the workmen, can never be recalled. Another spirit may be given by another time, and then a new building; but the spirit of the dead workman cannot be summoned up, and commanded to direct other hands, and other thoughts. . . . What copying can there be of surfaces that have been worn half an inch down? The whole finish of the work was in the half inch that is gone; if you attempt to restore the finish, you do it conjecturally; if you copy what is left, granting fidelity to be possible . . . how is the new work better than the old? There was yet in the old *some* life, some mysterious suggestion of what it had been, and of what it had lost; some sweetness in the gentle lines which rain and sun had wrought.

Hardwick Hall and Drayton Hall still give us that "mysterious suggestion" of what they had been. Hardwick Hall is owned by the British National Trust whose long experience in preserving historic houses has taught them the virtue of leaving things as they are—to preserve houses not as museums but as homes, lived in if possible by the families traditionally connected with them. They would like the caller to feel like a private visitor who has arrived while the family is out. A house, as the British Trust puts it, "enshrines that delicate personal art of living." Visitors should "be able to absorb this atmosphere at their leisure." The word "restoration" hardly enters into the British Trust's vocabulary. Conservation, preservation, and maintenance are the key words. And preservation is considered even more important than access. At Hardwick Hall, for instance, curtains and blinds are only opened on special occasions lest sunlight harm the priceless Elizabethan tapestries and needlework. "Preservation, as we have seen, is for all time, whereas access arrangements are changeable and should be secondary to preservation," is how the British Trust puts it.

In 1967, Charles Ravenswaay, who was chairman of a seminar on "Planning for Preservation" during a workshop jointly sponsored by the American

Van Cortlandt Manor House

Cliveden

National Trust and Colonial Williamsburg, stated that "It is highly desirable that some exceptional buildings be preserved intact, without restoration, as surviving documents of a period or region. Simply protecting them from deterioration may sometimes prove to be the best solution."

And when the National Trust took over Drayton Hall in 1974, a committee of architects was appointed to advise on its preservation. The committee stated in its initial report that the force of Drayton Hall's "expression in its existing state does not require either amplification or refinement. Any changes of any kind would inevitably obscure rather than clarify its worth as architecture." Ruskin would have agreed.

Hardwick Hall

Derbyshire, England

. . . There the imagination was free indeed—freer than in our own day, when it is burdened by too great a weight of knowledge, and hemmed in by the harsh realism of an age of machinery.
      G. M. Trevelyan

Very few houses really capture the imagination and when one does, it is invariably because an extraordinary individual has left something of herself or himself—a ghost if you will—to wander within its walls and down its garden paths. It is almost always the personal that inspires and delights us. Perhaps one of the most romantic houses in the world belonging to this particular genre is Hardwick Hall in Derbyshire, England. It is a house of great romantic beauty appealing to the poetic imagination much as Venice does. But it is also the most undilutedly English of all the great Elizabethan houses and a splendid summation of the romance, arrogance, and inventiveness that marked the last years of Elizabeth's reign. By no means the least of the wonders of Hardwick Hall is that it has preserved so much of its original appearance and so many of its Elizabethan furnishings that within its tapestried rooms it almost seems possible for a susceptible modern mind to reach an imaginative comprehension of those strange Elizabethans whose lives and ways are so remote from ours. But very likely, as Virginia Woolf once commented, our fancy picture of what it pleases us to call Elizabethan life would rouse the ribald merriment of the Elizabethans. Nevertheless Bess of Hardwick, the incredible Elizabethan who built Hardwick Hall, has managed to cross the centuries in the shadowy recesses of that magic house to tell us something about the intimate tastes of her day and something, too, about her lusty and exuberant age.

The outside of Hardwick Hall with its great mullioned windows, its flat roof, and six crested towers, is pure adventure but the mood of the inside is both sober and splendid. The great bare stone stairways winding mysteriously through the house, the quiet rooms, occasional expanses of unadorned whitewashed walls, rush matting on the floors, lend Hardwick's interiors almost a monastic air. But there is also the splendor

of great faded tapestries, many of which Bess bought for the walls they cover, magnificent inlaid chests, marquetry tables, carved cupboards, and everywhere the exquisite needlework, some of which was made at Hardwick including pieces that bear Bess's own initials, ES. We know from an "Inventorie of the Plate and other Furniture of howshold stuff" drawn up in 1601 that there was very little furniture in Hardwick's rooms in Bess's day. Many of the pieces now in the house belong to the 17th century. In the 75-foot-long, two-story-high entrance hall, for example, the 1601 inventory lists "three long tables and six formes" (or benches), as the only furniture. And in the incredibly romantic High Presence Chamber on the top floor, where Bess had her masques and other entertainments, the furniture was limited to a few "farthingale" chairs and stools.

Bess was undoubtedly responsible for much of the splendor and sobriety as well as the adventure of Hardwick Hall. It was probably that her sense of drama drove her, in the middle of building, to order "eight windowes for two of the turrets" to be "highed" still further.

By some miracle, Hardwick Hall has come down to us almost exactly as it was when Bess left it to her favorite son, William Cavendish, first Earl of Devonshire, nearly four centuries ago. It thereby passed into the powerful Cavendish family whose vast estates and great houses include Chatsworth, which even before 1700 became the favorite Derbyshire seat of Bess's descendants. Thus changing fashions passed Hardwick by and it remains today one of the least altered of Elizabethan houses inside and out. It is like a huge storehouse preserving the taste of Bess of Hardwick. She, no doubt, intended it to be just that, for Bess knew what she wanted and generally got it. Room after room with its plaster decoration, its paneling, its richly tapestried walls, its full-length portraits, its furniture—strike a decidedly authentic note. It is that most rare and important of historic houses—an "original" come down to us with little change, an invaluable record of its time.

In 1959 Hardwick Hall passed into the

From the northwest.

*West front showing the aptness of the old
rhyme: "Hardwick Hall, more glass than wall."*

care of Britain's National Trust and it remains today not only "the supreme triumph of Elizabethan architecture" but the supreme triumph of Bess of Hardwick.

Of Husbands and Houses

Bess was born in 1520, the daughter of John Hardwick who owned the manor of Hardwick and lived in a minor manor house. At the age of 13 she married Master Robert Barlow, 14, first of her four husbands. He died almost immediately and when she was 27 Bess became the third wife of Sir William Cavendish. She had six children with him and started to indulge the passion for building that was to make her a legend. She &persuaded her second husband to buy the Chatsworth manor in Derbyshire and immediately began to build. When Sir William died in 1557, the new Chatsworth had not gotten very far, but he left Bess a woman of considerable wealth and she spent many years finishing and furnishing it. Almost nothing, incidentally, remains today of Bess's Elizabethan Chatsworth, which was torn down by the fourth Earl of Devonshire in order to erect the Palladian house now on the site.

Bess married her third husband, Sir William St. Loe, in 1559 and within five years he too was dead. She was then in her mid-forties and set out to find still another husband. Her choice was George Talbot, sixth Earl of Shrewsbury, by far the wealthiest and most powerful of all her husbands. They were married in 1568 and, perhaps to make trebly sure of keeping such riches in the family, Bess arranged for two of her Cavendish children to marry two of his. The Earl was her last husband but Chatsworth was by no means her last house.

Queen Elizabeth, who took a great interest in the love affairs of her nobility, was very pleased when Bess married the Earl of Shrewsbury. Soon after the wedding the Queen appointed Shrewsbury the jailer of Mary Queen of Scots with whom, during his long guardianship of her, Bess was often in intimate contact. From her royal prisoner Bess acquired a large part of her appreciation of the decorative arts. As a young girl Mary Stuart had been brought up in the luxury and elegance of the French court of Henry II, where French Renaissance art was at a high level. During the early years of Mary Stuart's captivity with the Shrewsburys, Bess spent many hours doing needlework with her and some of the results are still to be seen at Hardwick Hall.

The Earl separated from Bess in 1583, after she had started a rumor of a liaison between him and Mary, and in spite of many attempts by Queen Elizabeth to bring them back together, they were never reconciled.

The Earl could not forgive his wife who had called him "knave, fool, and beast to his face, and mocked and mowed at him." He might well have been a bit of a fool, judging by some contemporary accounts, but he did not forget the unseemly insult. During the last years of the Earl's life Bess spent most of her time converting the old manor house at Hardwick into a mansion fit for herself and her granddaughter, Arabella Stuart, who had a serious claim as a successor to the English throne. Bess had bought her childhood home in 1576 from her brother and proceeded to reconstruct it. Today it is a ruin, but it was obviously large and lavish and gave Bess another lesson in the art of designing great houses which was to have its grand culmination in the new Hardwick Hall only 100 yards from the old. There were undoubtedly imperfections in the remodeled old hall, but in his *Memoirs of the Family Cavendish* (1708), Bishop White Kennett tells us that "The old house at Hardwick had one room of such exact proportions and such convenient lights it was thought fit for a pattern for Blenheim."

When the sixth Earl of Shrewsbury died in 1590, Bess became extremely wealthy and in a position to carry out her most ambitious building venture of all—the construction of a new Hardwick Hall which would surpass all the great Elizabethan houses that had been "a-building" in recent years up and down the English countryside. Apparently she lost no time. The Earl died on November 18, 1590, and by December 15th of that same year, the accounts show that the foundation of the new hall was laid.

Bess was 71, with apparently no lessening of her vigor, ambition, or inventiveness, when she started the new Hardwick Hall. In 1594 she moved in, and it must have been plain to all who saw that proud and romantic house that she had accomplished her aim.

The Wit of the Fox is Everywhere on Foot

Elizabethan architecture of the late 1580s and 90s was as modern and different from the castles of the recent past as it possibly could be. The Elizabethans were enamored of anything that was new, and there was much that was new about their lives. They no longer needed to build their houses for defense but for the conduct of a civilized life in which ladies and gentlemen shared alike. The Middle Ages seemed to them chaotic and irrational or, as the Queen put it, "In those days force and arms did prevail; but now the wit of the fox is everywhere on foot."

During the 45 years of her reign, Elizabeth did very little building as a matter of

(Above and opposite page) The staircase threads ingeniously and romantically through the house.

policy or, as Sir Nicholas Bacon boasted, she did not construct "gorgeous sumptuous superfluous buildings." The gentry, however, felt no such restraint, at least those who were in—the leaders of the Protestant elite who were anxious to demonstrate their pride in their great country houses. They were often self-made men not bound by tradition. They wanted to show off their wealth and position. "Each one desireth to set his house aloft on the hill, to be seen afar off, and cast forth his beames of stately and curious workmanship into every quarter of the country," is how William Harrison put it in his *Description of England* (1587).

The Elizabethans built profusely and on a palatial scale but they built in relative isolation. They had very little contact with the art and architecture of Renaissance France and Italy, which partially explains both the provincialisms and great originality of their own building. The novelty, daring, and unity of late Elizabethan architecture, according to architectural historian Mark Girouard, would have been impossible if England had been exposed to the full blast of the Renaissance. He calls it "one of the curiosities and triumphs of European art." The Elizabethans, he points out, felt the same way about their houses as they did about their clothes. "They thought a great deal about dress. They spent extravagant sums on it. But they did not write or read books on the theory of costume. They seldom discussed clothes in letters to their friends. And they did not ask their tailor to dinner."

There was, in fact, no such thing as an architect in Elizabethan England, certainly not in the modern sense. Building a house involved the interaction of a large number of people—the builder, friends of the builder, a variety of craftsmen, and so on. The plan might come from one source and details from others. A craftsman might supply designs for individual features which were often derived from foreign pattern books but he wasn't generally very careful about making exact copies. As Sir John Summerson says, "Although foreign fashions in ornament, and sometimes in plan, were excitedly adopted, they were adopted for the intrinsic pleasure they gave rather than any sense of apprenticeship to foreign achievement greater than their own."

Occasionally patrons, such as Bess of Hardwick, designed their own houses. Or, as the chronologist William Harrison put it, "divers men being bent to buildinge, and have a delectable view in spending of their goodes by that trade, doo dailie imagine new devises of their owne to guide their workmen withall."

The craftsmen were generally the greatest influence on the interiors, but they had little education, no social standing, only a very superficial knowledge of Renaissance architecture, and are rarely known to us by name. But, as Girouard says, among them were men of independent and original ideas, "and it is probably largely due to this class that Elizabethan architecture is, at its best, more than a provincial shake-up of ill-digested foreign ideas."

Robert Smythson was one of the very few Elizabethans who operated more or less as an architect does today. He is known to have designed Sir Francis Willoughby's Wollaton, which is similar to Hardwick in many important ways—one reason why the general design of Hardwick has often been attributed to him. Girouard, in his book on Robert Smythson, gives several other convincing reasons for this attribution, but he admits there is no evidence to connect any of Hardwick's interior detail with Smythson. Moreover, as strong a case as Girouard makes for Smythson as Hardwick's designer, he agrees that Bess must be reckoned with. She was not, as he says, the sort of person to leave the details of her house to others. He believes that many of the idiosyncrasies of its planning are probably due to her—placing the main rooms on the top floor, varying the heights of rooms beneath one roof line, using a cross-hall which had not appeared in any previous house, the unique stairways—and it is some of those idiosyncrasies that give Hardwick its great romantic appeal.

One enters the great two-story entrance hall at ground level under a gallery supported by a screen of classical columns. Contrary to previous custom, the hall runs through the center of the house from front to back and thus made Hardwick's symmetrical plan possible. It is hung with tapestries above the wainscot like most of the rooms in the house and is probably where Bess's household and estate servants dined. On one side of the hall is the kitchen and offices, on the other side nurseries and servants' rooms. The more intimate family rooms were on the floor above where the dining room, or the "Low Great Chamber" as it was called in Bess's day, is linked to the withdrawing room through the hall gallery. The bay window in the dining room may have been where some of Hardwick's famous embroidery was made by Bess's ladies. The withdrawing room is hung with Flemish tapestries described in the 1601 inventory as "six pieces of tapestry with personages and my ladies arms in them." Bess's own bedchamber and maid's room are off the withdrawing room. Although the chapel is now on this floor, it originally rose two stories from the ground level as the hall does.

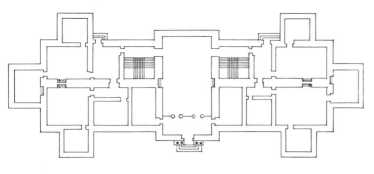

A variant plan for Hardwick, by Robert Smythson
(in the R.I.B.A. Drawings Collection)

First Floor (Family Apartments)

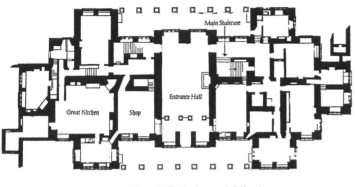

Ground Floor (Hall, Kitchen and Offices)

14

Second Floor (State Apartments)

15

(Left) Entrance door to the High Presence
Chamber. Stags over door support the
Schrewsbury arms.

(Above) Plans of the house.

(Below) View of the High Presence Chamber
which Sacheverell Sitwell calls the most
beautiful room in all of Europe.

Bess of Hardwick as the Countess of Shrewsbury.

Detail of the colored plaster frieze in the High Presence Chamber represents Summer.

(Opposite page) The Long Gallery on the top floor runs the entire length of the east front of the house. The walls are hung with the famous Gideon tapestries which Bess bought for the purpose.

On the top floor are the great state rooms which best illustrate Hardwick's special quality. The High Presence Chamber on one side of the house is where Bess would occasionally receive distinguished guests and dine in state. It leads into the withdrawing room, then into the state bedchamber with its own servant's and inner room. The Long Gallery runs the entire length of the east side of the house. While the state bedchamber, or "Best Bedchamber" as Bess called it, was reserved for the grandest guests, it was mainly kept to symbolize its owner's prestige and to complete the usual sequence of state rooms—from presence chamber to withdrawing room to bedchamber.

Lightsome, Airy, and Spiritous

In the last analysis, it is Bess's house and it is an Elizabethan house and could be none other. No one could have been a more typical Elizabethan. She possessed the Elizabethans' ambitions, their love of display, their directness, even their coarseness. It was an affluent and mobile society and Bess rose to its top. The Elizabethans put their money into art and ostentation—jewels, plates, extravagant clothes, and especially into beautiful buildings in which to display the pride and pageantry of their lives. Their houses, above all, were status symbols. That, of course, was one of the motivating forces behind Bess's long passion for building. In the 1790s Edmund Lodge probably summed up this eminent Elizabethan pretty well when he described her as a:

> woman of masculine understanding and conduct, proud, furious, selfish, and unfeeling, she was a builder, a buyer and seller of estates, a money-lender, a farmer, and a merchant of lead, coals, and timber; when disengaged from these employments she intrigued alternately with Elizabeth and Mary, always to the prejudice and terror of her husband.

Hardwick Hall is not an extravaganza as some Elizabethan houses were. From the outside it is what Professor Nikolaus Pevsner calls it: "an admirable piece of design and architectural expression; no fussing, no fumbling, nor indeed any flights of fancy." It stands on the flat top of a hill, large and symmetrical, self-assertive and severe, its huge and rhythmical windows distinguishing it from all other Elizabethan houses, as do Bess's proud and ostentatious initials ES (Elizabeth Shrewsbury) which top its towers on all four sides.

Actually the exterior (except for those arrogant initials) reveals a certain modesty that is not in keeping with Bess's immodest characteristics and thus adds credence to the Smythson attribution. But the interior is full of that dramatic sense that was both a mark of the Elizabethans in general and Bess in particular. From room to room and floor to floor, there is a variety of spatial adventures and exciting plays of light and shadow which owes something to the Elizabethan love of music as well as drama. The angles and shifting of the great stone staircases create romantic patterns of light and shade. There is also a wonderful sense of changing light as one goes up the various levels of the house. The ground-floor rooms seem low and dark; the rooms above are higher, lighter, and more spacious; and the great rooms on the top floor are tremendous in size and flooded with light. Most Elizabethans who had anything to say about the interiors of a house insisted that ceilings and windows should be high so that the rooms were "lightsome, airy, and spiritous." And there is a charming account of the Queen's reception at Kenilworth in 1575 in which the writer describes:

> the stately seat of Kenelwoorth Castle, the rare beauty of bilding that his Honor hath avaunced; all of the hard quarry-stone; every room so spacious, so well belighted, and so hy roofed within; so seemly too sight by du proportion without: a day tyme, on every syde so glittering by glasse; a nights, by continuall brightnesse of candel, fyre, and torchlight, transparent thro the lightsome wyndz, as it wear the Egiptian Pharos relucent untoo all the Alexandrian coast; or els (too talk merily with my mery frend) thus radiant az though Phoebus for his eaz woold rest him in the Castl, and not every night so travel dooun unto the Antipodes.

A preoccupation with the play of light was a key feature of Elizabethan interiors. Those elaborate plaster friezes were designed for candlelight, as John Buxton reminds us in *Elizabethan Taste*, "when ribs and medallions and pendants would be alive with the constantly moving shadows." Ceilings, too, were designed to "interrupt and diversify the varying light, to use, not to eliminate shadows" as our flat modern ceilings do. This was also true of the squares and lozenges of paneling and the elaborate marble chimney-pieces. A play of light and shadow is also seen in the contrast between light-absorbing tapestries and polished marble or wood. In their gardens, too, the Elizabethans played with patterns of light and shadow in their fountains, topiary, and statues.

Hardwick's High Presence Chamber which Sacheverell Sitwell has called "the most beautiful room, not in England alone

The Green Velvet Room takes its name from the magnificent bed hangings. The tapestries depict the story of Adam.

"The fancie of a fowler and other personages"—needlework panel.

but in the whole of Europe," presents one of the most enchanting examples of changing light and shadow in its marvelous colored plaster frieze. Abraham Smith, Bess's chief plasterer, was responsible for this unique frieze with its forest scenes, strange animals, and figures which may have inspired Pevsner's remark that the detail at Hardwick was "coarse but jolly work." On the walls of the High Presence Chamber hang the early 15th-century tapestries depicting the story of Ulysses for which the room was designed. Also in this room (although it was in another room in 1601) is the walnut table inlaid with chessmen, dice, and musical instruments which was made for the marriage of Bess's son Henry Cavendish and Grace Talbot, Shrewsbury's daughter. The Cavendish and Shrewsbury arms appear at the top with the words:

> The redolent smell of Eglantyne
> We stags exalt to the devine

In the 1601 inventory this table is described as "the inlayde table in the window." The "farthingale" chairs which appear in that inventory are still in the High Presence Chamber and still covered with their original 16th-century needlework. Even the rush matting on the floor is of the same weave that has always been there.

While the whole interior of Hardwick is exuberant with the fantasy of a rich imagination, the High Presence Chamber and the Long Gallery, both on the top floor, are the most impressive rooms in the house to a modern eye. They must have fulfilled Elizabethan requirements too, judging by Sir Henry Wotton's dissertation on the *Elements of Architecture* in which he speaks of "that agreeable harmony between the breadth, length and height of all the rooms of the fabric, which suddenly, where it is, taketh every beholder by the secret power of proportion." Wotton also charmingly suggests that "the entertaining rooms should appear fit for the welcome of cheerful guests."

Many have called the art of decoration in Elizabethan England coarse, which is probably true compared to what was being done on the continent, but at the same time it is the coarseness or the exaggeration of a stage set—more notable for its effect than for its subtleties. The Long Gallery at Hardwick is a case in point. It is an unbelievable, almost awesome space with its three immense bay windows. It runs the entire length of the east front of the house (166 feet or 53 meters), and the walls are hung with the magnificent Gideon tapestries which Bess bought in 1592 from the heirs of Sir Christopher Hatton, Queen Elizabeth's Lord Chancellor. She paid 35 pounds 15s 9d, an

End view "when the house shuts up narrow and bears down with the race and speed of a ship in full sail."

*View from roof looking toward entrance
gateway and country beyond.*

enormous price at the time, but she insisted on a 5 pound rebate because the Hatton arms had to be replaced by those of Hardwick. Along the back wall facing the windows are two immense chimney pieces of alabaster and colored marbles.

Keeping warm in those great draughty Elizabethan country houses was an important factor in their decoration. The fireplace was a focal point of every room. Tapestries were hung on the walls for their warmth as well as for their decorative qualities. The Long Gallery, which was peculiar to England, must have been designed with the English climate in mind, for it provided the Elizabethans with a place to walk up and down and take their exercise on cold days. It was also found to be an ideal place for hanging those many Elizabethan portraits of family and friends. In Ben Jonson's *Poetaster*, Albius tells his wife not to hang pictures anywhere but in the gallery for "tis not courtly else." The Elizabethans rarely had any pictures except portraits. In the 1601 inventory made by Bess there were about 70 portraits at Hardwick and less than 10 other pictures. Nudes, incidentally, were not particularly to the Elizabethan taste. "Mediterranean classicism had not yet divested our furred and farthingaled shapes," says Buxton, "and the nude figures that we sometimes see carved by Elizabethan fire-places look as if they had gone there to keep warm."

Elizabethan bed hangings should also be mentioned as both a decorative asset and a means of keeping warm.

Magnificentia Clarissima Fabricatrisa

During the last years of her life, Bess planned her tomb, erecting a monument with her prone effigy in a red mantle over a black gown with a hart at her feet. A long Latin inscription records the names and titles of Bess's four husbands and her six children, while she gives herself the proud title of *magnificentia clarissima fabricatrisa* of Chatsworth, Hardwick, and Oldcotes. The latter was a house she built for her son William toward the end of her life, but it was torn down early in the 18th century.

Bess died at Hardwick on February 13, 1608, at the age of 88. It was one of the severest winters in England's history, which gives credence to a legend that has come down in the Cavendish family that "it had been prophesied to her that she would never die as long as she was building." The hard frost of 1608 stopped her building and she promptly died.

It has often been said but it bears repeating: those high Elizabethan houses with their tall windows are curiously modern and could have been precursors of our 20th-century skyscrapers. Some of the factories built in the early part of this century also might be derivations, albeit disenchanted ones, of Hardwick. But in the last analysis, Hardwick Hall and *The Faerie Queen* are unlike anything else ancient or modern. They are self-confidently English.

Hardwick Hall can, as Girouard says, "be called a house of great romantic beauty, or a ruthless admirable and uncompromising design; a perpetual delight, so simple is it, so ingenious, so obvious, so effective, as one walks round and watches the masses group and regroup, contract and spread out, advance and fall away, shifting from the full weight and splendour of the main elevations to the view from the side, when the house shuts up narrow and bears down with the race and speed of a ship in full sail." In all it is a superb Elizabethan performance.

Drayton Hall

Near Charleston, South Carolina

Two-story portico with its superimposed Doric and Ionic orders stems directly from Palladio.

. . . architecture inevitably reflects the deeper beliefs of an age; it bears witness to current feeling about nature, about society, about the very possibilities of human improvement.   Lewis Mumford

About the time Benjamin Franklin was inventing his stove and the wealthy merchants of Newport were building their foursquare timber-framed houses close to the street, Drayton Hall was being constructed on the banks of the Ashley River surrounded by hundreds of acres of marsh and woodland. This remarkable plantation house stands today in lonely grandeur amid the somber beauty of live oaks—an almost untouched legacy from the 18th century and a splendid reminder of life in the southern colonies. Drayton Hall could hardly have been imagined by the house carpenters of the north, and in the sophistication of its design, it is even far ahead of contemporary great houses on the James and Potomac.

A proud brick mansion with its two-story Palladian portico, its expansive planning, and rich ornamentation, Drayton Hall bespeaks the hospitality and opulence of the Low Country society that impressed so many 18th- and 19th-century travelers such as the Englishman John Lawson who, as early as 1700, noted that "the Gentlemen seated in the country are very courteous, live very nobly in their Houses, and give very Genteel entertainments to all strangers and others that come to visit them."

Drayton Hall was built between 1738 and 1742 by John Drayton, a member of the King's Council and the third generation of Draytons who emigrated from Barbados in 1679. His son William Henry Drayton was born at Drayton Hall in 1742 and later became the state's Revolutionary Chief Justice and a delegate to the Continental Congress. Drayton Hall remained in the family for more than 200 years, and like the Low Country in which it stands, there is an aura of timelessness about it that is almost magical. One senses the long generations of Draytons who were born there, lived there, married there, and died there; the great festive parties that were given there while

candlelight cast flickering shadows on its plastered ceilings and on the glittering guests. Writing in the December 1825 issue of *Harper's New Monthly Magazine*, Constance Fenimore Woolson tells us that many people in Charleston still remembered

> the stories told by their fathers and mothers of the dinner parties and other entertainments given at Drayton Hall, when carpets were laid over the broad flights of steps at both entrances and out to the carriage-ways, that the ladies might alight and enter without endangering the satin of their robes."

While Drayton Hall lacks the plantation buildings that once surrounded it, the dependencies that once flanked it, and the furniture that once adorned it, it is the only complete 18th century plantation house remaining on the banks of the Ashley. Such modern amenities as plumbing, electricity, gas, water, and heat have never been installed. This great plantation house stands today basically as it was constructed, and in all its loneliness and emptiness, it tells its story far more convincingly than if it were dressed up according to 20th-century ideas, no matter how enlightened they may seem. Drayton Hall carries with tremendous dignity that which Ruskin called "the golden stain of time."

The southern aristocrats of the 18th century could and did import most of their furnishings and their arts from England. Their plantation houses—the one thing they could not import—are the only certain indication of their taste. Their houses, moreover, were the real heart of the Carolina society.

Although Drayton Hall miraculously survived the ravages of the Civil War as well as the Revolution and the War of 1812, it was threatened by 20th-century development. To save the mansion and its surrounding grounds, the National Trust and the Historic Charleston Foundation leased the house and 632 acres from the Drayton family in 1973 with an option to purchase. In 1974, following a successful fund-raising drive by the two groups, the National Trust acquired title to Drayton Hall thus opening the way

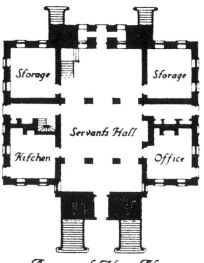

Basement Floor Plan

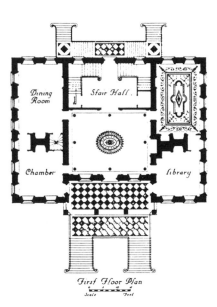

First Floor Plan
Scale   Feet

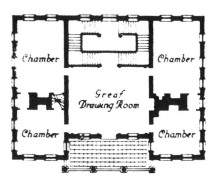

Second Floor Plan

Floor plans of the basement and first and second floors. The Ionic room is in the upper right of the first floor plan.

for preserving the natural and cultural characteristics that formed a historic landscape. The tidewater area in which Drayton Hall stands still retains its 18th- and 19th-century characteristics. It is easily identifiable as a region of plantations and rice fields. An early 18th-century parish church, an old fort, the live oaks, and the river itself make it a rare historic and cultural region.

In 1975, the South Carolina Department of Parks, Recreation and Tourism purchased a 485-acre tract of the Drayton Hall land from the Trust to be developed as a recreation area that will complement the mansion—thus ensuring the general character of the environment. Rural preservation in the past, as planning consultant Ann Satterthwaite points out in *Historic Preservation* (July–September 1973), "has concentrated not on the amenities but on the spectaculars such as the Yosemites, Grand Canyons, and threatened ecological areas such as Dismal Swamp." Too often, moreover, houses that were originally country houses have been preserved out of the context that was their raison d'être. With 20th-century development houses closing in on them, they are a historic anachronism—like Paul Revere in a New York subway.

Because of the importance of preserving this irreplaceable landmark, the Trust appointed an advisory committee of architects to study preservation concepts in order to establish a policy that will be followed by the Trust in the future. The advisory committee—made up of four architects, two in private practice and two with architectural schools—studied the entire site because, as they put it in their initial report:

> Upon visiting Drayton Hall one cannot fail to be impressed with an almost overwhelming sense of mystery and loneliness. Certainly the mansion in its unique state of survival is the prime element creating this feeling; however, the environment also contributes strongly to this atmosphere. . . .
>
> To assure that Drayton Hall remains the "special place" that it is today, sensitive master planning must be undertaken.

In their evaluation of the mansion itself, they agreed that

> Drayton Hall is in many respects the most interesting and probably the finest early Georgian building in America. Its survival in an almost untouched state through earthquake, war, affluence, and poverty was extraordinary, and puts a heavy responsibility on the National Trust to preserve both its clear architectural values and the even more un-

usual purity of its condition. Certainly its importance lies in the full discipline of architectural history, rather than any regional or cultural historic significance, and its preservation must be undertaken with recognition of its overriding consequence as an architectural document. It would be an irreparable mistake to confuse its clear statement with any modern philosophy of restoration. The force of its expression in its existing state does not require either simplification or refinement. Any changes of any kind would inevitably obscure rather than clarify its worth as architecture.

Drayton Hall's worth as architecture, nevertheless, can only be enhanced by its rural setting which must also be kept intact. In *English Country Houses*, Victoria Sackville-West observes that "the house is essentially part of the country, not only *in* the country, but part of it, a natural growth."

Where Art and Nature were Happily Combined

Life at Drayton Hall was always intricately interwoven with its natural environment, and the mansion was always considered an element in that environment rather than an isolated piece of architecture as a later John Drayton makes clear. In *A View of South Carolina; as respects her National and Civil Concerns*, which he wrote in 1802, Drayton explains the genesis of the great plantation houses along the Ashley:

> . . . gentlemen of fortune were invited to form these happy retreats from noise and bustle; the banks of the Ashley, as being near the metropolis of the state was first the object of their attention. And here elegant buildings arose, which overlooked grounds, where art and nature were happily combined. Gardeners were imported from Europe; and soon the stately laurel, and the soft spreading elm, shot up their heads in avenues and walks; while they were occasionally clasped by the yellow jasmine, or crimson woodbine. Soon the verdant lawn spread forth its carpet, contrasted with hedges, gravel walks, terraces, and wildernesses. And nature drawn from her recesses, presented landscapes, diversified and beautiful, where winds had not long before shook the trees of the forest, or savages had roamed, impatient of government and control.

Art and nature are still happily combined at Drayton Hall. The Low Country in which it stands, moreover, is still recognizable as the "Country of Stately Wood, Groves, Marshes and Meadows" abounding "with variety of brave Okes as Eye can behold,"

The east or "river" facade would have given river-borne visitors their first view of the plantation house.

The double mahogany stairway in the paneled stair hall has a grandeur unknown in the colonies at the time.

that Robert Horne described as early as 1666 in his *Brief Description of Carolina*.... After extolling the uncommon lushness and other advantages of that "fair and spacious Province," Horne goes on to say,

If therefore any industrious and ingenious person shall be willing to pertake of the Felicities of this Country, let them imbrace the first opportunity, that they may obtain the greater advantage....

If any Maid or single Woman have a desire to go over, they will think themselves in the Golden Age when Men paid a Dowry for their Wives; for if they be but Civil, and under 50 years of Age, some honest Man or other, will purchase them for their Wives....

The Draytons, who came to the Carolina province not many years after Horne penned his encomium, were apparently among those "industrious and ingenious persons" willing and able "to pertake of the Felicities of this Country," for it didn't take them long to be numbered among that "clique of merchant-planter-politician families who," Samuel Gaillard Stoney tells us in *Plantations of the Carolina Low Country*, "were making and marrying themselves into being a sort of Venetian aristocracy." Long before the Revolution the Draytons belonged to the small group of Low Country gentry whose lavish patronage managed to impart to Charles Town's social life, in the words of Carl Bridenbaugh, "a surface brilliance and blithe insouciance that never failed to inspire strangers to superlatives."

In 1798, John Davis, a young Englishman, obtained a position as tutor in the family of Thomas Drayton (William Henry's half brother) where he "enjoyed every comfort that opulence could bestow," he informs us in his *Personal Adventures and Travels of Four Years and a Half in the United States of America*. He spent the winter months with the family at Ocean Plantation near Coosawhatchie and moved to Drayton Hall in May. Although Davis found the "solitude of the woods" at Ocean Plantation "rather dreary," he couldn't say enough for "the polite attention of an elegant family." Drayton's table, he tells us,

was sumptuous, and an elegance of manners presided at it that might have vied with the highest circles of polished Europe. I make the eulogium, or rather, exhibit the character of Mr. Drayton, in one word, by saying, he was a gentleman; for under that portraiture I comprehend whatever there is of honour....

In May, Davis continues,

Mr. Drayton and his family exchanged the savage woods of Coosawhatchie, for the politer residence of their mansion on Ashley river. In our migration we formed quite a procession. Mr. Drayton occupied the coach with his lady and youngest daughter; and I advanced next with my fair pupil in a chair, followed by William Henry [Drayton's 14-year-old son] on a prancing nag, and half a dozen negro fellows, indifferently mounted, but wearing the laced livery of an opulent master....

In the venerable mansion at Ashley river, I again directed the intellectual progress of my interesting pupils, and enlarged the imagination of William, by putting Pope's version of the Odyssey into his hands, which I found among other books that composed the family library. He had before read the Iliad....

From Ashley river, after a short residence, we removed to Charleston which was full of visitors from the woods, and exhibited a motley scene. Here was to be perceived a coach, without a glass to exclude the dust, driven by a black fellow, not less proud of the livery of luxury, than the people within the vehicle were of a suit made in the fashion. Such is the pride of the people of Charleston, that no person is seen on foot unless it be a mechanic. He who is without horses and slaves, incurs always contempt.

In July the Draytons moved to Sullivan's island to "avoid the fever, which every summer commits its ravages at Charleston." Davis informs us further that "No families are more migratory than those of Carolina. From Sullivan's island we went again to the mansion on Ashley river, where I had invitations to hunt, to feast, and to dance...."

Such was the peripatetic and pleasure-fraught life of the planter aristocrats who, it should be mentioned, also went on Grand Tours of England and the continent to bring home the symbols of cultivation from abroad. And they were no less diligent in pursuing the pleasures of life. Dancing and horses, it has been said, often took precedence over politics. J. Hector St. John de Crèvecoeur found the inhabitants of Charles Town "the gayest in America . . . the centre of the beau monde" and "always filled with the richest planters in the province, who resort hither in quest of health and pleasure." The climate, the American farmer informs us,

renders excesses of all kinds very dangerous, particularly those of the table; and yet, insensible or fearless of danger, they live on and enjoy a short and a merry life. The rays of their sun seem to urge them irresistibly to dissipation and pleasure; on the contrary, the women,

from being abstemious, reach to a longer period of life and seldom die without having had several husbands. An European at his first arrival must be greatly surprised when he sees the elegance of their houses, their sumptuous furniture, as well as the magnificence of their tables. Can he imagine himself in a country the establishment of which is so recent?

Dr. Johann Schoepf was also struck by the southern aristocrats: "their manner of life, dress, equipages, furniture, everything," he concluded "denotes a higher degree of taste and love of show, and less frugality than in the northern provinces." And Charles Woodmason, who was later to become a missionary for the Church of England, reacted to the wonders of the Low Country with Augustan lines worthy of Pope:

What! tho' a second Carthage here we raise,
A late attempt, the work of modern days
Here Drayton's seat and Middleton's is found,
Delightful villas! be they long renown'd.
Swift fly the years when sciences retire,
From frigid climes to equinoctial fires
When Raphael's tints, and Titian's strokes shall faint,
As fair America shall deign to paint....
Domes, temples, bridges, rise in distant views,
And sumptuous palaces the sight amuse.

Woodmason's lines appeared in London's *Gentleman's Magazine* in 1753.

Palace and Gardens

Drayton Hall is a remarkable symbol of that affluent society that brought forth such oft-repeated words as opulence, pride, luxury, gaiety, and hospitality. The sophistication of its design and superb decorative elements have made many suspect that it must be the work of an important architect. Perhaps some day research will reveal who created this evocative architectural symbol of a society that has never been equaled in America. But does it really matter? It is true that he provided an ideal setting for that aristocratic, opulent, and hospitable life but isn't it the playwright who inspires the set designer's magic?

The garden that once embellished the river side of Drayton Hall was admired by many including the Duc de la Rochefoucauld, who described his visit there in his *Travels through the United States of North America, 1795, 1796, 1797*:

We stopped to dine with Dr. Drayton of Drayton Hall. The house is an ancient building, but convenient and good; and the garden is better laid out, better culti-

*The heavy splendor of the carved
wooden cornice, the Doric pilasters,
the overmantel, and the plaster ceiling
decoration, make the great hall a
memorable interior. The overmantel is
a free adaptation of an illustration in
Kent's* Designs of Inigo Jones. *The
ceiling design is based on stylized tobacco leaves and dates from the
1860s.*

vated and stocked with good trees, than any I have hitherto seen.

It was through the garden that the majority of visitors would have approached Drayton Hall since the most efficient means of travel was by river. Plantation houses invariably faced the rivers—the bearers of their produce and the path to the outer world. And thus they had a "river" facade and a "land" facade rather than a front and back. Drayton Hall's "river" facade is dominated by a classical pediment. The entrance door and three windows above it are framed by pilasters and pediments executed in carved Portland stone imported from England. The most striking feature of the "land" facade is its projecting two-story Palladian portico with Doric and Ionic columns also of Portland stone. Many examples of such porticos are shown in Andrew Palladio's *I quattro libri dell' architettura* published in Venice in 1570. Similar porticos appeared later on a number of Low Country houses but Drayton Hall seems to be the earliest example of this type of Palladian villa in America. It was Drayton Hall's two-storied portico that moved a reporter to speak with respect of "the Honourable John Drayton, Esqr's Palace and Gardens" in the *South Carolina Gazette* of December 2, 1758.

From the river side one enters the stair hall with its divided flight of stairs echoing those outside. Behind the stair hall is the great hall. On the right is the dining room and a chamber, on the left the Ionic room and library. Above the entrance hall is the great drawing room with its ten Corinthian pilasters. The kitchen and service quarters are in the high basement, the plan of which was also inspired by Palladio's *I quattro libri dell'architettura*.

The great hall with its full-paneled walls, ornamented ceiling, elaborate cornice, and majestic proportions, reflects the new Palladian revival that was in full flower in England under the influence of Lord Burlington and his villa at Chiswick (see page 77). The handsome overmantel was undoubtedly inspired by a mantelpiece at Houghton Hall in England illustrated in William Kent's *Designs of Inigo Jones* (1727). The magnificent double flight of stairs in the stair hall is still another Palladian idea unlike anything in America at that time.

The architectural roots of Drayton Hall, like so much in the Carolina colony, are plainly English and its early neo-Palladianism is excellent proof of how much closer in time the southerners followed the pace of classical evolution in England than did the northern colonists. But, more than anything else, Drayton Hall is a southern house. It has all of the tone of the south.

Oddly enough, the John Drayton who

(Top) The design of the plaster ceiling of the small drawing room (or Ionic room) on the first floor is an adaptation of the leaf motif that appears in the top panel of the overmantel. (Above) The decorative plasterwork of the Ionic room ceiling is simple but effective.

built this original and influential mansion seems to have been the least of the Draytons. He was, according to his memorialist, "a man of indifferent education, of a confined mind, proud and stingy." If we are to believe the writer, we also learn that "such was his character he lived in riches—but without public esteem. He died in a Tavern, but without public commiseration." He married four times and disinherited his celebrated son William Henry who, unlike his father, was well educated at Balliol College, Oxford.

Toward Keeping Magic Intact

The National Trust and Historic Charleston Foundation agree that the main objective is to preserve the house and the parkland around it with a minimum of changes. The architects advisory committee in its initial report on the preservation of Drayton Hall was even more emphatic about leaving the house as it is.

To begin with the committee advocated a thorough research program that would provide on-going study for the next five to ten years. This would not only include an exhaustive research of the Drayton family and its associations with Drayton Hall, but a study of plantation culture through the 18th and 19th centuries as expressed at Drayton Hall, and an archaeological study to determine "the original grades around the house, evidence of outbuildings, appurtenances, roads, walks, gardens, etc." The architects also advised a search over the entire property for evidence of the evolving use of land.

The report called for architectural research that would involve a thorough analysis of the structure "to determine its construction sequence, stylistic and structural characteristics." The architects emphasized, however, that this research "should be with non-destructive techniques, leaving all existing elements in place. The architecture should be studied as finished surfaces, not as a study of construction techniques. Where elements must be disturbed for proper stabilization and/or maintenance," they added, "the opportunity presented by their displacement should not be lost for more detailed analysis of the

structure beneath. The fabric should be subjected to complete mortar and paint analysis. The capabilities of advanced techniques, such as X-ray and chemical analysis should be used."

Specific suggestions for carrying out the preservation of the house included an analysis of the structure and reinforcement where necessary for anticipated loads. But, said the architects, "where such reinforcing might be obtrusive, the loads must be limited." Necessary repairs of unobtrusive elements, such as service stairs, "should be made of materials suited to the job, and be clearly identified." Exterior fabric, the architects advised, "including the stone steps should be repaired as required, giving full consideration to retaining patina and natural growth of lichen. . . .

"Existing interior finishes should be stabilized and left as they are." All finishes, the architects added, "should be fully analyzed to determine color, media, and application. Board ceilings on the second floor should be left as they are."

The architects made a point of stating that no mechanical systems of any kind— heating, cooling, ventilation, plumbing, electricity—should be installed other than alarm systems.

"Displaced original decorative items which can be reset in their original locations, such as bits of carving, dentils, Delft tile fireplace linings, etc. should be restored." They also pointed out that no repair of hardware or anything else should be done "beyond cleaning up finishes, etc. and preserving from future damage."

As for the furniture, the report suggested that only enough original Drayton Hall furniture should be returned "to give a sense of scale to the interior. The preservation is not concerned with people, family, or a way of life. No attempt should be made to furnish the house completely, nor any room therein. Pieces should be selected for their scale and appropriateness, rather than any inherent or associative values."

In conclusion, the architects stated:

This committee strongly feels that the only proper approach to the preservation of Drayton Hall is one of the sensi-

tive, intelligent stabilization of the house as it now exists. The foremost purpose of this exercise is to clarify and maintain the architectural values of the structure. We must fully exploit its potential as an architectural document.

Certainly most architects and historians visiting Drayton Hall will appreciate the philosophy of preservation thus exercised. But it is important also to consider the desires and needs of the average citizen visitor. These should be fulfilled in an educationally interesting manner through a well developed interpretive program at a site remote from the mansion itself. . . .

Writing in *Country Life* (August 1, 1974), John Cornforth expressed the hope that Drayton Hall would not be made into a house museum of the usual type "for it still has the feeling that the Draytons have just gone, leaving nothing to come between the present and the past."

The great plantation house surrounded by live oaks and quiet marshes is surely haunted by the past as is the country in which it stands, and it is this haunting quality that makes so many people not want a blade of grass or a particle of dust disturbed. A house museum, it has been said, if it is to function properly should convey the sense of a different reality—the reality of another time. Drayton Hall, with which time and the weather have played all sorts of pictorial tricks but only to refine it, does that to perfection. The sensitive and carefully thought-out preservation philosophy set forth by the architects advisory committee recognizes that rare quality and should go far toward keeping it intact.

The designer of Drayton Hall deserves to be remembered but perhaps it is enough that his masterpiece can move men more than two centuries and innumerable generations after he planned it. And if the good advice of the architects advisory committee is followed, Drayton Hall will reveal its magic to many more generations to come. But in the final analysis, such a house, as Henry James said of one of England's great country houses, "is really, *au fond*, an ineffaceable image; it can be trusted to rise before the eyes of the future."

The great drawing room on the second floor with its ten Corinthian pilasters and its crested overmantel is almost as impressive a space as the great hall below it. Tongue-and-groove wooden ceilings throughout the second floor replaced the original plaster ceilings when the house was reconditioned after the Civil War.

Hunter House

Newport, Rhode Island

The graceful front door surmounted by carved pineapple pediment is an outstanding example of the classic details with which wealthy merchant princes enriched their mansions.

Old houses were scaffolding once and workmen whistling.　　　T.E. Hulme

Newport is many things to many people. To some it is the fabulous 19th-century summer resort with ponderous pavilions and the Ten Mile Drive. To others it is the home of international yacht races. To a few it is the old colonial town where Washington not only slept but danced the minuet with Newport's internationally accredited belles, where Rochambeau had his headquarters during the Revolution, where Gilbert Stuart spent his youthful years, where the Townsends and Goddards turned out their distinctive cabinetwork, and where the 18th-century "Quaker grandees" of Rhode Island fashioned their houses as well as their lives with extraordinary taste.

The real essence of Newport seems to be secreted in the old part of town, where simple wooden houses with gambrel roofs and beautiful doorways are clustered near the bay, while the 19th-century ocean-front castles serve as a dazzling facade for those who cannot sense the more delicate atmosphere of the 18th-century community. Nevertheless Newport's two personalities with their sharp architectural contrasts eminently highlight two brilliant facets of the American dream. On the one hand is the simple natural grace of the intellectually minded 18th-century Quaker community, on the other is the self-conscious braggadocio of the money-minded late 19th-century resort. Henry James conveys the climate of Newport in 1870 when he speaks of "the beautiful idle women, the beautiful idle men, the brilliant pleasure-fraught days and evenings." In 1780 the Comte de Ségur wrote that Newport "offered delightful circles composed of enlightened and modest men and of handsome women."

From America's "first architect" Peter Harrison who designed some of Newport's 18th-century gems to Richard Morris Hunt who was responsible for some of the 19th-century's ocean-front extravaganzas, Newport has an extraordinary heritage spanning three centuries of American architecture. And architecture, John Ruskin reminds us, "is to be regarded by us with the most serious thought. We may live without her, and worship without her, but we cannot remember without her."

But it is the city's colonial riches that offer us such unexpected bonanzas for our lagging memory. In a country like America where cities can hardly be recognized from one generation to another, we can only call it a lucky quirk of history that Newport remains today one of the most completely preserved colonial towns, boasting some 400 structures built before 1800 and more early public buildings than in any other community in America.

An antique shabbiness obscured most of them until the middle of this century when a few people recognized their rarity. Mrs. George Henry Warren, founder of the Preservation Society of Newport County, was one of them. A summer resident of Newport, she liked wandering around the old colonial town and glimpsing the brilliant story lurking behind the shabby but still proud exteriors. She often talked about it with John Howard Benson, famous Newport calligrapher who worked in his ancestor's 17th-century shop. One day Benson told her that the 18th-century house at 54 Washington Street was going to be torn down. New York's Metropolitan Museum of Art was interested in buying the interior paneling but a purchaser might still save the entire house. Mrs. Warren persuaded her husband to buy it with the idea of keeping the house intact until some historical society might take it over. No one, however, seemed to be interested in "just another old house." Thus Mrs. Warren created the Preservation Society of Newport County in 1945, not only as a means of restoring the Hunter House but with the overall objective of interesting Newport citizens in recognizing the value of preserving all the town's irreplaceable riches. Unlike Williamsburg, says Mrs. Warren, they had no "angel" so the Preservation Society's philosophy is "to make it happen through the interest of the people themselves."

Beguiling Women, Diligent Men

One can't imagine a more likely environment in which to produce the necessary vision for meeting such a chal-

(Above) View from street. (Right) First floor plan. The northeast parlor is to the right of the front door, the southeast parlor to the left. The dining room is behind the southeast parlor.

lenge than the one that nurtured those hardy merchant princes who turned a wild strip of island into one of the five colonial cities large enough to be classified as such (Philadelphia, New York, Boston, Charleston, and Newport), and by the middle of the 18th century had won for their little island city the honor of being the cultural center of the American colonies.

We can assume, however, that not only the diligence and daring of its men but also the beauty and charm of its women contributed to the commercial and cultural greatness of 18th-century Newport. And perhaps these unique commodities were the result of the tolerance of its citizens, who from the beginning believed that everyone should worship as he pleased. It is notable that crime appeared later in Newport than in the other colonial cities. Not until 1749 did the town think it necessary to appoint three citizens "to inspect into Nucenses," and apparently these were no more serious than when it was reported that "divers Sorts of Linnen have been taken from the Lines whereon they were hanging." Other "Nucenses," oddly enough, were caused by traffic accidents such as the time in 1743 when the government considered it necessary to confiscate cart and oxen of a careless driver who had run over "a pleasant young Child."

A Lusty City with Lovely Doorways

In 1748 Deputy Governor Jonathan Nichols purchased the waterside lot along with all "buildings and edifices thereon erected . . . the wharfs, the fish, etc." Nichols was a prosperous merchant, the owner of at least one privateer, and the proprietor of White Horse Tavern which sold "all sorts of Strong Drink." Nichols probably built the house at 54 Washington Street (then Water Street) between 1748 and 1754. It was purchased in 1756 by Colonel Joseph Wanton, Jr. who later became Governor. It is generally assumed that some time after 1758 Wanton enlarged the house and gave it the character it has today. He also bought mahogany furniture from Job Townsend, as the latter's account books show, and was probably responsible for the unusual paint decoration in the northeast parlor.

During these years Newport was at the height of its importance and glory, a lusty colonial city with a forest of masts in its harbor and lovely doorways facing its streets. The Redwood Library which opened in 1750 was the first and long remained the finest colonial monument to letters. In 1754, Newport was the scene of the first lectures on anatomy to be delivered in the New World by Edinburgh graduate Dr. William Hunter whose son was to give the Hunter House its present name. Between 1726 and 1763 six extraordinarily fine buildings were put up. Three of them—Trinity Church, the Sabbatarian Meeting House, and Colony House—were designed by Richard Munday who called himself "housewright"; and three were by amateur architect Peter Harrison—Redwood library, the Brick Market, and Touro Synagogue. The taste in building, as Carl Bridenbaugh puts it, "that caused Newporters to applaud the superb architecture of Richard Munday and Peter Harrison reflected itself in their private buildings. For proportion, pure detail, and beauty of line, they had few American equals."

The hospitality of Newport's gentry to strangers was also celebrated according to one traveler who described them as "extremely genteel and courtly in their manners." These were the families whose fortunes had been made at sea and who tended to expend their wealth on graciously paneled and elegantly furnished interiors rather than the exterior of their houses.

When the Revolution broke out, Colonel Wanton's loyalist sympathies made it "convenient for him to go to New York" and the house was confiscated by the British a few years later. When the friendly French forces under Rochambeau arrived in 1780, Commander of the French fleet Admiral de Ternay was quartered in the house at 54 Washington Street and died in one of its bedrooms.

The house sold at auction in 1805 to William R. Hunter from whom it takes its name. A brilliant lawyer and son of the anatomist Dr. William Hunter, the new owner was also the brother of the three Hunter belles who had charmed and delighted the gallant young French officers in 1780–81.

In 1804 Hunter married Mary Robinson, a Quaker girl from New York and relative of the Thomas Robinsons who also lived on Washington Street. The couple moved into the house in 1805 and lived there until 1826 when Hunter went to Washington as Senator from Rhode Island, and advertised the house for sale in the *Newport Mercury* as an Estate consisting "of large lot, an ample elegantly furnished Dwelling house in perfect repair, a suitable Garden etc. . . . If not sold, it will be let for the Summer. It is a most elegible residence for a Southern Family."

Around 1759 Newport's fine climate had begun to attract wealthy West Indians and South Carolinians during the summer

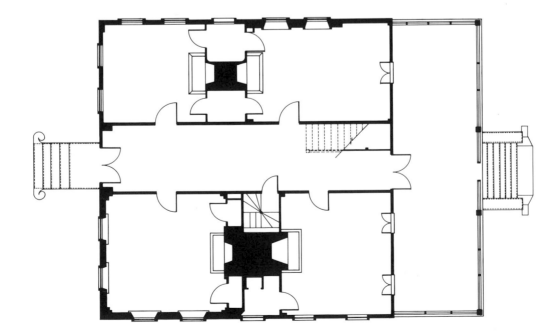

Northeast parlor. It was in such paneled and candlelit parlors that Rochambeau's aristocratic officers wooed the belles of Newport. "The Inventory of Jonathan Nichols, Esq., late of Newport, deceased, taken September 14, 1756," listed among other things: "One Easie Chair and 8 bottoms for Comm £30, 1 Easie Chair £40, Bed and Furniture £140."

months. But even though Crèvecoeur found the climate and gardenlike beauty of Newport impressive enough to call it the Montpellier of America, the house remained untenanted. In 1834 Hunter was appointed Chargé d'Affaires and later United States Minister at the Court of Dom Pedro the First, Emperor of Brazil. He returned to Newport in 1844 and died there in 1849. The house later became a boarding house and in the 1870s was turned into a convalescent home.

Yankee-style Trompe l'Oeil

During the restoration it was found that the exterior of the house was apparently left unpainted for many years, since the remaining old split and shiplapped clapboards on the north side were weathered a dark gray underneath the paint. An off-white next to the wood was probably put on early in the 19th century. This was the color selected to repaint the restored house because of the impracticality of stripping the old paint and leaving the wood exposed. Early records indicate, however, that most 18th-century houses were allowed to weather or were painted barn red. But by 1780 an officer in Rochambeau's army noted in his diary that the exteriors of Newport houses were "painted in divers colors," which "gives a variety pleasing to the eye."

Hunter House is built on the typical mid-18th-century floor plan—a wide hall running through the center with rooms opening on either side—and although its interiors are outstanding for their great quantity of bolection molded paneling, its exterior is not unlike most of the three-story frame houses that made up what travelers called the beauty of the little community. James Birket, a visitor to Newport in the 1750s, noted that:

> The houses in general make a good appearance, and also are as well furnished as in Most places you meet with, many of the rooms being hung with printed Canvas and paper, etc. which looks very neat. Others are well wainscoted and painted as in other places.

The Hunter House hallway is typically colonial with its low carved archway set in scroll brackets and the staircase behind it. There has been some conjecture that the staircase with its curved and ramped rail and richly carved balusters arranged in sets of three on each step was taken from Malbone, a Newport house that burned in 1766. It shows signs of having been planned for a building with higher ceilings and may have been cut down and installed by Colonel Wanton.

The wainscoting in the hallway has been repainted its original blue-green color found under many coats, and the walls above are whitewashed although they originally may have been hung with "printed Canvas."

The northeast parlor on the right of the hallway is perhaps the most interesting room in the house. Its paneled walls are ornamented by Corinthian pilasters set on high pedestals. The room is further distinguished by lovely shell cupboards that flank the fireplace and have four carved cherub heads set in the spandrel of the arches.

After the rooms had been stripped of their incrustations of paint, some interesting information about the original finishes came to light. The parlor was taken back to the natural wood and it was found that the first color was a reddish tone which had been applied with a powdery paint that came off almost completely when the second level of paint, a greenish putty color, was removed. This putty color appeared on all the walls and doors while the pilasters and baseboards were painted to simulate black marble veined in gold. The cupboards were originally painted a dark blue-green, which was duplicated during the restoration, and the cherub faces in the arch spandrels were polychromed naturalistically. The two angels at the left of the mantel retain their original 18th-century color and the others were returned to their naturalistic polychromed effect.

After the paint had been removed there was also evidence that the cupboards and paneling had been made for different places. Nevertheless the cupboards, glazed cupboard doors, angel heads, and the marbled decoration were all part of the room when it received its first covering of greenish putty color paint and it seems likely, as Antoinette Downing and Vincent Scully say in their *Architectural Heritage of Newport*, that "Joseph Wanton installed some of the various parts, and supervised their decoration soon after 1758." Downing and Scully also suggest that the room's third level of paint, a sand color which covered the whole room except for the mahogany window seats, may have been contemporary with the painting of the Colony House Chamber in 1784, also a sand color.

A map made by Ezra Stiles in 1758 indicates that the southern part of the house was added after that year. But if Colonel Wanton enlarged the house, the interior woodwork belongs to an earlier period and it is possible that he installed some of the paneling from earlier Newport houses as well as the stairway.

In addition to the trompe l'oeil marbleizing in the northeast parlor, the Hunter

Winged cherub head in arch spandrel of cupboard.

Marbleized Corinthian capital of one of the pilasters in the northeast parlor.

The central hallway has carved archway typical of colonial houses. Portraits of Joseph Wanton and his wife Mary by John Smibert face each other across Newport pieces they would not find unfamiliar.

(Right) Close-up of the mahogany staircase with its richly carved twisted balusters. (Far right) Dutch tiles surround fireplace in "walnut" parlor, so-called because paneled walls are "grained" to simulate walnut. Panel over the fireplace was scraped down to the original finish and the rest of the room painted to match it. The painting of Dr. William Hunter's spaniels is thought to represent Gilbert Stuart's first commission and has always been owned in the Hunter family. Adding to its interest is the Goddard table in the background.

House boasts three "grained" rooms creating an effect, as one observer put it, that is "sober, matter-of-fact, and rich, like the house itself." Although graining and marbleizing were not unusual ways of enhancing the architectural effect of 18th-century interiors, the Hunter House with its marbleized parlor decoration and three "grained" rooms is exceptional. The paneling in the southeast parlor was "grained" to simulate walnut, the dining room and northwest chamber to simulate cedar. In each room the graining has been duplicated, and a small section of the original has been preserved. During the restoration of the White Horse Tavern, also owned by Jonathan Nichols, a room was found on the second floor that had been "grained" in an identical color and pattern as the Hunter House dining room indicating that it may have been done by the same craftsman.

Colonel Thomas Wentworth Higginson, who boarded in the Hunter House in the middle of the 19th century, writes in *Malbone* (a story of the Newport house that burned in 1766):

I know no finer specimen of these large colonial dwellings in which the genius of Sir Christopher Wren bequeathed traditions of stateliness to our democratic days. Its central hall has a carved archway; most of the rooms have painted tiles and are wainscoted to the ceiling; the sashes are red cedar, the great staircase mahogany; there are cherub's heads and wings that go astray and lose themselves in closets and behind glass doors; there are curling acanthus-leaves that cluster over shelves and ledges, and there are those graceful shell-patterns which

one often sees on old furniture, but rarely in houses . . . the western entrance, looking toward the bay is surmounted by carved fruit and flowers, and is crowned . . . with pineapple in whose symbolic wealth the rich merchants of the last century delighted.

The finely carved scroll and pineapple pediment that Colonel Higginson mentions is now on the front door of the restored Hunter House and gives us our first suggestion of the taste and hospitality that were hallmarks of the period. It originally belonged to the waterside entry but was discarded in the 1870s when the house became a convalescent home and structural changes were made. Fortunately the pediment was preserved and installed on the street doorway. The only clue to the original front doorway was Colonel Higginson's reference to "its Ionic cornice."

Swell'd-Front Chests and Desks

When the physical restoration of the house was complete, the Preservation Society wisely decided to furnish it with Newport pieces of the period—the kind of things that would have furnished such a house in the 18th century. The flowering of Newport cabinetmaking was chiefly due to the talents of the Townsend family, and the Goddards who were allied with them through apprenticeship and marriage. It was they who developed the famous block or "swell'd"-front chests and desks which have been called the "most distinctively American product in woodwork especially when surmounted by the shell." From the ledger of Job Townsend, Jr., we learn that these cabinetmakers made all kinds of furnishings from wooden houses to birdcages. On one occasion Townsend sold a coffin for a Negro slave and "two Roller pins" to J.R. Rivers. Another time he made a "Corner Cubbord" and three tables for the barber Benjamin Dunham for which he received in payment "A year's Shaven, a Cutt Wigg, a foretop to the Wigg," and 24 feet (7.3m) of mahogany.

There were 14 Townsends and five Goddards who followed the "Art, trade, and mystery" of cabinetmaking before 1800. Because they often cooperated with one another it is not always easy to ascribe a certain piece to one man. Apparently all of them, at one time or another, had a hand in creating the superb furniture that makes Newport stand out as an important cabinetmaking center. It is known that John Goddard, the first of that name, manufactured many inexpensive tables and chairs for export to the southern colonies and West Indies, but in the 1760s he began making the "swell'd"-front secretaries and

kneehole desks which were "Costly as well as ornamental."

It was with such fine pieces of furniture that the merchant princes of the 18th century furnished their houses along with silver by Newport craftsmen; family portraits by such Newport limners as Gilbert Stuart, Robert Feke, and John Smibert; and clocks by William Claggett.

The Hunter House was opened to the public in 1953 entirely furnished with products made by Newport craftsmen, a loan exhibition which was said to represent the largest collection of Newport items ever assembled in one place. When the furniture, silver, paintings, and pewter had been placed in the various rooms, says Ralph E. Carpenter, Jr., in *The Arts and Crafts of Newport Rhode Island, 1640–1820*, published by the Preservation Society as a permanent record of the exhibition,

the affinity between house and furnishings immediately became apparent. The sometimes robust furniture of the Townsends and Goddards looked completely "at home" in the rooms where raised panels were surrounded by bolection molding. The spiral fluted drops of the staircase were reflected in the spiral fluting of one of the beds and several tables. All in all, house and furnishings complemented each other.

While many of the exhibition pieces were returned to their owners after the show, some were left on extended loan. These are supplemented each summer with other loans of Newport pieces from museums and private collections. Thus an ever-changing exhibition of Newport's 18th-century arts and crafts are seen against the kind of background they were intended for. "Newport building, like Newport furniture," as Antoinette Downing puts it, "developed a quality of intrinsic richness wherein the ornament became an inseparable part of the whole." Hunter House offers visual proof of her words. The study and decoration of its graceful rooms with their Newport furnishings has done much to bring to light the kind of decoration and furniture in fashion when first Jonathan Nichols' and later Joseph Wanton's cargo-laden ships tied up to the Hunter House wharf.

Through one of those ironies of fashion Newport is better known today as the glamorous playground of the blasé than for its wealth of reminders of a rich chapter in American history. But anything, as Henry James says of Newport's old houses, "that has succeeded in living long enough to become conscious of its *note*, is capable on occasion of making that note effectively sound."

ARMS OF VAN CORTLANDT. *G. KANE.*

Van Cortlandt Manor House

Croton-on-Hudson, New York

The Van Cortlandt coat of arms, painted in oil on a wooden panel and signed "G. Kane" hangs in the hall.

As they built, they made, used, and left behind them records of their thinking. . . . Whatever the character of the thinking, just so was the character of the building.

Louis Sullivan

"If there be any terrestrial Canaan," wrote the English traveler Daniel Denton around 1670, " 'tis surely here where the land floweth with milk and honey." He was speaking of the Hudson River Valley—a region whose milk and honey had previously been dicovered and made ample use of by the Dutch patroons whose great river estates had been granted to them by the West India Company. Another enthusiastic Englishman proclaimed "the air of the province is very good. . . . A sober Englishman may go into it and live there and come out of it again without any seasoning or other sickness caused meerly by the Country." Even the British emissary who later handled the surrender of Burgoyne's army on the Hudson found it necessary to expiate "with taste and eloquence on the beautiful scenery," before getting down to the more mundane business of surrender.

And still today Henry Hudson's "Great River of the Mountains" conveys a delightful visual impression as it winds through its mountain-hemmed valley dotted with the lush estates of tycoons and titled ladies, divinities, and descendants of early families.

When the English took New York in 1664, manorial grants were made to induce the settling of new territory. In 1677 Stephanus, founder of Van Cortlandt Manor, took out a license from Governor Edmond Andros for the purchase of Indian rights to land in the Croton area. His father Oloffe Van Cortlandt, the first of the family in this country, had come from the Netherlands in 1639 in the service of the West India Company, and was accounted the fourth richest man in New York when he died in 1684. It was Oloffe who adopted a family coat of arms composed of four windmill sails between five mullets. Painted on wood in the 18th century, it now hangs in the Manor house hallway.

In 1683 Stephanus bought a large area north of Croton and south of Peekskill from the Indians. In 1688 he purchased the property on which the Manor house now stands. The original part of the house, which was probably there at the time, served as a lodge and trading post for about 63 years. In 1697 the patent for the "Lordship and Manor of Cortlandt" was granted to Stephanus.

Around 1749 the Manor house was enlarged and prepared as a permanent residence. Pierre, Stephanus' grandson, had married Joanna Livingston in 1748 and the young couple moved to Croton in 1749 to make it their permanent home for more than half a century. During these years the Van Cortlandt Manor house was at the height of its social, political, and economic significance. The Hudson's first literary figure, Cadwallader Colden, who spent a night there in 1753 remarked that "young Pierre and his charming wife keep up the hospitalities of the house equal to his late father."

The Van Cortlandt family occupied the stone Manor house for more than two centuries, one of the longest such records in America. Miss Anne Stevenson Van Cortlandt, the last descendant to live there, died in 1940. In 1953 John D. Rockefeller, Jr., purchased the house to preserve and restore it to its 18th-century appearance. The restoration was done by a staff of experts under the direction of Colonial Williamsburg's resident architect A.E. Kendrew. In 1959 it was turned over to Sleepy Hollow Restorations, Inc., to administer as a house museum.

It was decided to restore the Manor house, gardens, and ferry house to their appearance in the decade immediately following the Revolution because in 1790 the Manor house "was an outstanding architectural example of which few remain in original form; the Van Cortlandt family was most active at this period in affairs of national importance; and the Manor as an economic unit enjoyed its greatest prosperity and influence." The architectural staff further stated that its decision was based on the feeling that "the presentation of accumulated culture including many generations and historical periods has been much less effective than the portrayal of a single important age. . . . The story of life in the late eighteenth century will prove more effec-

The Manor house as it appears today—an outstanding example of a Dutch-English farmhouse.

(Below Left) Ground floor plan. The large room on the left is the kitchen and the old parlor is on the right. The milk room runs across the back. A brick paved piazza is on three sides. (Below Right) First floor plan. A double flight of steps gives access to the porch. Flanking the central hall is the parlor on the right and the dining room on the left. Behind the parlor is the northeast chamber.

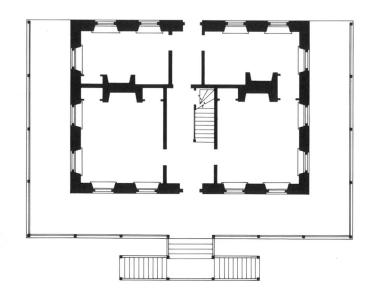

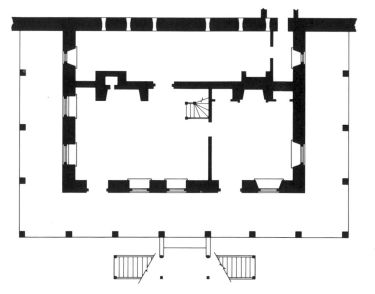

tive than an attempt to show the changes over a period of two hundred years."

Five years of research in historic records and the family papers, and archaeological investigation of the grounds, not only helped establish the original structural details of the house but provided much information about the life of the family and Manor life in general.

Patriarchal Simplicity

The Van Cortlandt family played an important role in colonial life and the American Revolution and entertained many distinguished visitors but in spite of the aristocratic and political distinction of the life of its occupants, the Manor house is notable for the simplicity of its design. It has the air of a Hudson Valley farmhouse and is far more simple than most of the surviving manorial mansions of its day. The interior paneling and furnishings, however, while unpretentious, are equal to the finest. Indeed the house seems a perfect reflection of Pierre Van Cortlandt's character as he was described in his later years by the Reverend J.B. Wakely:

> . . . there was much of patriarchal simplicity about him. Though of a wealthy and aristocratic family, he was as simple and artless as a child, while he was dignified as a grand old Roman . . . a complete gentleman of the old school in his manners. . . .

Local legend says—and New York State abounds in legend—that the earliest portion of the Manor house was built as a fortress against Indian attacks. Although a series of apertures in the 2½-foot thick walls of the house were thought to be loopholes for musketry, the barrel of an 18th-century musket does not fit them. More likely they were for ventilating raw furs.

Unlike the frame houses built by the New England colonists such as Hunter House in Newport (page 43), the Dutch settlers usually built their houses of stone. The Van Cortlandt house, however, with its brick piazza and raised porch—a style more usual in the south—is the only example of its kind in the Hudson Valley. Its exterior walls combine red and yellow brick, brownstone, and fieldstone. By framing door and window openings with brick in a kind of quoined treatment, these early Hudson Valley builders did away with the laborious task of stone cutting around door and window jambs.

An 1841 engraving of the Manor house shows it with dormers, the two-story porches, and the same roof line. The porches extended around the sides to meet the wings on the east and west, and a double flight of

The parlor is on the second level of the Manor house. The New York Chippendale tea table and sofa have been in the family since the 18th century. The Chinese export porcelain tea set belonged to Anne Stevenson Van Cortlandt (Pierre II's wife). Portraits (c. 1720) are of Anne's grandparents Caleb Beck, Sr., and his wife Annetje. There is a bill of sale dated New York, August 11, 1809, for the French Empire mantel clock purchased by Pierre II for $170. The three Sheraton side chairs were made in New York about 1790.

The so-called Old Parlor is on the ground floor. A New York 18th-century oval table with Hudson Valley pad on disc feet is surrounded by four Queen Anne country chairs. Over the mantel hang the antlers of a pet deer which belonged to Pierre's brother John. The curtains are of 18th-century blue-and-white resist-dyed fabric as are the chair cushions.

Abraham Van Cortlandt (1713–1746) was painted in the 1720s by an unknown Hudson Valley artist. Abraham was Pierre's brother, and his portrait now hangs in the hall. The drapery in the portrait inspired the design of the parlor curtains.

steps in the front gave access to the upper porch. The east wing was built about 1810, but maps made in 1836 and 1837 show the house plan before the west wing was built and the porch on this side extended the full width of the house. During the restoration, the dormers and both wings were removed, the side porches carried the width of the house as they were built originally, and the double flight of steps shown in the engraving were reconstructed.

When the wings were removed, original windows were revealed and repaired. The removal of the wings also brought to light some of the original unchanged pointing of the stone walls which served as a guide for pointing all the stonework. A pair of the original paneled shutters were discovered and used as models for the rest of the shutters of the house.

At some time in the 18th century the north wall of the house was raised about four feet, and the front slope of the roof was carried higher up and further back thereby altering the pitch and ridge position. The earlier roof line can still be seen on the chimney. Because these changes were made in the 18th century they have been kept.

Fragments of the original shingles which were found under the later roof were painted red. This color has been duplicated for all the Manor's restored roofs.

The construction of the porches is an integral part of the framing of the house and was evidently contemporary at least with the raising of the stone house walls from a one-story level to their present height. They may have been built even before Pierre Van Cortlandt made the house his permanent home. All the wooden elements of the house were studied to determine the 18th-century paint colors. Porch posts, balusters, and railings were white. Door frames were a light gray and the two original shutters were painted a dark gray blue. Handrails, steps, and downstairs doors were chocolate brown with the upper panels picked out in white. All these colors have been reproduced.

3 Barrels Pork and 12 Chairs Blue

During the Revolution, Pierre and his family played active roles in the fight against England and the making of the new nation. Many Van Cortlandt relatives were loyalists and although Governor Tryon visited Croton in 1774 to urge Pierre to remain loyal to the King with offers of land and a title, as well as a commission in the British Army for his son Philip, both refused.

In 1775 Pierre was commissioned a Colonel of the Third Westchester County Regiment. He served as a member of the Second, Third, and Fourth Provincial Congress. In July of 1777 he was elected Lieutenant

Governor of the state and remained in that post for 18 years. Philip received his commission in 1775 and served in most of the important actions of the war.

Van Cortlandt Manor was located in the area known as Neutral Ground which was subject to attack by both British and American soldiers. Thus in 1776 the Van Cortlandts moved north of the American lines, first to the family's Peekskill house known as the "upper manor," and later to Rhinebeck. They took their choice possessions with them and inventories taken at the time provided valuable information about their household belongings. One list of articles sent "by waggon" to Rhinebeck, April 3, 1777, includes such items as "3 Barrels Pork," "1 Desk & BookCase," "1 Case Looking Glasses," "1 Case Gin," "2 Chests of Drawers," "5 Feather Beds," "2 Carpets," "The Settee & 12 Chairs Blue," "1 Dining Table." The latter is the fine mahogany William and Mary gateleg table that has always been one of the treasures of the Manor house and is now in the dining room.

After the war Pierre and his family returned to the Peekskill house. They went there, Pierre II explained later, because

> the Old Manor House at Croton was not in a situation to take my Mother & family there as the House had been occupied by our Army as an Outpost—the Tories having taken away every door and Window. . . .

There is a paper in Pierre Senior's handwriting labeled "House and farm at Croton, Losses during the Revolution," which gives specific information about damages to the house and outbuildings.

The house and barn, according to family papers, were repaired around 1784, and the restored house today probably closely resembles that "Old Manor House at Croton" after the windows and doors were replaced, new mantels installed in the main rooms, and it was generally repaired for occupancy. Since most of the original woodwork remained, the design of the paneling and other interior treatments were readily established, and the original paint colors, including the marbleized flooring in the parlor, could be reproduced.

Many of the present furnishings in the house have come down in the Van Cortlandt family including an amazing amount of personal items such as Pierre Van Cortlandt's razors. ". . . the patrons, and indeed all the landed proprietors," wrote Mrs. Pierre Van Cortlandt III when describing the furnishings in the homes of Manor families, "gloried in the solid magnificence of their household furnishings." Mrs. Grant, an English woman who spent two winters in

(Above) The kitchen on the ground floor features many Van Cortlandt family possessions including the long pine sawbuck table with X-shaped supports peculiar to New York country tables. It stands in its old central place surrounded by a collection of country Queen Anne rush-bottomed Hudson Valley chairs. The Dutch kas holds an array of pewter plates.

(Left) One of the Queen Anne Hudson Valley rush-bottomed chairs with pad on disc feet appearing in the Manor house and ferry house. Each chair has its own personality.

Pierre Van Cortlandt I by John Wesley Jarvis in the Museum of the City of New York. It is almost identical to the portrait which hangs in the Van Cortlandt parlor.

Portrait of Joanna Livingston Van Cortlandt as an old lady painted by Ezra Ames after her death.

the 1760s with Pierre's aunt Mrs. Philip Schuyler in Albany, observed in her *Memoirs of an American Lady* that "valuable furniture, though perhaps not very well chosen, was the favorite luxury of these people . . . and the mirrors, the paintings, the china, but above all the state bed, were considered as the family zeraphin . . . secretly worshipped. . . ."

Benjamin Franklin Slept Here

The lower entrance to the house leads across the brick paving of the piazza through double Dutch doors (the 1785 replacements of those removed during the Revolution), and into the Old Parlor, one of three rooms on the ground or sunk story. Since the Old Parlor was probably used as a sitting-dining room in Pierre and Joanna's day that is how it has been restored. The paneling and two cupboards flanking the fireplace are painted their original putty color while the cupboard interiors are painted a warm orange red frequently found in Dutch interiors. The whole room, in fact, is characterized by the sturdy simplicity one associates with the Dutch.

To the left of the Old Parlor is the kitchen, which Mrs. Grant might have beeen describing when she wrote that the winter kitchen in the Schuyler house was in "a sunk story immediately below the eating parlor where it increased the general warmth of the house." The Van Cortlandt kitchen has whitewashed walls and gray painted woodwork and is equipped with many of the utensils that have always belonged to it. It was in this kitchen fireplace that foods raised within the Manor confines were prepared for family and guests. Washington Irving's Knickerbocker in *Knickerbocker's History of New York* called the fireplaces in such kitchens "of a truly patriarchal magnitude, where the whole family, old and young, master and servant, black and white, nay, even the cat and dog enjoyed a community of privilege."

On the first floor, the central hallway runs the width of the house and is divided into front and back sections by a low arch. Double Dutch doors in the front open onto the second-story level of the porch and similar doors in the back open onto a cobblestone terrace at ground level. The staircase in the front hall has balusters of a robust profile. Its detail is typical of the work of early mid-18th-century less sophisticated builders. The original 18th-century balusters had been removed in the 19th century and the present ones were modeled after those in a house of the same period in Kinderhook, New York. Old graining to represent a reddish wood was found on all the original woodwork in the hall and has been restored.

Both the parlor and the dining room, on either side of the hall, sometimes served as bedrooms but they have been restored and furnished as a formal parlor and dining room. In her description of the Schuyler house, Mrs. Grant says it

contained no drawing-room; that was an unheard of luxury . . . and in the eating room, which, bye the bye, was rarely used for that purpose, were some fine scripture paintings; that which made the greatest impression on my imagination, and seemed to be universally admired, was one of Esau coming to demand the anticipated blessing. . . .

Benjamin Franklin, to mention but one of many distinguished guests known to have visited Pierre and Joanna, stayed at the Manor house in May of 1776, and according to family tradition, he slept in the southeast room which is now the parlor. It has been noted that during this visit one of the children brought in the thorns of prickly pears to be used as pins. Franklin supposedly remarked that the "colonists will certainly succeed if they can grow their own pins."

Three of the parlor walls are plastered and the fourth is paneled from floor to ceiling. The mantel, installed after a fire early in the 19th century, is flanked by a round-topped cupboard on one side and a closet on the other with a round top above its door to balance the cupboard. It is all painted a warm putty color and the cupboard interior is the same Dutch red found on the cupboards in the Old Parlor. The floor, painted to simulate alternating squares of black and gray marble, reproduces the original floor treatment found in the closet. The curtains in this room were patterned after the drapery in the portrait of Araham Van Cortlandt which hangs in the hall. They are of French 18th-century blue silk bourette, scalloped and edged with gold braid. The windows have deep window seats, paneled reveals, and are fitted with Venetian blinds painted the color of the woodwork. Most of the windows in the house must have originally had Venetian blinds since Philip Van Cortlandt's inventory lists 15 separate window blinds and specifically states that three of them were wooden.

Whenever possible throughout the house the original furniture known to have been there during Pierre and Joanna's lifetime has been brought back, or furniture associated with the family has been installed. Other pieces were selected because of their 18th-century date, their Hudson Valley and New York provenance, or because of similarity to furnishings the Van Cortlandt family is known to have possessed.

In her account of the furnishings in the homes of manor families, Mrs. Pierre Van

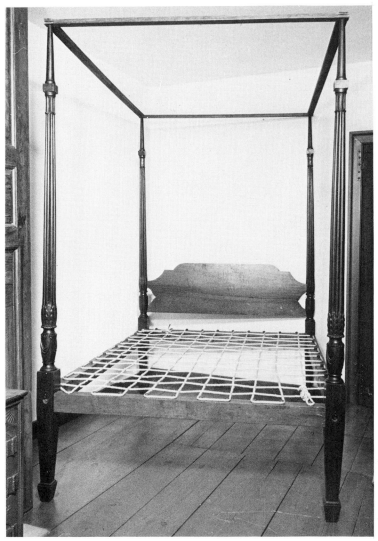

Mahogany 18th-century chest-on-chest has carving closely related to that of the dressing table. It was willed by a Van Cortlandt descendant to Sleepy Hollow Restorations after the house was restored.

Late 18th-century New York four-post mahogany bed attributed to Duncan Phyfe's shop has always been in the possession of the Van Cortlandt family. It is in the northeast chamber.

This mahogany 18th-century Philadelphia Chippendale dressing table with panels of fretwork carving across the front and sides came down in the family of Cornelia Beekman, Pierre's daughter, and was acquired for the Manor house from one of her descendants.

Cast-iron stove in early Adam style was, according to family legend, supposed to have inspired the Franklin stove.

The ferry house.

The ferry house barroom, where tavern cheer would have been dispensed to travelers as well as local gossipers, features a large round 18th-century hutch table with Hudson Valley shoe feet surrounded by Windsor chairs made in the vicinity of Kingston in the late 18th century. The pewter dresser found near Rensselaerwyck is filled with English and American pewter, the common tableware of the day.

Cortlandt III tells us that "the furniture of the well-to-do people was massive and costly and that of the plain people good and made to last." She mentions the parlors with their turkey carpets and mahogany tilt-top tables, the "cupboards set in the walls" that "held china, which was often very beautiful, especially that of the favorite Lowestoffe and Chinese makes."

Back of the parlor is a small chamber which was used in the 19th century as a library with Gothic Revival arches and shelves. After they were removed, the original paneled mantel breast and other woodwork was almost intact but somewhat scarred from vandalism during the Revolution. When it was cleaned, a painted walnut grain finish was uncovered and restored. In this room is a cast-iron stove which was evidently admired by Franklin during his 1776 visit because it is a family tradition that he developed his concept of the Franklin stove from it. Franklin's book on stoves, however, was published in 1744. The stove was discovered within a fireplace during the restoration.

Lady Gardeners in an Earthly Paradise

The Manor, like others in the province, represented a completely self-sufficient community. The main house was surrounded by many small buildings including a school, mills, store, carpenter shop, blacksmith shop, icehouse, barns, cowshed, beehouses, smokehouse, tenant house, ferry house, along with orchards and gardens. (While the ferry house and ferry, which served north-south travelers across the Croton River until the early 19th century, were owned by the Van Cortlandts, they were leased to Manor tenants to operate.) The office where Pierre administered all these Manor holdings has been reconstructed on its original foundations adjacent to the house.

Joanna's role in Manor activities was closer to home. In the worlds of the Reverend Wakely she "was a model wife, a model mother, and a model Christian; she made the Manor House an earthly Paradise." She was also an expert gardener as were many of the Dutch housewives in the province. In her *Memoirs of an American Lady*, Mrs. Grant tells us something about the Hudson Valley's 18th-century gardeners:

> . . . not only the training of children but of plants, such as needed peculiar care or skill to rear them was the female province. . . . A woman in very easy circumstances, and abundantly gentle in form and manners, would sow, and plant, and rake incessantly. These fair gardeners too were great florists: their emulation and solicitude in this pleasing em-

ployment, did indeed produce "flowers worthy of Paradise."

Joanna's rectangular flower beds lining the "long walk," which leads from the main house to the ferry house, have been restored and planted with the kind of flowers that her solicitude must have produced.

But while the Van Cortlandts led a busy country life, it was also a gracious and hospitable one. They were of the wealthier class—"that is to say," as Washington Irving's Knickerbocker puts it, "such as kept their own cows, and drove their own wagons." Actually Pierre and Joanna were probably among the earliest commuters between Westchester and New York, making frequent trips by sail, wagon, or on horseback, and their guests were among the most distinguished of their time.

The Ferry House

The Van Cortlandt ferry, about a thousand feet from the Manor house, was the only means of crossing the Croton River without a long detour. Although the law required that a ferry keeper provide shelter for persons using the ferry service, accommodations of 18th-century ferry houses were, from all reports, very primitive. Madame Knight, a hardy New Englander writing of her horseback journey to New York in 1704, gives us a vivid picture of the inconveniences to be found in such places:

> From hence we Hasted toward Rye . . . and so riding till about nine at night, and there arrived and took up our Lodgings at an ordinary, wch a French family kept. Here being very hungry, I desired a fricasee wch the Frenchman undertaking, managed so contrary to my notion of cookery that I hastened to Bed supperless;—arriving at my apartment found it to be a little Lento Chamber furnisht amongst other Rubbish with a High Bed and a Low one, a Long Table, a Bench and a bottomless chair,—Little Miss went to scratch up my Kennell wch Russelled as if shee'd bin in the the Barn amongst the Husks, and suppose such was the Contents of the tickin—Nevertheless being exceeding weary, down I laid my poor Carkes . . . and found my covering as scanty as my Bed was hard. Annon I heard another Russelling noise in Ye Room—called to know the matter—Little Miss said she was making a bed for the men; who, when they were in Bed, complained their leggs lay out of it by reason of its shortness.—poor I made but one grone, which was from the time I went to bed to the time I Riss, which was about three in the morning, setting up by the Fire till light. . . .

Another traveler reporting a journey taken in 1744 said that although he went to bed alone in a room,

> When I waked this morning I found two beds in the room, besides that in which I lay, in one of which lay two great hulking fellows, with long black beards, having their own hair (rather than shaved for wigs) and not so much as half a nightcap betwixt them. I took them for weavers, not only from their greasy appearance, but because I observed a weaver's loom at each side of the room. . . .

The Van Cortlandt ferry house—a story-and-a-half brick fronted building with wide overhang and brick end chimneys—was probably built in the early part of the 18th century. There is evidence that originally you entered a single room with a steep staircase leading to the upper floor. In the latter part of the 18th century it was divided into two rooms with a hall and stairway between—and so it has been restored.

Because the ferry house was leased to a succession of tenants who brought and took away their own furniture, no inventories of actual furnishings have come to light. A thorough study, however, was made of inventories for other 18th-century New York ferry houses and Van Cortlandt Manor tenants. Thus while the various rooms in the restored ferry house are furnished with such typical Hudson Valley 18th-century country furniture as hutch tables, Windsor chairs, stoneware, pewter, rush-bottomed chairs, and the inevitable Dutch kas (cupboard), it is undoubtedly far more fully equipped and orderly than any weary 18th-century traveler could possibly imagine. Nevertheless the simple painted furniture and homespun flavor of the ferry house interiors along with the more formal Manor house interiors offer today's visitors the unusual opportunity of viewing two facets of 18th-century Hudson Valley Dutch modes of life—the simple and the sophisticated.

After Pierre and Joanna returned to the Manor farm in 1803, they spent the remaining years of their lives there. Joanna died in 1808 and Pierre in 1814. Writing to his sister Mrs. Philip van Rensselaer about the death of their father Philip says:

> He is at rest, I trust, in Paradise, and his advice I pray the Lord to enable us to keep constantly in mind. He said "Love each other and put your trust in your Saviour; he never will forsake you. My Redeemer has been my friend and supporter upward of ninety years, and will continue to be so although my struggles are hard, yet ere long I shall be happy," in short, he was all love—all resignation.

Cliveden

Germantown, Pennsylvania

Exterior and one of the dependencies. The Pennsylvania stone house, says Struthers Burt, is "the most quiet, the most four-square, the coolest, the warmest, and the most dignified house in America."

I cannot but think it an evil sign of a people when their houses are built to last for one generation only. There is a sanctity in a good man's house which cannot be renewed in every tenement that rises on its ruins: and I believe that good men would generally feel this; and that having spent their lives happily and honorably, they would be grieved . . . to think that the place of their earthly abode . . . with all the record it bare of them, and all of material things that they loved and ruled over, and set the stamp of themselves upon—was to be swept away. . . . I say that if men lived like men indeed, their houses would be temples—temples which we should hardly dare to injure. John Ruskin

When the spires of churches were beginning to vie with the masts of sailing ships to ornament Philadelphia's skyline, Benjamin Chew decided to establish a country seat in nearby Germantown. The result of that decision is Cliveden, one of America's distinguished Palladian houses.

In 1763 Chew purchased land in Germantown just six miles from the burgeoning Quaker city where he was an eminent jurist and, in the words of his friend Governor John Penn, "the ablest man in the country." He started to build Cliveden in 1764. It was finished three years later and the Chew family lived there, with the exception of an 18-year period, until October 1971. In 1972 the National Trust acquired Cliveden from Samuel Chew, sixth generation descendants of its builder.

The Chew family's long tenancy of Cliveden sets them apart from most Americans who rarely remain in a house for one generation, let alone six. The mobile society that has existed in America from its beginning is not conducive to establishing ancestral homes. This characteristic shocked such early travelers to these shores as the Frenchman Moreau de St. Méry who noted in the 1790s that Americans:

cling to nothing, attach themselves to nothing. There is plenty of evidence of this among country dwellers. Four times running they will break land for a new house, abandoning without a thought the house in which they were born, the

church where they learned about God, the tombs of their fathers, the friends of their childhood, the companions of their youth, and all the pleasures of their first society. . . . Everywhere, even in Philadelphia, which is America's outstanding city, everything is for sale, provided the owner is offered a tempting price. He will part with his house, his carriage, his horse, his dog—anything at all.

Not the Chews. All six generations who lived at Cliveden have been conscientious preservers of the house, its furnishings, and thousands of Chew papers which document the lives of the family and the building of their house. The Chews possessed a great sense of history. In addition to keeping all the building documents and family papers, they made notations about almost everything that happened from births, marriages, and deaths to minute facts about their possessions. There is, for example, a chatelaine and watch with a 1755 hallmark still in its original box. Inside the watch case is a carefully printed Chew notation stating that it was given to Benjamin Chew's bride in 1757.

The Chews, moreover, have always made every effort to preserve the house as Benjamin Chew knew it. Between 1958 and 1972 Samuel Chew even removed a number of later furnishings and other objects while retaining those its builder knew. It can be argued, of course, that Cliveden is especially Benjamin Chew's story and should reflect his life and time even if it loses some of its credibility as an ancestral home. Benjamin Chew (1722–1810) was part of that inspired society of men who, during the late colonial and early Federal period, possessed not only great wisdom but a high degree of culture and taste. And Philadelphia was the center of that culture. Few cities anywhere in the world could boast the galaxy of intellectual and civic leaders produced by that young city in the decades before the Revolution.

On the other hand the story of a house and its furnishings is in large part the history of all its owners. This is particularly true of Cliveden which was lived in for more than two centuries by one family. A mingling of its 18th-, 19th-, and 20th-century furnish-

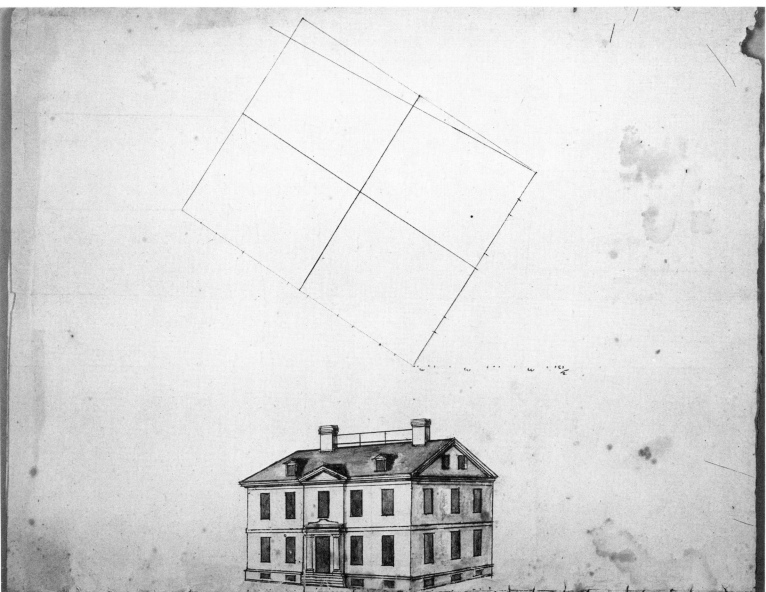

(Above) Engraving of Kew Palace, from which Cliveden's design evolved.

(Right) This Chew plan is close to its final form.

(Opposite page: top) One of the Chew drawings showing the elevation with the dependencies as they were beginning to acquire their present form. (Bottom) Drawing, probably by Chew, is thought to be the only colonial architectural drawing done in perspective.

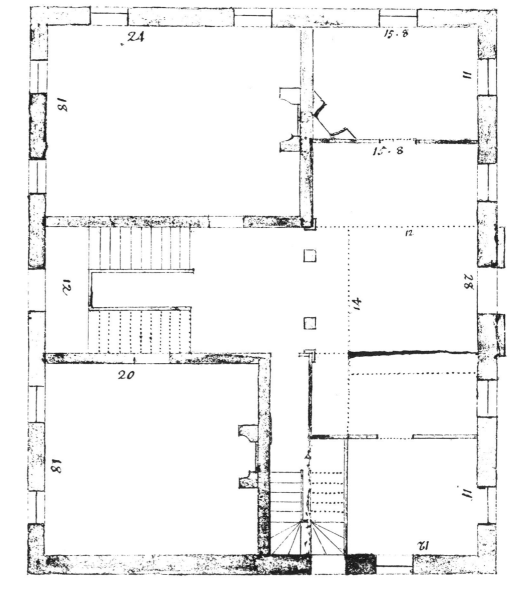

Roof detail with urns ordered from England.

ings would only enhance its appeal as the living document of history that it surely is.

Cliveden, in any case, meets every requirement for preserving a historic house. It is important for its architectural, its cultural, its social, and its historic significance.

The Dulce and the Utile

Benjamin Chew was born and reared a Quaker in Anne Arundel County, Maryland. When he was 10 the family moved to Philadelphia and at the age of 15 he entered the office of Andrew Hamilton to study law. When he was 21 he went to London to finish his law education at the Middle Temple.

A letter Chew wrote much later to his future son-in-law who was then studying at the Inns of Court, gives us insight into the writer's character both as a man and a lawyer:

> . . . Every lawyer . . . should be well versed in human nature. This kind of knowledge can never be acquired from books; mixing with the great world is the only school to learn it in. Again, what you see and hear in such a place as London will not only open your mind and enlarge your ideas, but furnish you with a fund of agreeable conversation to the end of your days; for you are to qualify yourself for the gentleman as well as lawyer. . . .
>
> Let me caution you, however, not to risk your health by too sedentary a life and intense application. . . . Mingle the *dulce* with the *utile*, and let your time be divided between the Law, History, Belle Letters, Society, and exercise, and learn to profit by the views and foibles of others, and by copying the virtues and manners of those worthy of imitation. Remember an excellent and useful rule you have often heard me mention [he gives the Latin]: Know a man perfectly before you make him your confidant. Be courteous and civil to all; speak ill to none; but above all let your actions in public and private life bespeak you an honest man, truly called by Pope the noblest work of God. . . .

In 1747 Chew married his cousin Mary Galloway and they settled in Dover. In 1754 they moved to Philadelphia and the first Mrs. Chew died the following year. In 1757 he married Elizabeth Oswald and his only son, Benjamin, was born in 1758.

It was during these years that the fame of the legendary "Philadelphia lawyer" became firmly established and Chew's ability, learning, and success was a factor in establishing it. He was appointed Attorney General of Pennsylvania in 1755 and Chief Justice in 1774. He was the Penns' legal adviser and one of the five commissioners from Pennsylvania who signed the Mason-Dixon survey. As his fortune and distinction increased Chew decided, like many 18th-century Philadelphians who followed the English pattern of gentility, to establish a country seat. Chew concurred with the prevailing taste to the point of naming his country seat after Cliveden, country seat of the late Frederick Louis, Prince of Wales, and father of George III. Kew Palace, moreover, which William Kent designed for the same Prince of Wales around the middle of the 18th century, was the inspiration for Cliveden's design. An engraving of Kew Palace from *Gentleman's Magazine* of August 1763 is among the architectural drawings in the Chew papers.

But while these 18th-century Philadelphians often took their ideas from English country houses, they used native stone, indigenous wood, and locally baked brick, along with their own good taste to make their houses a distinct product of the Philadelphia area. The local master builders, as the Bridenbaughs put it, "breathed life into the dead forms of the manuals by means of their active and vigorous concepts of function, structure and material." These men did unconsciously what Emerson told a later generation of architects to do:

> Study with hope and love the precise thing to be done by him, considering the climate, the soil, the length of the day, the wants of the people, the habit and form of government.

Chew started to build Cliveden in 1764 on 11 acres of land he purchased for £650. Cliveden's master carpenter was Jacob Knor who was also the carpenter for the main building of Germantown Academy (1760). Another Germantown craftsman John Hesser was the mason, and some of the finer stone cutting was done by Caspar Guyer. How much Knor had to do with the design of the house is not known but Cliveden seems to have been mainly Chew's creation. A number of plans and elevations for it survive and some of them are certainly by Chew who, in any case, took a very personal interest in the construction of his house. Most of the houses erected in the area around Philadelphia in the 1760s and 1770s reflected to an extraordinary degree the tastes and interests of their owners. "To their preoccupation with music and the theater and their patronage of education, literature and painting," as the Bridenbaughs put it, "these gentlemen of leisure and experience now added an intelligent and very personal interest in the style and process of building." They "either became amateur architects themselves or, more usually,

Profile of Benjamin Chew.

(Top) The handsome entrance hall is separated from the narrower stair hall by a columnar screen. It has been suggested by Nancy Halverson Schless that the inverted T shape of Cliveden's plan was probably derived from one of Colen Campbell's own unexecuted designs illustrated in his Vitruvius Britannicus (volume 2, 1717). (Above) The Doric entablature contributes to the dignity of the entrance hall.

commissioned master builders to construct homes for them in accordance with their own ideas or what they had seen on their travels."

Private Equipages and Cosmopolitan Tastes

Philadelphia itself was less than a century old when Chew built Cliveden but in population it was the largest community in America. Its literary and artistic life was as active as its scientific life. It led the colonies in medicine and law. Its craftsmanship was famed throughout the colonies and its tolerance hardly less so. In 1786 Jefferson noted that "The city of London, tho' handsomer than Paris, is not so handsome as Philadelphia."

But while these wealthy Philadelphians were not averse to equipping themselves with fashionable appurtenances in their town and country houses, the Quaker tradition restrained them from too great a show of luxurious living. Chew's Quaker background is often apparent. When he ordered the urns for the roof of Cliveden from Bristol, England, he wrote his Quaker neighbor William Fisher in December 1766:

> I have shown the pattern of the urns sent over by Mr. Pennington to the knowing ones among us and have fixed on No. 2 only that it is to have little or no carve work as most suitable to the plainness of my building.

And in 1773 Josiah Quincy, who did not approve of the high living of the Carolina planters, noted that:

> The Philadelphians in respect of the bounty and decency of table are an example to the world, especially the American: with the means of profusion, they are not luxurious; with the bounties of earth and sea, they are not riotous; with the riches of commerce and industry they avoid even the appearance of epicurean splendor and parade.

One hallmark of Philadelphia's upper gentry, however, was their "private equipages." A list published just before the Revolution numbers 84 families with such equipages and Benjamin Chew was among the eight exalted coach owners.

The Philadelphians were probably the most traveled and cosmopolitan of the colonists. Study in England and the Grand Tour were almost invariably a part of the education of the "scions of Philadelphia wealth and gentility." When attending the First Continental Congress in 1774 John Adams noted this cosmopolitan aspect of Philadelphians and compared it with "the want of address" in his fellow Bostonians.

He comments on the "freedom of ease and behaviour" of the "nobles of Pennsylvania," and attributes the Bostonian's lack of the "exterior and superficial accomplishments of gentlemen" to the "little intercourse we have with strangers, and . . . our experience in the world."

There could not be a better example of the cosmopolitan and exemplary gentry of Philadelphia than Benjamin Chew. His cultivated tastes were tempered by his Quaker background. He read the classics, collected a library, and took a great interest in his gardens and orchards as most Philadelphians did. Cliveden boasts the only 18th-century law library that survives in its original setting. In addition to Benjamin Chew's books, it includes those of his son and grandson. Cliveden's extensive grounds, moreover, are still shaded by trees and decorated by marble statuary that were placed there by Benjamin Chew. The entire composition—stone house and tree-filled grounds—is a splendid remnant of Penn's "green countrie towne."

Benjamin Chew's finished mansion cost £4/718/12/3. The family moved in an 1767, and while they retained their townhouse, Cliveden was often the pre-Revolutionary setting for the Chews' illustrious company. Washington and Adams undoubtedly dined there. In October 1774, Adams' diary records a dinner with "Mr. Chew, Chief Justice of the Province," and although the entry probably refers to the Chew's townhouse, it is a good indication of how Benjamin Chew and his family lived:

> We were shown into a grand entry and stair-case, and into an elegant and most magnificent chamber, until dinner. The furniture was all rich. Turtle, and every other thing, flummery, jellies, sweetmeats of twenty sorts, trifles, whipped sillabub, floating island, fools etc. and then a dessert of fruits, raisins, almonds, pears, peaches, Wines most excellent and admirable. I drank Madeira at a great rate, and found no inconvenience in it. . . .

But the festivities were not to last for long. In July of 1777, Chew and Governor John Penn along with other Crown office holders, were "enlarged upon parole" in "the back country" of New Jersey. Less than a year later Chew was released and permitted to return to Philadelphia. But while he was away Cliveden had been the scene of important fighting during the Battle of Germantown and suffered what might have been its destruction.

Cliveden was damaged but not destroyed. When Chew returned home, he found his country house "an absolute

The Philadelphia sofa and rococo looking glass in the parlor have been in the Chew family since the 18th century.

(Above) The imposing fireplace, mantel, and projecting chimney breast in the parlor are flanked by two small rococo looking glasses. (Right) Detail of the marble-faced parlor fireplace. There is a Philadelphia sideboard in the parlor with a marble top that matches the marble of the fireplace.

(Opposite page) The fireplace wall in the dining room is paneled in an early 18th-century style. The dining room furniture is of the Federal period.

wreck, and materials are not to be had to keep out the weather." He sold the property in 1779 but repurchased it in 1798 and it remained in the family until the National Trust acquired it in 1972.

Palladian Palace to Fieldstone Vernacular

Chew may have used Kent's Palladian Palace at Kew as the starting point for the design of his country seat, but he went on from there and the final result bears little resemblance to the English palace. No one could possibly mistake Cliveden for anything but a Philadelphia house constructed some time before the Revolution. Its Palladianism is a colonial interpretation of Palladio's theories—an elegant Grandma Moses of Palladian architecture if you will—with its roof urns, its baroque dormers, its Doric doorway and its classic pediment crowning the central bay. Cliveden's ashlar facade is of native gray Germantown stone, its sides of stucco, and its back of pointed fieldstone as described by the Swedish botanist Peter Kalm when he visited Germantown in 1748:

> Most of the houses were built of the stone which is mixed with glimmer, and found every where towards *Philadelphia*, but is more scarce further on. . . . Each house had a fine garden.

While Cliveden belongs to the period of Philadelphia's greatest colonial houses which, as Professor Robert C. Smith puts it, "offer the invigorating contrast of Palladian sobriety side by side with baroque or rococo details of decoration," it still suggests the old fieldstone vernacular.

There is an almost complete record of the building of Cliveden among the vast collection of family papers gathered by the Chews over the centuries (some 200,000 manuscript pages with half dating before 1830). They comprise an architectural and cultural story that is unique among surviving 18th-century Delaware Valley houses. The building accounts include bills for every detail of Cliveden's construction. There are bills listing such items as "for painting a carpet 22 yds," "for painting 4 bettsteads," and for "5-12 bushels of hair." There are bills from the master carpenter, the stone mason, the carvers, among others. There are architectural drawings that show the evolution of Cliveden from the engraving of Kew Palace to the finished house.

Chew made three plans for Cliveden. The five-part Palladian plan of Kew was first cut down to a three-part Palladian house. Another drawing further reduced the three stories to two. The dependencies were originally placed on either side of the main block and later set back to form a

court at the rear of the house. The gabled end is to the front in many of the drawings although as finally built, the main house has its gables at the sides as in most colonial houses. The fully developed pediments in its end gables are all that Cliveden retains of the Kew model.

Cliveden's front door leads into one of the most imposing spaces in colonial architecture—an entrance hall (16 x 27 feet or 4.8 x 8.2m) that not only impressed 18th-century visitors but has impressed many since. Lighted by two windows flanking the doorway, it is separated from the narrower stair hall by a screen of four Doric columns which with their entablature repeat the classic details of the front door. In the Chew papers is a bill dated December 1766 for "glueing and fluting 116 ft. of columns" of the Doric entablature. There are two small square rooms on either side of the entrance hall and two larger rooms—the parlor and dining room—on either side of the stair hall in the rear. The arrangement of the Cliveden rooms is based on Georgian precedent and obviously planned for a gentleman of wealth and importance.

Cliveden must have served admirably as the notable social center that it was. This is where Benjamin Chew's son and daughters often entertained.

Don't do anything that can't be undone

From almost the beginning the Chew restoration philosophy has been to retain as much as possible of Benjamin Chew's era and succeeding generations of Chews have gone to extraordinary lengths to carry out that objective. Some time before 1856 a two-story addition was put on the back of the house in such a way that it left the exterior wall of the 18th-century house intact. Even a pair of outside shutters are still in place. The original pedimented window on the stair landing was replaced by a mirrored door leading to the addition. A bathroom was suspended on columns so that light could still come into the parlor below. It probably was, as Cliveden administrator Raymond Shepherd says, "one of the most expensive bathrooms ever installed." But all the additions could be removed with little difficulty leaving the 18th-century house as it was when Benjamin Chew built it. No 20th-century preservationist could find fault with the preservation practices of those 19th-century Chews. *Don't do anything that can't be undone* is one of the main tenets of today's preservationists.

The Chews were no less protective of the 18th-century interiors of Cliveden. The plaster walls were not painted until about 30 years ago because that is the way Benjamin Chew knew them and neither did they want to disturb the cannon ball scars left by the Battle of Germantown. A section of the wall in one bedroom has always been left unpainted so as not to cover up a British soldier's drawing of his girl in blood done during Cliveden's occupation by the British.

The National Trust is essentially carrying on a Chew philosophy of preservation while emphasizing Cliveden's continuing history as a house—a house that reflects the lives of the later as well as the early generations who lived there. Cliveden is that rarity in America—a house that has been lived in by one family for 200 years. It represents a case study of careful and thoughtful preservation throughout those 200 years. That it survives at all is remarkable and the Trust is aware that it should tread lightly. We know very little about houses such as Cliveden. Most of them have disappeared. That in itself makes its continuing preservation of paramount importance.

The decisions as to whether to leave things as they are or return them to another period are not always easy. The Trust hopes to reproduce the original "graining" of the staircase, for example. Although it was not grained when they took over the house, there was plenty of precedence for such a decision: it had been regrained by three generations of Chews.

Before anything was done, family records, inventories, photographs, as well as outside sources were studied. Comparisons were made with other houses of approximately the same age. In one instance, a family photograph and a comparison with other Germantown stone houses helped determine the kind and color of mortar to use when repointing Cliveden's facade. The photograph taken on the front steps of Cliveden in 1871 clearly showed raised mortar that was absolutely white, which was consistent with the other houses studied.

A paint analysis was made of all painted surfaces inside and out. Whenever a paint surface is restored both prime and finished coats are tied in with the Munsell color system.

Before and after any work is done on the inside or outside of the house it is photographed and described. This is done in order to provide any future restorer with sufficient evidence to return the house to another period just as the Chews did when they added the 19th-century wing. "Philosophies change," as Shepherd puts it, "what is trash in one period is valuable in another." The Trust also keeps a description of all materials used in restoring anything from paint to stone work along with an explanation of why they were used.

An unrestored sample is left wherever possible. In one of Cliveden's bedrooms a section of the wall has been left unpainted and a piece of the wallpaper that was put on 25 years ago has been saved so that a future restorer can choose his period and have the evidence to re-create it.

Among the 18th-century furnishings at Cliveden are outstanding pieces by Philadelphia craftsmen, some of which are undoubtedly those admired by John Adams. There is a superb sofa in the parlor made by Thomas Affleck for Governor John Penn which was probably purchased by Chew when he bought Penn's townhouse on Third Street in 1771. Cliveden also boasts a serpentine chest bearing the label of its maker Jonathan Gostelowe, which is matched by a notation of cash expenditure for £6/13/9 on February 12, 1772, and signed "J. Gostelowe." Carved rococo looking glasses by Philadelphia craftsman James Reynolds are

The painting of Cliveden during the 1777 Battle of Germantown was done by E.L. Henry long after the event. It hangs in the entrance hall.

also among Cliveden's fine assemblage of 18th-century furnishings. Six of these looking glasses are known to exist and five are at Cliveden.

A file compiled for every object at Cliveden includes a description, a photograph, and a conservation report. Such information should go a long way toward providing the future with what Shepherd calls "a chance to prove us wrong."

One Well-Bred Noble of the Land

"If men lived like men indeed," as Ruskin said, "their houses would be temples—temples which we should hardly dare to injure." Six generations of Chews believed this. They recognized what Ruskin called "the sanctity in a good man's house" and it seems likely that Benjamin Chew's many friends—Philadelphia's "men of distinction" as well as foreign visitors—would agree. The Duc

de la Rochefaucauld Liancourt who was in Philadelphia in the 1790s, writes on December 5, 1794:

> Received a call from Mr. B. Chew. The bearing, the manners of this man continue to please me very much. . . . We talked about the negroes. He rather seems to me to have some of the prejudices common to owners of slaves, but in reality not many, and in his conversation he shows a great depth of kindness and naturalness. . . .

A year after his death, Joseph Dennie's *Port Folio*, the leading American literary periodical, had this to say of Benjamin Chew:

> . . . In addition to his more substantial qualities and acquirements, Mr. Chew's taste was cultivated and refined, his conversation easy and animated, his deport-

ment graceful and pleasing, and his will not infrequently playful and sparkling. His elevated rank in society, the style of affluence in which he lived, and the public stations which he so long continued to fill, led him of necessity into frequent entertainments. On these occasions the most sprightly and engaging display of convivial qualities was tempered by an observance of the strictest decorum. Hence he knew how to partake of the pleasures and mingle in all the revelry of the table, without either descending from his dignity or forfeiting for a moment his title to respect.

. . . Were titles and honors hereditary in the United States, a stranger on entering Mr. Chew's dwelling and being personally introduced to him in the bosom of his family, would have been ready to exclaim "This is one of the ancient and well bred nobles of the land."

Palladian England and Federal America

Chiswick

Castletown

Andrea Palladio, the 16th-century architect who designed his lovely villas for the noble families of the Veneto, has probably influenced more buildings throughout the Western world than anyone else. In Anglo-Saxon countries alone Palladian houses range from such small country dwellings as Thomas Jefferson's simple Edgemont outside of Charlottesville, Virginia, or Lord Burlington's miniature villa at Chiswick to such grandiose country seats as Castletown in Ireland. It may seem strange that Palladian ideals have had their greatest appeal in the Anglo-Saxon world, but as Professor Nikolaus Pevsner points out, Palladian "orders" are reasonable and rationalism is an Anglo-Saxon trait. Just as the Anglo-Irish aristocracy found an answer in Palladio's theories so did Thomas Jefferson's democracy, although their answers were understandably different. The Irish Palladian house was pompous and far more impressive in size than its American counterpart. To Jefferson the Palladian house was symbolic of a new nation's aspirations.

Inigo Jones first introduced England to Palladian ideas early in the 17th century but it was under the patronage of Lord Burlington in the 18th century that the Italian architect's theories really captured the Anglo-Saxon imagination. The quality of civilization reveals itself best in the arts and perhaps this was particularly true of architecture and literature in England's Augustan age. Like the heroic couplet, the Palladian villa is intellectual not emotional. And as James S. Ackerman has noted, there was a cerebral, abstract quality in Palladio that appealed to a similar quality in Burlington as well as his fellow countrymen who took so eagerly to his Palladian suggestion. It was not by chance then that Lord Burlington with his Palladian villa and Alexander Pope with his Augustan lines set the pattern for English taste for the 18th century.

Burlington, the English noble, and Jefferson, the American democrat, were intellectual theorists, as Peter Quennell, says of Pope, but their theories would not have carried much weight had they not also been equisitely accomplished artists who molded the discordant materials of life into forms of classic elegance.

America after the Revolution was no longer just another corner of the Kingdom. Its people thought of themselves as Americans rather than Virginians, Carolinians, Pennsylvanians, or New Englanders, and they consciously looked for an architecture to express their common values. They couldn't, however, completely escape their Anglo-Saxon background. For all his professed love of the French, Jefferson had more in common with such Palladian-minded Englishmen as Lord Burlington. The villas Jefferson designed for himself and his southern neighbors were inspired by many of the same motives that inspired Lord Burlington.

The sporadic Pallandianism of pre-Revolutionary days (Drayton Hall and Cliveden in the previous section for example) was directly, if sometimes primitively, derived from England's Palladian revival. But in the postwar period such a man as Jefferson looked squarely at the rationalism of Palladio as an expression of the freedom of thought and imagination of American democracy. Palladio's buildings are "sober and disciplined," in the words of Rudolf Wittkower, and at the same time "noble and grand." Jefferson believed in the

Edgemont

The Octagon

beauty of discipline, the wisdom of rule by law rather than men. Palladio himself thought his principles derived from eternally valid natural laws and so did Jefferson.

But while those postwar Americans found one architectural answer (and by far the most enduring one) in the Palladianism of Jefferson, they found another in the Adamesque-Federal style that derived from Robert Adam's ideas. The latter was particularly the style of the mercantile class who came to the fore after the Revolution and whose wealth made possible the Adamesque-Federal townhouses in Boston, Salem, New York, and even the new Federal city on the Potomac. This was where William Thornton designed the Octagon for Virginia aristocrat John Tayloe III who also "engaged in the manufacture of iron, in ship-building, and in various other enterprises." The style that Adam evolved, however, had a lot in common with Burlington's Palladianism although it was more delicate in conception.

It was mainly the plantation owners, not surprisingly, who patterned their dwellings after the Palladian villa, which had been designed for an economic and social situation nearly identical to their own. Palladio's clients, as Ackerman has pointed out, "were country gentry in much the same way that British squires and American plantation owners were. The country landowner in eighteenth-century Anglo-Saxon culture, like his predecessor in the Veneto of the sixteenth century, was economically tied to the land as overseer of the crops and the herds, but a classical education and the ambitions of a Humanist gave him city tastes."

The restored Palladian houses in this section should reveal to a modern eye why Palladio's ideas have been such a long-lasting influence in the Anglo-Saxon world. The reasonableness of the antique orders were to Palladio, as to Burlington and Jefferson, the expression of a law of nature in architectural terms. They were, moreover, manifestations of the innate taste of humanity in general. The noble grandeur of Castletown, the gemlike perfection of Chiswick, and the unaffected charm of Edgemont are three entirely different expressions of the Palladian spirit and that innate taste.

That Palladian villas and Adamesque-Federal townhouses are a more felicitous answer to living than say the pseudo-colonial development house or the impersonal apartment in a faceless high-rise is a fact with which the family living in the beautifully restored Jefferson-designed Edgemont would agree.

While three of the houses in this section have been restored as museums to reflect an early period in their history, they are also partly used for other related purposes. The ground floor of Lord Burlington's villa at Chiswick is the setting for architectural exhibitions relating to the villa and its restoration; Castletown serves as headquarters for the Irish Georgian Society; and a second-floor wing of the Octagon is used as an exhibition gallery. The fourth, Jefferson's Edgemont, has been adapted for modern living while retaining the original intent of its architect. Edgemont is that fortunate house still intimately in touch with the daily activities of those who live in its rooms. And houses, as Francis Bacon tells us in his *Essay on Building*, "are built to live in not to look on."

Chiswick
Near London, England

The portico.

The head not the heart, held the easy flow of the language and the precise unfolding of the thought within the confines of the heroic couplet.   James S. Ackerman

Lord Burlington is not an easy man to know. He wrote few letters. He was reticent, almost secretive. Neither did his contemporaries have much to say about the man, although they admired him for his patronage of the arts, for his collections, for his taste, and for his genius. And above all they admired his houses and his influence on 18th-century architecture. The Palladian movement in England, as Sir John Summerson has pointed out, "could hardly have attained the momentum it did without the intervention of one particular personality whose name soon became identified with the movement—the Earl of Burlington." We know his style but not his heart.

He was a true classicist—dignified, remote, detached, restrained, lacking emotion—the complete opposite of the romantic exuberance of the earlier Elizabethans or the later Victorians. And yet Burlington—like Alexander Pope, his neighbor at Chiswick and confrere in taste-making—had his romantic side. Pope's poetry and Burlington's architecture are the essence of classicism, but their gardens were pure romanticism. Pope had his fanciful grottos and Burlington his cascades and serpentine paths—"prospects to excite not only the eye but the imagination." It was, in fact, these two men—Pope, the advocate of reason, and Burlington, the advocate of the cubic simplicity of Palladian architecture—who introduced the first picturesque gardens to England.

To learn something about Lord Burlington, we should take our cue from Pope. "I need not be put in mind of you," he wrote to Burlington, "by the traces of your art, your building or your gardens: but so it is that a good writer is not more remembered by his works, than you by yours." It is, then, from his building and his art that we can best discover this 18th-century prophet of taste and architecture. And the villa at Chiswick designed by Burlington for his own use might be expected to be pecu-

liarly personal in its expression of his taste. It is also expressive of the spirit of an age in which architecture has rightly been called the mistress-art.

Burlington believed, as Jefferson did later in the century, that Palladio's rules of architecture were somehow the answer to the good life—that finely proportioned buildings and beautifully laid-out gardens had a spiritual and philosophic, as well as esthetic, value. Palladian architects and Augustan poets shared the same theoretical concepts.

Burlington, Belov'd of Ev'ry Muse

Richard Boyle, Third Earl of Burlington, was 10 years old in 1704 when he succeeded to his title and inherited estates in Ireland and Yorkshire, at Chiswick and in London. The arts appealed to the young lord—poetry, music, painting, sculpture, and architecture. "Burlington, belov'd of ev'ry Muse," is how the poet John Gay put it.

In 1714 he made his first Grand Tour to the continent—an important part of the education of any well-born young gentleman of wealth—and shortly after his return to England he acquired the two folios that were to make architecture the particular focus of his future development: Colen Campbell's first volume of *Vitruvius Britannicus*, and Nicolas Dubois' translation of Giacomo Leoni's four-volume treatise on *The Architecture of A. Palladio.* Campbell intended to launch a new style of architecture in England by reviving what he called "the antique simplicity," and reverting to the authority of Inigo Jones. This appealed to Burlington who set out to make himself the patron of the new style.

In a letter Pope wrote in 1716 to the portrait painter Charles Jervas he says:

> my Lord Burlington desires you may be put in mind of him. His gardens flourish, his structures rise, his pictures arrive, and (what is far nobler and more valuable than all) his own good qualities daily extend themselves to all about him.

And so we can assume that Burlington's way of life was taking shape. His first architectural venture was to employ Colen

The main or east front faces a square courtyard. The elaborate double staircase leads to the portico and is flanked by statues of Palladio on the left and Inigo Jones on the right. The two-story portico is surrounded by Corinthian columns at the villa's main level. The chimney stacks on either side of the lead-covered octagonal dome are imitation obelisks.

The double staircase on the garden (west) side was reconstructed on its original foundation. The three Palladian windows are like the restored windows on the villa's north and south sides. The central window opens to form a doorway into the gallery. The villa never had gutters or rainwater pipes, in keeping with Palladian models, but a concealed gutter was added during the restoration for practical purposes.

Campbell to remodel Burlington House, the townhouse his grandfather had built in Picadilly. He was also apparently adding to the Jacobean Chiswick House which he had inherited and was later to be replaced by the famous villa, and he was designing a Palladian Bagnio for the Chiswick garden. Colen Campbell included an engraving of the Bagnio in the third volume of his *Vitruvius Britannicus* and described it as "the first Essay of his Lordship's happy invention."

When Burlington set out on his second cultural tour in 1719 he knew exactly what he wanted to do—study Palladio's buildings at first hand. And when he returned he brought back not only the first of many copies of Palladio's book that were to become part of his library, but also the versatile Yorkshireman William Kent who was to become part of his life. Thus "the Apollo of art," as Horace Walpole put it, "found a proper priest in the person of Mr. Kent."

Kent was a painter when Burlington discovered him. He had spent some time in Italy where he studied painting and also learned to denounce the art and architecture of his native land or, as he called it, the "damned gusto that has been with us for this sixty years past." The "damned gusto," of course, referred to the near-baroque architecture perpetrated by such architects as Vanbrugh and the great Sir Chistopher Wren. Kent was outspoken and uninhibited, quite the opposite of the cool impassive Burlington. It must have been an extraordinary relationship—Kent, the unrestrained Yorkshireman of humble birth who "often gave his orders when he was full of claret" and spent much of his time lolling under the trees at Chiswick consoling himself with "syllabubs, damsels, and other benefits of nature," and the taciturn noble patron who was content to play his harpsichord in his Chiswick library. While Burlington "lacked finesse but had learning, Kent lacked depth but abounded in fertile imagination," which, as James Lees-Milne has suggested, probably accounts for the long productive relationship that had such far-reaching consequences for architecture as well as landscaped gardens.

Kent became something of a rage in London soon after Burlington installed him at Burlington House where he was to remain until he was transferred to the Burlington family vault. Kent was a much sought-after decorator who could paint a ceiling, design a chimney-piece, a chair, a garden, or a dress with equal skill. Horace Walpole tells us that:

> two great ladies prevailed on him to make designs for their birthday-gowns. The one dressed in a petticoat decorated with columns of the five orders; the other

like a bronze in a copper-coloured satin with ornaments of gold.

Kent, in Sir John Summerson's words, was "the Palladians' star performer."

It was after returning from his second Grand Tour at the end of 1719 that Burlington, with Kent as his collaborator, embarked on his plan to continue the Palladian ideas that Inigo Jones had begun in the previous century. He assembled a group of artists and architects who shared his convictions, or to whom he imparted his ideas, and soon became the central figure of the neo-Palladian vogue that for the next 50 years added so many classic houses and romantic landscapes to the British countryside.

In 1721 Burlington married Lady Dorothy Savile, the daughter of the second Marquess of Halifax and the possesser of a fiery temper. When Lady Burlington died at Chiswick, Horace Walpole informs us that even on her deathbed "in the Corner room in the new House hung with Brussels tapestry," beneath the portraits of herself, the Duchess of Somerset, and Pope, the irascible lady "breaks out all over in—curses and blasphemies."

A Temple of the Arts

In the copy of *Palladio* Burlington brought back from Vicenza he had noted his impression of the 16th-century architects's famous Villa Capra (the Rotonda) that served as the general plan for the villa at Chiswick:

> This is the only house in Vicenza that is quite finished by Palladio, and one plainly sees, by the ornaments and exquisite taste that is in the most minute part of it, that he executed his design without restraint.

After a fire destroyed parts of the old Jacobean house at Chiswick, Burlington decided to start the new villa. It was not intended to be a substitute for the old house to which it was connected by a link building, but to serve as a place in which to entertain his friends and to house his ever-increasing collections of art and books—a place of the spirit rather than the flesh.

It is a mistake to think of the Chiswick villa as a replica of Palladio's Rotonda. While Burlington used the design of the Rotonda as his starting point, he introduced many entirely new and personal elements. Actually the only common denominator in the two plans is a central room under a dome with stairways in the angles. Burlington has replaced the Villa Rotonda's circular central hall with an octagonal one. The form of the Chiswick dome also differs from the Rotonda's. It is higher and its base is penetrated by four large Roman segmen-

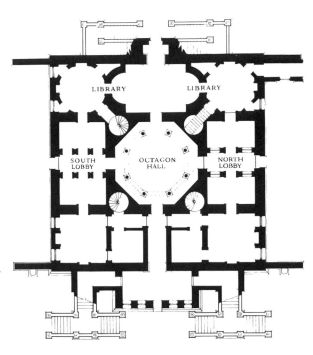

Ground floor plan.

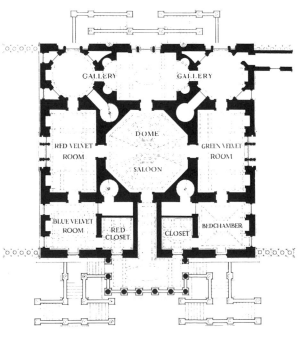

First floor plan.

tal windows, which provide the central room with plenty of light and thereby counteract the usual criticism of lack of light in the symmetrical Palladian plan. The central room of Palladio's Rotonda, moreover, is approached through four passages from four identical porticos. Burlington's octagonal central domed room is approached through a single portico and one paneled passage. There is also a variety of room shapes at Chiswick not to be found in the Rotonda. The latter is symmetrical around both north-south and east-west axes. The Chiswick plan is symmetrical only around the main axis, which runs through the house from portico to garden.

Burlington's experimentation with space extended to the ceilings where he introduced domes and half-domes coffered in the style of Roman public buildings. The variety of these Roman ceilings adds to the general effect of richness and grandeur without overpowering the villa's small scale. It is no wonder that Burlington's play upon spatial forms has been called his most individual contribution to British architecture.

The decorative elements in the villa's rooms (borrowed from Palladio, Scamozzi, and Inigo Jones) probably were the work of Kent as was much of the garden with its temples, statues, cascades, and serpentine paths. Contemporary documents, however, make it clear that Burlington was responsible for the main outline of the villa and most of the interior. In any case, the minuteness of the scale of the rooms and the grandeur of their baroque and mannerist elements are combined with extraordinary skill and taste and are unlike anything else Italian or English. In 1732 Sir Thomas Robinson reported that "both within and without it is a fine bijou, and much beyond anything of the villa kind I ever saw in my life." Horace Walpole admired the Chiswick villa as a "model of taste" but he did find fault with some of the interior treatment as having "too many correspondent doors in spaces so contracted; chimneys between windows, and, which is worse, windows between chimneys." Such arrangements, however, were not unusual in the symmetrical Palladian plan. The contemporary architect Robert Morris stated that uniformity was essential to interiors and should determine the position and number of doors. If real doors were out of the question, false ones should be introduced.

Today's visitor to Lord Burlington's miniature villa on the Thames finds it a subtle experience to pass from one space into another—from the high central domed saloon with its richly decorated tiers of octagonal panels decreasing in size as they near the top, through one of its four pedimented

(Above) The Blue Velvet Room's doorways with their carved and gilded pediments are surmounted by round panels containing a portrait of Pope painted by Kent on the left and one of Inigo Jones by Dobson on the right. The ceiling is one of the most elaborate in the villa.

(Opposite page) In the center of the Blue Velvet Room ceiling is an allegorical figure of Architecture crowned with a Corinthian capital and flanked by cherubs carrying drawing instruments.

(Top) The main rectangular section of the three-part gallery has apses at each end leading into two tribunes, one circular, the other octagonal. On the inner wall are two reproductions of the gallery's original mirrors. The original porphyry vases flank the Palladian window. The door on the right leads into the domed saloon. (Above) The gallery's octagonal section is less than 15 feet (4.6m) in diameter but contains six doors, a window, and a chimney-piece with a carved overmantel and mirror, as well as decoration in its upper part.

doors into the gallery with its painted ceiling and long vista, and then into the red, green, and blue rooms along the periphery with their intense colors and opulent ceilings. "Oh, those English, with their placid exteriors and all that passion underneath," is how the restored villa struck English author Ian Nairn. In any case the theatrical effect of the Chiswick interiors are the first example of the happy collaboration between Burlington and Kent.

Restoration of Chiswick's Ordered Opulence

After the death of Lord Burlington in 1753, the estate went to the husband of his daughter, Lord Hartington, later the fourth Duke of Devonshire. In 1788 the fifth Duke employed James Wyatt to demolish the Jacobean mansion and enlarge the villa. Two wings designed to harmonize with it were added on the north and south sides.

During this period the beautiful Georgiana, Duchess of Devonshire, gave many of her celebrated parties at the villa, several Tsars of Russia were entertained there, and the Prince of Wales (later King Edward VII) spent numerous summers there. The Chiswick story, in other words, had become more social than architectural.

Eventually in 1892 the Chiswick art treasures were moved to Chatsworth and other Devonshire family seats. The house became a private lunatic asylum and one can't help wondering what effect all those chaste proportions and baroque details had on the lunatics.

In 1928 when the estate was about to be acquired for a building development, it was purchased by the Middlesex County Council and subsequently handed over to the Ministry of Public Building and Works (now the Department of the Environment), which has been responsible for its meticulous restoration and continuing preservation.

Fortunately for architecture if not for society the Wyatt wings were found to be in such a state of disrepair they were removed. It was then possible to restore the original character of the villa that did so much to proliferate England's Palladian architecture and make it an idiom of strength. No less a Palladian than Thomas Jefferson, incidentally, deplored the Wyatt wings which he felt spoiled the effect of the miniature villa.

The Palladian windows on the north and south sides had been removed for the Wyatt additions but enough evidence was found in the structure and in documentary sources to make their accurate restoration possible. The staircase on the garden side had also been demolished during the 18th-century alterations but again it was possible to accurately restore it with the aid of contemporary illustrations and the discovery of much of its carved stonework which had been re-used elsewhere. A drawing by Burlington of the chimney stacks was used as a basis for their reconstruction.

The tall octagonal domed saloon has been scrupulously restored to its 18th-century opulence. On each wall is a large picture in an ornate gilded frame from Lord Burlington's original collection. Classical busts on brackets between the doorways are replacements of the originals. The domed saloon is flanked by identically shaped rectangular spaces—the Red Velvet Room on one side and the Green Velvet Room on the other, names inspired by their original velvet wallcoverings. Flock paper was used in the restored rooms to simulate the velvet. These rooms are lighted by the tall Palladian windows that were restored after removal of the Wyatt wings.

The Blue Velvet Room—a small square room in the corner left of the entrance—has one of the most elaborate ceilings in the villa resting on richly ornamented console brackets. Its three doorways all have carved and gilded pediments surmounted by round panels supported by cherubs and containing paintings of Inigo Jones and Pope. The latter was done by Kent as, presumably, was the paneled ceiling with its decorations of masks and cherubs on a blue-and-gold background.

The gallery on the garden side, unlike anything in Palladio's Rotonda, is an apsed rectangular space flanked by a circular section at one end and an octagonal one at the opposite end. The Chiswick gallery gains in grandeur what it lacks in size (the circular section is only 15 feet, or 4.5m, in diameter) by its division into three parts with a long view through the arches from one end to the other. Doorways, niches, statues have all been scaled down to fit the small space. The ceiling in the rectangular central portion is divided by richly decorated beams into nine panels. Eight of them are conventional designs by Kent. The central panel—a painting of warriors resting in an Italian landscape—was attributed in early documents to Veronese but it is more likely a copy of a work by that artist scaled down to fit the panel. A large Palladian window on the outer wall leads to the restored garden staircase.

Although furniture was never plentiful in the ordered opulence of Palladian interiors, there was obviously something to sit on in Chiswick's gallery. In one of many letters Lady Burlington wrote to her lord about the decoration of the rooms, she discusses fabrics for the gallery cushions. Instead of the velvet that had been suggested, she thought

William Kent's sketch of the villa's portico.

The Inigo Jones gateway north of the villa was brought there in 1736 from Beaufort House in Chelsea and is inscribed with these lines by Pope: I was brought from Chelsea last year / Batter'd with wind and weather; / Inigo Jones put me together; / Sir Hans Sloane let me alone; / Burlington brought me hither.

a rich damask would be as handsome and less expensive. Besides, she adds, "in any velvet that is much used, there will be always the print of people's sitting." In the end she selected a velvet damask, "The ground is gold colour, & ye flowers a bright crimson."

When furniture did exist in Palladian interiors it was architectural in character and usually designed for its particular place as another dimension of the decorative interior details. Kent undoubtedly designed most of the Chiswick furniture.

The raised main floor of the Chiswick villa with its intercommunicating rooms—the Italian *piano nobile*—is where Burlington entertained and displayed his art. His own private domain was on the ground floor. It was probably in his library under the gallery that he read proofs of Pope's *Dunciad*, which he had offered to submit to a lawyer so that the poet would not be open to charges of libel. Burlington's large library included the work of many poets as well as his illustrated volumes on architecture, ancient and modern. In one of his two copies of Inigo Jones' *Vitruvius*, Burlington wrote: "This book belonged to Inigo Jones and the notes are of his hand writing."

The restored ground-floor area is used for exhibitions of architectural drawings from the Burlington-Devonshire collections formed by Lord Burlington and housed partly at Chatsworth and partly at the Royal Institute of British Architects. These vast collections provided much of the documentary evidence for restoring the villa.

Too Large to Hang on a Watch

Lord Burlington's fine bijou, in all its regained splendor, makes it easy to understand why it sometimes amazed and sometimes enchanted his contemporaries. "I assure you," Pope writes Burlington in 1732, "Chiswick has been to me the finest thing this glorious sun has shin'd upon." Sir John Clerk thought that it was "rather curious than convenient." And Lord Hervey could only exclaim, "House! Do you call it a house? Why! it is too little to live in, and too large to hang on one's watch."

Lord Burlington built his ornamental villa at the height of the Augustan age. Pepys had died in 1703, Boswell was not born until 1740, and Pope was preeminently the poet of the age just as Burlington was its architect-patron. Both molded the discordant materials of life to forms of classic elegance. It was Burlington who is most often credited with the taste that brought Augustan domestic building to the height of splendor and the villa at Chiswick is, as Horace Walpole called it,

"his model of taste."

After the middle of the century there was a reaction to Burlington's influence, and while lesser architects continued to build Palladian houses in England they misunderstood the spirit of Burlington's creation. They failed to comprehend that the house, as Burlington developed it, was an object within the landscape. Pope and Burlington between them have rightly been given credit for inspiring the enthusiasm for landscape gardening and rural beautifying which not only gave so many great houses their serene undulating parks but transformed the whole English countryside.

It was Pope who, while paying tribute to Burlington's taste, predicted the vulgarization of his style. He writes in his *Epistle to Lord Burlington* published in 1731:

> You show us, Rome was glorious, not profuse,
> And pompous buildings once were things of use.
> Yet shall (my Lord) your just, your noble rules
> Fill half the land with imitating fools:
> Who random drawings from your sheets shall take,
> And of one beauty many blunders make;
> Load some vain church with old theatric state,
> Turn arcs of triumph to a garden gate;
> Reverse your ornaments, and hang them all
> On some patched dog-hole eked with ends of wall;
> Then clap four slices of pilaster on't,
> That, laced with bits of rustic, makes a front.
> Shall call the winds through long arcades to roar,
> Proud to catch cold at a Venetian door;
> Conscious they act a true Palladian part,
> And, if they starve, they starve by rules of art.

The world of Burlington and Pope was one of order, grace, dignity, enlightenment, and intellect. The readers of Pope's poetry would have been ashamed, as Peter Quennell has pointed out, "had they failed to recognize one of the classical references with which he winged his modern satires." A classical education and the Grand Tour undoubtedly played a major role in developing English artistic taste in circles where social distinction and political importance predominated. Nor had taste yet been vitiated by mass production. The middle classes followed the manners and morals of the nobility and gentry just as they followed their taste in architecture, in furniture and furnishings. There was a steady accumula-

tion of large estates and a tremendous amount of building, much of which was by no means picayune. Blenheim was designed to rival Versailles. Defoe, in his *Tour Thro' the Whole Island of Great Britain* (1724–27), speaks of his difficulty in recording his progress adequately because of the "abundance of matter, the growing buildings, and the new discoveries made in every part of the country."

Those self-possesed and self-confident aristocrats, moreover, exchanged ideas with the greatest generosity. It was not unusual to provide a friend with plans for his house or the services of his gardener as Jefferson

Engraving of the Ionic Temple, the Obelisk, and orange trees in the original garden designed by Kent. In 1732 Kent wrote Lord Burlington: "Your building at Chiswick is very pretty and ye oblisk looks well."

did in Virginia later in the century (page 99). There was also a fraternal give and take among the sexes. The women wrote books, made contributions to medicine, played cricket and hunted. A foreign traveler noted that "they do whatsoever they please and so generally wear the breeches . . . that it is now become a proverb that England is the hell of horses and the paradise of women." One need only remember Lady Mary Wortley Montagu, brilliant and outspoken friend of the Augustan wits, to know that those bluestockings did indeed do whatsoever they pleased. The 18th-century gentry, too, unlike their descendants,

considered it *de rigueur* to keep a mistress. There were many illegitimate children roaming around the great country seats and no one thought much about it.

The Palladian house was perhaps above all symbolic of the art of living as envisaged by the 18th-century gentry who may have been the last humans to believe in the possibility of perfection. We may prefer our haphazard, more practical way of life and the organic architecture that suits it, but we can't help admiring the beautifully proportioned and chaste perfection of a classic Chiswick villa designed not so much to house the flesh but the spirit of man.

"Burlington approached his task," as Rudolf Wittkower has written, "not from a purely pragmatic point of view, but brought to bear upon it the convictions of his life, his ideals and beliefs—in short, everything he stood for, and all he most valued in life." The style he revived and re-edited to suit his generation was a true Augustan work of art—as much a literary as an architctural and horticultural composition. And his house tells a similar story. The taste and refinement are there and so is the decorum. It is Benjamin's Chew's house but it also retains the spirit of his many descendants who took such wise care of it.

Castletown
County Kildare, Ireland

Portrait of Speaker Conolly by Charles Jervas hangs in the dining room.

I know of no civilization whose central stem has not been the country-house and estate—I believe that the best all-round type of human being needs, like a tree, a certain physical scope and amplitude in which to grow.
Arland Ussher

Sean O'Faolain in his autobiography *Vive Moi!* remembers as a small boy visiting his uncle who was "the gatekeeper of a gentleman's country house in Celbridge . . . whose pillared gates faced the end of the village street. . . . On top of each pillar was a lion with a bare-breasted woman's head. A long, long, long avenue, linden-lined, led to a big, big house with hundreds of windows. I know now that was a very famous and splendid building: Castletown House. . . ."

If any country can be said to have two faces it is Ireland. Wild, irrational, proud, mystical, and whitewash-simple on one hand; elegant, ordered, cultured, and socially conscious on the other. A land of saints and bards, of mists and sunshine, of rocky coasts and vast pastures, of rich folklore and down-to-earth politics. But nowhere are Ireland's two faces more evident than in its houses—whitewashed thatched cottages and ruined Norman castles jutting out of the wild landscape as opposed to spacious classic Georgian mansions presiding over clipped green lawns. The mansions are almost entirely the result of the Anglo-Irish aristocracy who were in the ascendancy during the 18th century and probably gave Ireland a greater concentration of civil gifts than any previous or later colonizers. They were responsible for Ireland's first important domestic architecture. They brought about a material culture and a style of living that was highly social and utterly foreign to the individualistic Irish who distrust society and the law-driven material world. Culturally speaking, as Sean O'Faolain says, the Anglo-Irish created "modern Irish-thinking, English-speaking, English-writing Ireland." Politically and in the largest sense socially, he adds, "they were either wicked, indifferent, or sheer failures." He points to Dublin's "grace, roominess, magnificence, and unique atmosphere" as their "nearest-to-hand monument," but "all about the country they built gracious houses (each to be known to the native tenantry as 'The Big House') . . . which are the epitome of the classical spirit of that cultured and callous century."

But even when one is surrounded by the Georgian grace of Dublin, the older and less ordered Ireland is never very far away. The pure morning air is filled with the wild screech of seagulls mingling with the soft toll of church bells and the wilder shores are just beyond the city's doorstep.

Although it is true, as O'Faolain says, that the Anglo-Irish resided in Ireland—"their country, never their nation"—there were some members of that 18th-century enclave who were of native Irish stock, albeit of Protestant faith rather than the native Catholic gentry, who had been defeated at the Boyne in 1690 and utterly suppressed by the Anglo-Irish.

William Conolly, the builder of Castletown, was such a native Irishman. He was not only a Protestant and a devoted adherent of the English interest, he was also a self-made man. Conolly was born in 1662 in Ballyshannon, County Donegal, the son of innkeepers. But in an amazingly short time he rose to great wealth and influence. He became Chief Commissioner of the Irish Revenue in 1709, and Speaker of the Irish House of Commons in 1715, and was reputed to be the richest man in Ireland. Such a self-made man was a new type on the Irish scene, only made possible in the 18th century through the revival of economic life for which the Anglo-Irish were largely responsible. His talents for achieving both riches and public advancement, however, were bound to create enemies. In 1717 when he was named one of three Lords Justice, Sir John St. Leger, Baron of the Exchequer in Ireland, wrote to Lord Chief Justice Parker in England,

many people here, especially our quality and old gentry, are much offended at Mr. Conolly's being one of them; this gentleman was lately an attorney, his father keeping an ale-house in the north of Ireland, this being too notorious to be stifled, but by making long bills and good bargains, he is now reported to be worth eight thousand a year.

Front entrance: "a big, big house with hundreds of windows."

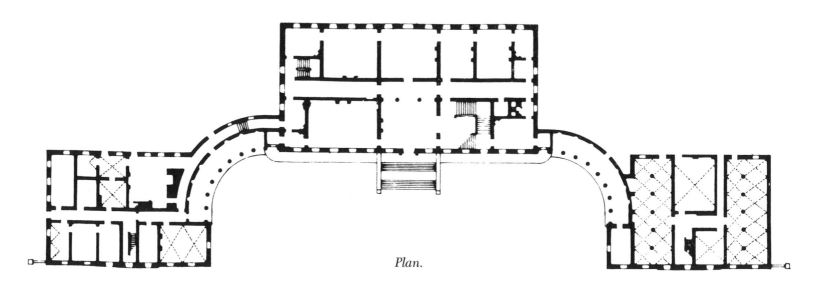

Plan.

Conolly's dealings in the purchase and sale of forfeited estates following the 1690 Rebellion earned him the title of a "cunning intreiguing spark."

In 1694 he married Katherine Conyngham, daughter of Sir Albert Conyngham, and thereby became allied with some of the most influential Portestant families in northern Ireland. William Conolly was, as Lena Boylan points out in her history of the Conolly family, a legend in his own lifetime and "his name became the silver spoon with which parents bestowed wealth and prosperity on their sons, and so we had Wm. Conolly Conyngham, Wm. Conolly Coan, and Wm. Conolly McCausland."

The Epitome of the Kingdom

In 1722 Speaker Conolly began to build his great mansion at Celbridge about 12 miles, or 19 kilometers, west of Dublin. In July of that year the Irish philosopher George Berkeley, Bishop of Cloyne, wrote to Sir John Perceval (later first Earl of Egmont):

> The most remarkable thing now going on is a house of Mr. Conolly's at Castletown.... It is to be of fine wrought stone, harder and better coloured than the Portland, with outhouses joining to it by colonnades.

To which Perceval replied:

> I am glad for the honour of my country that Mr. Conolly has undertaken so magnificent a pile of building, and your advice has been taken upon it. I hope that the execution will answer the design, wherein one special care must be to procure good masons.... You will do well to recommend to him the making use of all the marbles he can get of the production of Ireland for his chimneys, for since this house will be the finest Ireland ever saw, and by your description fit for a Prince, I would have it as it were the epitome of the Kingdom, and all the natural rarities she can afford should have a place there. I would examine the several woods there for inlaying my floors and wainscot with our own oak, and walnut; my stone stairs should be of black palmers stone, and my buffet adorned with the choicest shells our strands afford. I would even carry my zeal to things of art: my hangings, bed, cabinets and other furniture should be Irish, and the very silver that ornamented my locks and grates should be the produce of our mines. But I forget that I write to a gentleman of the country who knows better what is proper and what the kingdom affords.

In September, 1722, Berkeley again writes to Perceval:

The front entrance as seen from the west colonnade.

you will be surprised to hear that the building is begun and the cellar floor arched before they have agreed on any plan for the elevation or facade. Several have been made by several hands, but as I do not approve of work conceived by many heads so I have made no draught of my own. All I do being to give my opinion on any point when consulted.

Bishop Berkeley's information has proven to be accurate since the cellar of Castletown bears no relationship to the well worked out plan and facade above. But until recently the architect of that grandly conceived facade was not certain.

The Best Architect in Europe

The first indication of Conolly's intention to build is found in a letter Robert Molesworth wrote in June 1719, to the Florentine architect Alessandro Galilei who is best known for the facade of St. John-in-Lateran in Rome:

> Mr. Conolly is going on with his designs and no doubt will be glad of your advice now and then. And truly of all your Employers has shown himself most generous.

An earlier Molesworth letter of May 18, 1717, mentions that Lord Justice Conolly was about to bring to Ireland "the best Ar-

chitect in Europe." Galilei was in Ireland in the summer of 1718 and wrote to an Italian friend that he was designing a grand country house for an important political figure in Ireland.

But conclusive evidence that Galilei was Castletown's architect was recently discovered (by John Cornforth of the English magazine *Country Life*) in the diary of Lady Elizabeth Seymour, the future Duchess of Northumberland, who writes in 1763:

> To Castletown it stands on a flat the shell of the house is good it was designed by Gallini the Pope's architect who after built the Pope's Palace on Mount Palatine at Rome....

Galilei, then, was undoubtedly Castletown's principal architect. But the Irish Palladian architect Sir Edward Lovett Pearce also had a part in its design. Pearce, who was the architect of the monumental Parliament House in Dublin (now the Bank of Ireland) for which Speaker Conolly laid the cornerstone in 1729, apparently first acted as an agent to transmit Galilei's designs to Ireland. Later, however, he was probably responsible for the architectural treatment in the entrance hall and staircase hall, the Long Gallery in its original form, and the wings. The west wing contained the kitchen while the east wing served as the stables. This typically Irish arrangement of house

(Top) The soaring entrance hall with its noble Italianate lines was designed by Sir Edward Lovett Pearce when the house was built. (Above) The great staircase from the entrance hall. The grandfather clock (c. 1760) has a case surmounted by a ferocious mask and is a fine example of Irish carving.

and outbuildings sometimes called "the economic Palladian layout" is, says Desmond Guinness, Ireland's greatest single contribution to country house design.

And so Castletown's plan and facade, which James Reynolds has aptly compared with "a superb Junoesque woman," was by the Italian Galilei, but the Anglo-Irish Pearce designed much of the interior.

At some stage Pearce probably studied under his first cousin, Sir John Vanbrugh, of whose Blenheim Palace Professor Nikolaus Pevsner has said, "One does not know whether the Palladian villa with its wings or Versailles with its *coeur d'honneur* stands behind its plan." But there is no doubt that Castletown's ancestry is pure Palladian. It was, in fact, the first great Palladian house built in Ireland and seems to have set off a spate of Palladian building that continued throughout the century.

When the Irish Georgian Society acquired Castletown it was in a dilapidated state and the prey of vandals. There was no government organization to preserve historic buildings and there was no endowment for the house. Money was raised for essential repairs but the return of Castletown to its former splendor is largely the story of restoration by volunteers. The aim of the Society, explains Guinness, has been to return the house to roughly what it might have looked like in 1770 when it was at its height as a setting for the gaieties of the aristocratic Anglo-Irish society.

"The house was very empty at first," as Guinness puts it. "The capacious rooms have gradually been furnished with objects given or lent to Castletown." And the Society hopes that eventually the house will be a showcase of the best of Irish furniture, silver, and glass, as well as art and architecture.

Remarkable Follies and Wonderful Barns

When William Conolly died on October 30, 1729, the Conollys had already moved into Castletown although it was not finished. Even in 1732 the English traveler John Loveday noted that "ye inside be not finish'd throughout, for ye great Staircase is not yet begun, & some of ye Rooms have no Furniture."

Although Castletown never had its main staircase during the lifetime of Speaker Conolly's widow, she was responsible for building some unique architecture outside the house. In order to provide work for the poor she commissioned the German architect Richard Castle, another disciple of Palladio, to design a gigantic obelisk two miles north of the house and visible from it. "My sister is building an obleix to answer a vistow from the bake of Castletown House," is the way Mrs. Conolly's sister expressed it. The resulting "folly"—a remarkable structure consisting of a complicated system of arches and domes topped by a 140-foot-, or 42m, high obelisk—was restored by the Irish Georgian Society in 1968. Mrs. Conolly later commissioned what is known as the "Wonderful Barn" to answer another "vistow" from the rear of the house. This fantastic conical-shaped structure, which was used for storing grain, might easily have been designed by the French visionary architects Boullée or Ledoux. It bears, however, the inscription "1743 Execut'd by JOHN GLINN" of whom nothing is known.

Mrs. Conolly died at Castletown in 1752. Mrs. Mary Delany, the English-born aristocrat, whose memoirs and letters are a lively source of information about life in 18th-century Ireland, informs us,

> We have lost our great Mrs. Conolly. She died on Friday and is a general loss. Her table was open to all her friends of all ranks, and her purse to the poor. She was, I think, in her ninetieth year. She had been dropping for some years, but never so ill as to shut out company. . . . She was clever at business, wrote all her own letters, and could read a newspaper at candle-light without spectacles. She was a plain and vulgar woman in her manner; but had very valuable qualities.

Her nephew William and his family moved into Castletown but two years later William died. His only son Thomas was Castletown's heir but he was under age when his father died and the house was without a tenant for several years.

Always a Receptacle for Society

In 1758 Thomas married Lady Louisa Lennox, third daughter of the Duke of Richmond whose second daughter Emily was living near Castletown as Lady Kildare. There were four Lennox sisters, all of whom were noted for their beauty and intelligence. Lady Louisa was only 15 when she married, Thomas was 24 and, according to Lady Louisa's brother-in-law, Lord Kildare (later the first Duke of Leinster), they were "running about everywhere like mad people." He also notes that "she wants to buy every house she sees; but they are both so young that they don't know what they are about or what to do with themselves." Although Thomas preferred the racy life of London to settling at Castletown, they eventually moved in during October 1759— a date which marks the beginning of Castletown's liveliest and most interesting period.

Lady Louisa loved the house and immediately began making it what her sister

(Top) The magnificent cantilevered staircase of Portland stone with a brass balustrade sweeps through the lavish rococo plasterwork done by the Francini brothers. (Above) The stair hall looking into the entrance hall. Family portraits are incorporated in the Francini brothers' plaster decoration.

(Top) Compartmented ceiling and mantel in the red drawing room are typical of Sir William Chambers' work. Most of the furniture in this room, with the exception of the Irish carved table in the center, has always been in the house. (Above) The green drawing room reflects the neoclassical taste of Sir William Chambers. The walls were originally covered in green silk, bits of which are still visible around the edges. The ground floor rooms are planned en suite *as in an Italian palazzo.*

Lady Sarah Napier later described as "always the receptacle for society, comfort and friendship." Indeed under Lady Louisa's reign, Castletown became a favorite of the gay aristocratic Anglo-Irish society which, with all its faults, achieved distinction at home and impressed most visitors from abroad. "High living," Mrs. Delany complained, "is too much the fashion here." She adds,

> You are not invited to dinner to any private gentleman of £1,000 a year or less, that does not give you seven *dishes* at one course, and Burgundy and Champagne; and these dinners they give once or twice a week.

Bishop Berkeley wondered "whether any kingdom in Europe be so good a customer at Bordeaux as Ireland?" Lord Cloncurry compared the wit and pleasure of Dublin life with Paris. Horace Walpole noted in 1756 that "Ireland which one did not suspect, is become the staple of wit, and I find coins *bons-mots* for our greatest men." In *Dublin under the Georges*, Constantia Maxwell suggests that the sprightliness of Irish conversation "apart from racial considerations," might be explained by "the mixtures of ranks" which distinguished Dublin society. Politicians, soldiers, divines, and lawyers all rubbed shoulders in the great houses. Dr. Samuel Madden complained of "a passion for show" and too much "gaudy frippery" from France in his *Reflections and Resolutions Proper for the Gentlemen of Ireland* published in 1738.

Lady Louisa herself impressed most people with her great charm and gaiety and she could evidently break all the rules of "proper" behavior and get away with it. Her sister Lady Sarah writes:

> Louisa does not seek enlarging her acquaintance for she has so many more than she can manage (leading a country life) that she could not do at all but for the footing which her *peculiar* character has established, and which nobody but herself could venture at and indeed I believe tis because she *aims* at nothing, that so great an allowance is *given* her, for do you know that she scarce visits anybody nor does she receive visits dropping in at odd times, but she now and then goes to town, to see the world and there she says with such a civil good natured face that she is to blame, and tells the people it will be so good natured of them to shew forgiveness by coming and dining with her such a day that they come and they see that she has ten thousand occupations and enjoys her home, so that they go away pleased with their reception, and bid her never think of a formal visit; she

Lady Louisa's sumptuous Long Gallery is 100 feet (30.4m) in length. Over the double doors is a copy of "Aurora" by Guido Reni, and between them is a statue of Diana said to have been smuggled out of Greece in a coffin.

Print rooms were popular in the 18th century, and several still exist in England, but Lady Louisa's is the only one in Ireland.

Mid-18th-century Irish gaming table with its wildly grimacing carved head and exuberant carving is typically Irish. It was purchased by the Irish Georgian Society for Castletown.

takes them at their word upon condition and that they will come every now and then to dinner of a Sunday when she is always at home, so that she has contrived to pay no *visits*, be liked, be civil and to have no trouble, for she escapes cards on the excuse of Sunday. . . .

Lady Louisa's husband, however, was not so popular, at least not with her sisters who considered Thomas a silly tiresome boy and "toad-eater." "I can but think how miserable I should have been at Louisa's age to have had such a husband," notes her oldest sister Lady Holland. "I hope and believe she won't find it out ever." Apparently she never did. And poor Thomas was a bore as well as a toad-eater. "His jokes are very bad," complains Lord Kildare. "I am sometimes very uneasy, particularly when ladies are present, and lest they should not be understood he repeats very often the same thing." Nor did he distinguish himself politically although he was a member of both the English House of Commons and the Irish Parliament and held other important offices in Ireland. In *The Rise and Fall of the Irish Nation*, Jonah Barrington says that Thomas Conolly's "qualities were curiously mixed, and his principles as singularly blended; and if he had not been distinguished by birth and fortune he certainly would have remained all his life in obscurity."

Nevertheless he did leave his imprint on Castletown. Shortly after the young Conollys moved in they began remodeling the interiors. They made Castletown a splendid example of Ireland's Georgian houses which are so eminently suited to what Mrs. Delany called the "great sociableness" of Anglo-Irish society. The lofty ceilings, the great staircase, the charming plasterwork, and the rich carving are masterfully designed to create an exquisite backdrop for a way of life that was a work of art in itself. If it lacked depth it certainly had a bedazzling surface since the Georgians had the good judgment to employ the best architects and craftsmen of the day.

Italianate Outside, Irish In

Although Castletown from the outside, as John Cornforth notes in *Country Life*, "strikes visitors as the most unified and Italianate of Irish houses, the story of its fitting up is typically Irish in the way it proceeded by fits and starts." While the coffered ceiling and cornice in the stair hall date from the 1720s, the great cantilevered staircase was not installed until 1760. Its brass balustrade is signed "A. King Dublin, 1760," and there are bills of that year from Anthony King as well as from Vierpyl (the Dutch-Italian sculptor and stonemason who had recently settled in Dublin) for working on the staircase.

The charming rococo plaster decoration of the walls was done by the famous Francini brothers whose lavish plaster work adorns the walls and ceilings of many of Dublin's lovely Georgian interiors. The Francini brothers, who came to Ireland from Italy to execute one of the most beautiful of all ceilings for Lady Louisa's brother-in-law Lord Kildare at Carton, probably started work at Castletown in 1759 when Lady Louisa wrote to Lady Kildare: "Mr. Conolly and I are excessively diverted at Francini's impertinence and if he charges anything of that sort to Mr. Conolly there is a fine scold in store for his honour." The records, however, show that only £100 was paid to "Frankiney Stucco man" in small amounts between September and December 1765. The human figures, which are a dominant feature of Francini plaster-work, have been described by Desmond Guinness as "orderly, stylized figures . . . not likely to misbehave when left to themselves," which was perhaps due to Irish persuasion rather than Italian desire.

While several ground-floor rooms and the bedrooms at Castletown have remained as they were in the 1720s, the two drawing rooms were probably remodeled by Sir William Chambers, English champion of Palladian architecture. Chambers also created the present dining room by throwing together two earlier rooms. Although he was never in Ireland, his work is well represented there. Vierpyl was his protégé and probably executed his designs. The Castletown dining room and the red drawing room have compartmented ceilings similar to others by Chambers and the chimney piece in the red drawing room was also probably a Chambers design and may be one that Lady Louisa mentioned as having been sent from England.

Ten-Thousand Occupations

In spite of all the architects and craftsmen who worked at Castletown, it is Lady Louisa's personality which gives its interiors their special charm and individualtiy. Fortunately Castletown's interior had hardly been altered since her day. Perhaps the Long Gallery—a feature of Elizabethan and Jacobean houses but rare in a house as late as Castletown—is Lady Louisa's masterpiece. It was designed by Pearce but, except for its compartmented ceiling, it had been left unfinished until Lady Louisa took over. In October 1774 she writes, "I have stayed here, chiefly diverting myself with the Gallery." The following June, it was being painted "in a most beautiful way" by Thomas Riley, a pupil of Sir Joshua Reyn-

The "Conolly Folly" commissioned by the Speaker's widow in 1740 "to answer a vistow at the bake of Castletown House."

One of the piers of the sphinx gates.

Lady Louisa walking with the keeper is by Robert Healy, 1768.

olds. But even after Lady Louisa had reported the Gallery was finished work went on. In the summer of 1776 she writes that "Mr. Riely goes on swimmingly in the Gallery but I am doing much more than I intended, that pretty grey, white and gold look that I admired in the ends of the room, did look a little naked by the painted compartments." She adds that "Mr. Riley has made some pretty slight sketches that end at the heads or the busts and are an addition but they made the stucco panels look so very bad that they are going to be knocked off smack smooth which I know you will approve of."

The bold colors and the enrichment of the ceiling make the Long Gallery an exciting space. The walls and centers of the ceiling panels are a bright lavender-blue. The background of the frieze is red. Riley's ornaments are in clear reds and greens. The large mirrors are an important part of the overall design and had to be ordered from France—"the French glasses are very bad and imperfect," Lady Louisa notes, "however they look handsome up." When the chandeliers arrived from Venice, she writes, "they are the wrong blue for the room." The Pompeian grotesques were derived from Raphael's cartoons in the loggia of the Vatican.

In 1778 the Gallery was finally finished and furnished, as one eyewitness reports, "in the most delightful manner with fine glasses, books, musical instruments and a billiard table." It was one of the most popular rooms at Castletown both with the family and guests. "In the gallery where we live," writes Lady Louisa, " 'tis the most comfortable room you ever saw, and quite warm; supper at one end, the company at the other, and I am writing in one of the piers at a distance from them all." Lady Sarah was also impressed with its versatility: "the Long Gallery divides the party so much one is capable of being very quiet at

one end, though there is *dancing* at the other."

The Print Room was perhaps even more Lady Louisa's personal creation. It was done before the Gallery and probably inspired it. Her own drawing for the Print Room is still at Castletown and she apparently did all the work herself from trimming and arranging the prints to attaching them to the walls. She writes to Lady Sarah in 1762: "I always forget to thank you my dear for the prints you sent me. . . . I have not had time to do my Print Room yet." She was still asking Lady Sarah for prints in 1768: "At any time that you chance to go into a Print Shop I should be obliged to you if you will buy me five or six large prints, there are some of Tennier's engraved by Le Bas which I am told are larger than the common size. If you meet with any pray send me a few."

Lady Louisa was continually making "pleasant improvements" in and out of doors through the last half of the century. Castletown's entrance gates were her final improvement. "The piers of Celbridge gate are finished," she reports in 1783. The gates were taken from a design in Sir William Chambers' *Treatise on Civil Architecture* (1759) and executed by John Coates of Maynooth. A bill for the "two sphynkes," which were later to be remembered by O'Faolain as lions "with a bare-breasted woman's head," is still at Castletown.

But Lady Louisa's happy life was not to last for long. The Irish Rebellion of 1798 made itself intimately felt at Castletown. On July 10th she writes,

> Our house is a perfect garrison, eighteen soldiers sleep in our saloon and we are all blocked up and shut up except by the hall door and one door to the kitchen-yard, and are frequently ordered all into the house upon the alarm being given of the rebels being near Celbridge. . . .

The Conollys had relatives on both sides and Lady Louisa, especially, was caught between her obligations as Thomas' wife (he was loyal to England) and her sympathy for the oppressed peasantry. But the greatest tragedy occurred when the Duke of Leinster's son Lord Edward Fitzgerald—a leader of the United Irishmen and Lady Louisa's favorite nephew—was betrayed and imprisoned. The story of his capture and Lady Louisa's visit to his prison deathbed is a well-known and moving part of Irish history.

In 1803 Thomas Conolly died. Lady Louisa continued living at Castletown and devoting her life to its upkeep and the welfare of her tenants. A steward of Castletown later remembered,

> often seeing her pass out of the garden to the house, dressed in her usual long, light-grey cloth pelisse, or surtout, having huge side pockets, and those pockets stuck full of the largest parsnips and carrots, their small ends appearing above; these being doubtless for the poor, who were permitted to come to the house two or three times a week for food.

"My headquarters are Castletown," Lady Sarah writes in 1811,

> which being a deserted palace, would fill me with gloom could I see those places where the happiest years of my life were spent, in a neglected state. But my dear, my perfect sister, who does all that is right and unites prudence with all her actions, spends the money she has allotted for its maintenance in doing all that is necessary rather than showy; so while it looks neglected, the essentials are all well done and as fires are necessary we live entirely on one floor, which makes it more connected and comfortable. But life there is perfect retirement, which is most comfortable to me, but broken into now and then by those we love, who come to dine and sleep at night.

In August 1821 Lady Louisa died sitting in a tent on the lawn in front of Castletown. "I do not get any idea of the beauty of my house if I live in it," she had said. "I get perspective and contemplation if I can gaze upon the house from a far off."

The house was essentially as Lady Louisa left it when the Irish Georgian Society took it over. Only minor changes were made during the 19th century. It did, however, need major repair work such as making the roof watertight, installing new plumbing and wiring. In some cases later layers of paint had to be stripped from walls and ceilings, paneling that had been infected with dry rot had to be replaced, and the staircase, which was found to be unsafe, had to be strengthened.

Had this great house not been saved in 1967, one shudders to think what might have become of it. Development houses encroaching on its lonely grandeur would surely be the worst ignominy and a sad thing to contemplate after all the loving attention lavished on it by Lady Louisa. For it is indeed one of those houses in which human desires and disappointments have left their unmistakable aura.

The Irish Georgian Society, through careful restoration and wise use, has brought back something of the gay activity so many mentioned during Lady Louisa's day. "Never was such activity or such good cheer," as Lady Caroline Damer puts it after a visit with Lady Louisa. "All is neat and clean, in spite of the vast rooms, and rackety servants."

The rackety servants are missing but the vast rooms are neat and clean and Lady Louisa's Long Gallery is often the scene of musical events and theatrical performances that bring back to Castletown some of the "great sociableness" mentioned by Mrs. Delany. When the famous 18th-century English actress Sarah Siddons was playing in Dublin, she gave recitations at Castletown, and Mrs. Siddons, not unlike many of today's visitors, "was full of the beauties of the house."

When a house becomes a museum, as Desmond Guinness has pointed out,

> its character is bound to change. For one thing, it will miss the ordinary comings and goings of family life. . . . In Russia and America, houses open to the public are not lived in as they are in England, and various attempts are made to give the impression that the owner has just rattled off down the drive in his coach and four. Flowers, books propped open by old-fashioned spectacles—Prince Yussoupoff's bedroom slippers even are ready for his return to his country house near Leningrad. All this helps to give an illusion that the house is lived in, and helps dispel the rusty atmosphere of the museum. Castletown has been brought to life in other ways . . . many theatrical performances, concerts, lectures and discussions have been held there.

Castletown is a proud symbol of Ireland's other face and offers impressive evidence that the Anglo-Irish could not have been wholly wicked. The Georgians, as Arland Ussher says in his fascinating book *The Face & Mind of Ireland*, "were more than mere roisterers; they were—many of them—builders, landscape-gardeners, fine speakers in public and writers in privacy. The evidence is in their mansions . . . in the lay-out of their estates, in their diaries. . . ."

(Top) The back steps before restoration. (Above) Volunteers on the front steps in 1967.

Edgemont

Near Charlottesville, Virginia

What still remains to be done is to carry the past in the marrow of our bones and as visual objects before our eyes and to go on from there in building, as Jefferson would say, an empire for liberty.   Sidney Hyman

The history of Edgemont is probably as strange as the history of a house by a famous architect could be. It was designed at the end of the 18th century by Thomas Jefferson—author of the Declaration of Independence, third president of the United States, and the country's first great native-born architect. But it was forgotten until 1936 when Virginia architect Milton L. Grigg and photographer Frances Benjamin Johnston happened upon it on a remote hillside not far from Charlottesville. The photographer was on a Carnegie grant to survey Virginia architecture and had enlisted the young architect as her guide because, as Grigg says, "she was a friend of my aunt's and I had made a study of Virginia houses."

When they discovered Edgemont it was in a dilapidated state, its hip roof covered with tin, an unsightly kitchen wing unbalancing its perfect symmetry, and a once-lovely garden all but obliterated. But Grigg was convinced. "This is Jefferson," he said. It was only a hope at the time, he admits, but to his great satisfaction he found Jefferson's plans and elevation for Edgemont in Fiske Kimball's *Thomas Jefferson, Architect.* Kimball, not knowing of its existence when his book was published in 1916, had tentatively identified the drawings as studies for rebuilding Shadwell, Jefferson's birthplace, which had burned in 1770. Grigg says one of his greatest thrills was writing to Fiske Kimball to tell him of his find.

After their dramatic discovery of Edgemont the first thing Grigg did was to have a plan made of it as a record of how they found it. Later he came across an insurance policy of 1797 with a description of the house built by James Powell Cocke in 1795 or 1796.

Edgemont was constructed on a hillside according to Jefferson's favorite formula and appears to be a one-story house in front but with two full stories in the rear. "All the new and good houses are of a single story.

That is of the height of 16. or 18. f. generally, and the whole of it given to rooms of entertainment," Jefferson wrote after his return from Paris in 1789 where he had admired the new French classicism.

With its four porticos through which one enters the main level of the house Edgemont is, like many of Jefferson's plans, based on Palladio's Villa Rotonda. Its front or west porch gives access to a wainscoted reception hall while the doors on the north and south open into a transverse corridor running the length of the house. An octagonal drawing room is opposite the reception hall and in the four corners are the master bedroom, guest bedroom, library, and dressing room. The basement or garden level is divided into an equal number of rooms with the dining room under the drawing room and the kitchen and sitting room on either side of it.

Edgemont is probably the only frame house Jefferson designed. Its exterior walls are of brick nogging covered with wide molded board siding painted to simulate stone. The quoins are also of wood. This is in the colonial tradition of imitating what was fashionable with the building technology available at the time. But most importantly, in appearance at least, Edgemont didn't contradict Jefferson's dislike of wood houses. In his *Notes on the State of Virginia* he wrote:

> A country whose buildings are of wood can never increase in its improvements to any considerable degree. Their duration is highly estimated at 50 years. Every half century then our country becomes a tabula rasa, whereon we have to set out anew, as in the first moment of seating it. Whereas when buildings are of durable materials, every new edifice is an actual and permanent acquisition to the state, adding to its value as well as to its ornament.

Certainly Edgemont does the latter with exceptional grace. It is only about 50 by 40 feet, or 15 by 12m, overall, but in its diminutive way it has all the elegance and dignity of a great country house.

James Powell Cocke, the builder of Edge-

Aerial view from the garden side.

Restored garden portico, right, and south porch, left.

Jefferson's drawing, which corresponds to Edgemont as it was built.

mont, was born at Malvern Hill on the James River. Around 1793 he moved with his family from Augusta County to Albemarle County where he built Edgemont on part of the land he had purchased some years before from Robert Nelson. Writing of James Powell Cocke and his homes in the *Virginia Historical Magazine* (January 1935) James Powell Cocke Southall, grandson of Cocke's youngest daughter, tells us that the countryfolk of the vicinity still say that "Edgemont was built for James Powell Cocke by Jefferson's own carpenters." This is not implausible since Jefferson did employ two master builders from Philadelphia, James Dinsmore and John Neilson, to work on Monticello. After having absorbed Jefferson's ideas they went on to build houses on their own which have sometimes been attributed to their mentor. The building of Edgemont, however, predates the arrival of these builders in Virginia—Dinsmore in 1798 and Neilson in 1804.

Southall's own idea was that Jefferson could have easily been Edgemont's designer. He argues in his article that Cocke and Jefferson were nearly the same age, both lived to be over 80, so that their lives almost completely overlapped. Jefferson in his young days probably had been a frequent visitor at Malvern Hill, and for more than 30 years he and James Powell Cocke were near neighbors in Albemarle. Thus, Southall concludes, it is reasonable to suppose they were close friends and that Jefferson designed his friend's house for him. No one, however, seems to have paid much attention to Southall's theory, and as he himself says, no reference to James Powell Cocke has ever been found in Jefferson's extensive correspondence. Nor has any yet been found except for one letter from Jefferson thanking Cocke for sending him fish to stock his pond at Monticello. Grigg believes that the physical closeness of the two Virginians made it unnecessary to correspond.

When Southall visited Edgemont in the early 1930s he tells us, the house was "rather desolate and forlorn in appearance, showing the effects of neglect and the ravages of time and," he adds, "it takes an effort of the imagination to reconstruct the picture it must have presented in the days when James Powell Cocke and his family lived there." Southall noted, however, that Edgemont was still a thing to be admired, that "the proportion and symmetry of the whole plan constitute one of the chief charms."

Putting Words In Jefferson's Mouth

This is as Milton Grigg and Frances Johnston found it a few years later—neglected

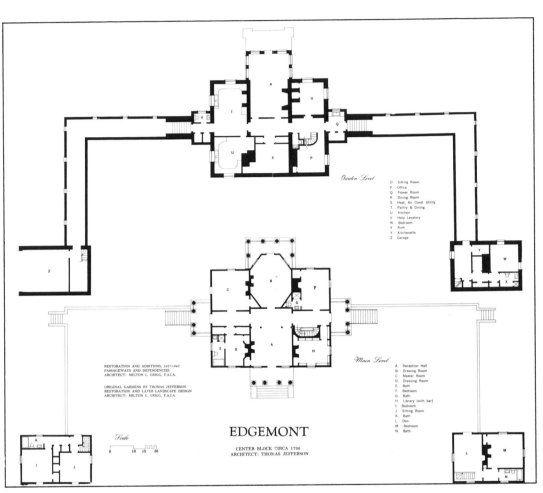

Garden Level

O. Sitting Room
P. Office
Q. Flower Room
R. Dining Room
S. Heat, Air Cond: Utility
T. Pantry & Dining
U. Kitchen
V. Help Lavatory
W. Bedroom
X. Bath
Y. Kitchenette
Z. Garage

RESTORATION AND ADDITIONS, 1937-1947
PASSAGEWAYS AND DEPENDENCIES
ARCHITECT: MILTON L. GRIGG, F.A.I.A.

ORIGINAL GARDENS BY THOMAS JEFFERSON
RESTORATION AND LATER LANDSCAPE DESIGN
ARCHITECT: MILTON L. GRIGG, F.A.I.A.

Main Level

A. Reception Hall
B. Drawing Room
C. Master Room
D. Dressing Room
E. Bath
F. Bedroom
G. Bath
H. Library (with bar)
I. Bedroom
J. Sitting Room
K. Bath
L. Den
M. Bedroom
N. Bath

Scale
0 10 15 20

EDGEMONT

CENTER BLOCK CIRCA 1796
ARCHITECT: THOMAS JEFFERSON

Plan.

(Top) Octagonal drawing room looking toward the garden. (Above) Heart pine flooring from the attic was used to panel the library.

and unkempt but still Jeffersonian.

Grigg was convinced it must be restored and was able to persuade his friend Dr. Graham Clark, then a medical student, to purchase it if Grigg would undertake its restoration. Their first objective was to restore the exterior of the house and the garden. Although the house was without its portico on the garden side, the foundation for it was there. The original portico may never have been completed or, Grigg suggests, a forest fire that had come close to the house on the garden side may have burned it and necessitated its removal. To reconstruct Edgemont's portico on the old foundation, Grigg based his design on a portico at Poplar Forest, the house near Lynchburg that Jefferson designed as his retreat. Grigg, however, insists on calling the Edgemont reconstruction a case of "putting words in Jefferson's mouth."

Removal of the kitchen wing, which had been added to the south side of the house some time in the 19th century, revealed the old wainscoting and the marks of the old porch. Traces of black paint were also found under the addition vouching for the truth of a weird interlude in Edgemont's history. It seems two sisters lived in the house during the 19th century and when one of them died the surviving sister carried her mourning to the point of painting the entire house black, inside and out.

Some of Edgemont's existing wood shingles served as patterns to reproduce the reinforced concrete shingles that were used to face the main house as well as the outbuildings.

Edgemont's 18th-century terraced garden had been laid out on five levels, one of which was a bowling green. Exploratory trenches revealed its contours along with the identity of some of the original plants including crepe myrtle, various hollies, and boxwood. These were duplicated and about 50 full-grown trees were transplanted from the surrounding woods to supplement those that were still there. The result is a charming example of a garden in the landscape style that Jefferson admired in England.

In 1941 both Clark and Grigg went into the service and the restoration was interrupted. When the war was over Clark moved to New York to study surgery, and in 1945, he put Edgemont on the market.

It was purchased in 1946 by Mr. and Mrs. William Snead, and again Edgemont had sympathetic tenants who asked Grigg to help them complete the restoration of the main house as nearly as possible to the way Jefferson designed it while adapting the interior to the requirements of a modern residence.

The Sneads, however, needed more

rooms. To add them to the main house would have meant finishing the attic, putting in dormers, and destroying the outline of the house as Jefferson designed it. Grigg's solution was both ingenious and in the Jefferson style. Excavations of the grounds had revealed that the garden and surrounding fieldstone walls were laid out in such a way as to indicate a secondary axis on either side of the house. This led Grigg to suspect that a second building phase had been anticipated in order to add two flanking dependencies—an office and service house—but was never carried out. Thus Grigg designed two flanking dependencies as he assumed Jefferson would have done, one as a servants' house, the other a guest house, and the resulting harmonious composition certainly would have met with Jefferson's approval. Nevertheless Grigg is careful to point out that the dependencies are merely "conjectural."

To provide communication between the main house and the dependencies Grigg hit upon another no less harmonious and no less Jeffersonian solution. He constructed underground connections from the ground floor of the main house to the basement of the dependencies as Jefferson had done at Monticello. In his book, *Thomas Jefferson American Humanist*, Karl Lehmann suggests that Jefferson's source for such below-grade passageways was the Roman villa where they are a typical feature. Called *cryptoporticus* they are described by Pliny in both his villas. The particular scheme at Monticello in which the tunnels are lighted by small windows in the upper wall fits Pliny's description of the *cryptoporticus* at his Laurentian villa. A similar scheme is preserved in many Roman villas and might have been known to Jefferson from etchings. Edgemont's underground connections have the small semicircular windows only on the garden side. The grade from the lawn on the other side is brought over to form the sodded roof of the passageways. Of Edgemont's underground passages, Grigg says, "once we got over the intellectual block of the dependencies, we feel we did what Jefferson would have done had he been faced with the same problem."

Vitruvius Americanus

While Jefferson was notoriously anti-British and often expressed a dislike of English architecture, it is impossible to escape the relationship of Jefferson's houses with the formal country houses of 18th-century England surrounded by their picturesque gardens, and most particularly with Lord Burlington's Palladian villa at Chiswick (page 77). Jefferson, the American democrat, and Burlington, the British lord, shared many of the same ideas. Both were disciples

(Top) Reconstructed Palladian screen separating reception hall from corridor. Drawing room is seen beyond. (Above) Hall on garden level.

Garden side as it was found in 1936. Part of the kitchen addition can be seen on the left. (Middle) View from the northwest in 1936. The front or west porch on the right gives access to the reception hall. (Above) South side after kitchen addition was removed.

of Palladio and delighted in the Palladian theory that the proportions of good building derived from the laws of nature. Both had an aversion to the baroque architecture of Wren, both built houses and laid out gardens, and both wanted to educate the taste of their countrymen with classic reproductions. Both men, moreover, considered themselves amateurs, and both provided their friends with plans for their houses.

There is a letter from Jefferson, dated August 19, 1796, to his friend Wilson C. Nicholas in which he says,

> I now enclose you the draught you desired, Which I have endeavored to arrange according to the ideas you expressed, of having the entry, not through a principal room as in Mr. Cocke's house, but at the cross passage.

This is interesting because it throws light on how Jefferson dealt with his client-friends and also because of the reference to Mr. Cocke's house which must have meant Edgemont with its transverse corridor and its main entrance into the reception hall.

Jefferson and Burlington were both classicists but while Jefferson was a literal classicist in his public buildings his classicism was much freer in his domestic buildings. Jefferson's houses were imaginative adaptations rather than literal translations. The plan of Edgemont is based on Palladio's Villa Rotonda just as Burlington's Chiswick is, but Edgemont is plainly an American creation consciously adapted to American soil and American ways. Architecture, as Karl Lehmann points out, was "the most articulate expression" of Jefferson's "admiration for antique civilization, for the freedom of thought and imagination which, he hoped, would finally be revived after a lapse of two thousand years."

Jefferson was the first American architect to knowingly reject the English tradition, as Burlington had done in England, and to seek instead an architecture appropriate to the new nation. And Edgemont is not only a splendid example of Jefferson's belief in the classicism of Palladio and the ancient Romans but also in the future well-being and taste of his countrymen. In 1786 he wrote to James Madison from France:

> You see I am an enthusiast in the subject of the arts. But it is an enthusiasm of which I an not ashamed, as its object is to improve the taste of my countrymen, to increase their reputation, to reconcile to them the respect of the world and procure them its praise.

Edgemont, like all Jefferson houses, is both romantic and rational. This it also shares with Chiswick, but Edgemont is disarmingly simple. It is exactly what its designer wanted American architecture to be—expressive of democracy. Edgemont is a livable house today. Chiswick is a showpiece. And thus they both have ever been.

In his *Notes on the State of Virginia* Jefferson wrote that it is "impossible to devise things more ugly, uncomfortable, and happily more perishable," than the houses in his native state, but he could not entirely break away from the American building tradition and the earlier colonial manner which he condemned. As Fiske Kimball points out,

> "Fortunately for him, perhaps, there was then, as always, no escape from the pervasive traditional style of the time. Sharing with other American buildings their materials, brick and wood, his works inherited unavoidably much of the homely domesticity and beautiful texture of their predecessors. It is this inevitable difference between Jefferson's intent and his results that permits the confusion of his work with the Colonial, and which at the same time makes it, like every attempted revival, a new creation. There is no mistaking it either for work of the Palladians or that of the French Romanists, it is an individual blend with native elements which make it, too, our own."

And this is particularly obvious at Edgemont. It embodies Jefferson's intention in its Palladian proportions, but the result is very much in the American tradition albeit a true Jefferson creation. Always Jefferson's classical devotion was invigorated with his native boldness and invention.

Jefferson had been interested in gardens and gardening since his youth and in the spring of 1786 when he was serving as Minister to the Court of France, he made a tour of English gardens with John Adams—a trip that must have made a far greater impression on him than he perhaps realized. A description of England written by a German lady during the same year of Jefferson's visit the affinity between Jeffersonian Virginia and Augustan England:

> Nature and man both enjoy noble freedom; the landscape over which hundreds and hundreds of fertile hills extend is set with splendid country houses of the great, and charming well-built farms.

Chiswick was on Jefferson's English itinerary but notwithstanding the fact that he undoubtedly owes the English architect-lord an unconscious debt, he had little to say about Burlington's ornamental villa on the Thames in his "Memorandums made on a tour to some of the gardens of England. . . ."

Chiswick—Belongs to Duke of Devonshire. A garden about six acres—the octagonal dome has an ill effect, both within and without; the garden shows still too much of art. An obelisk of very ill effect; another in the middle of the pond useless.

This, his total recorded response to the villa that Pope called "the finest thing this glorious sun has shin'd upon," might seem unappreciative to say the least until one realizes that Jefferson's notations about places he visited are just that—brief objective records of facts for his own future use. He himself explained that "my inquiries were directed to such practical things as might enable me to estimate the expense of making and maintaining a garden in that style." His personal reactions to places he visited are another matter and we will never know what they were unless he happened to express them in a letter where he was usually more expansive. It is in a letter written to his friend John Page after his return to Paris that Jefferson is quite explicit about his reactions to England:

The gardening in that country is the article in which it surpasses all the earth. I mean their pleasure gardening. This indeed went far beyond my ideas. The city of London, tho' handsomer than Paris, is not so handsome as Philadelphia. Their architecture is in the most wretched stile I ever saw, not meaning to except America where it is bad, nor even Virginia where it is worse than in any other part of America, which I have seen. The mechanical arts in London are carried to a wonderful perfection.

And of course Jefferson's famous letter written to the Comtesse de Tessé from Nîmes, gives us a charming insight into his admiration for ancient Roman architecture as well as the neoclassic architecture of Louis XVI's France:

Here I sit, Madam, gazing whole hours at the Maison Carrée, like a lover at his mistress. . . . The stocking weavers and silk spinners around it consider me a hypochondriac Englishman, about to write with a pistol the last chapter of his history. This is the second time I have been in love since I left Paris. The first was with a Diana . . . a delicious morsel of sculpture. . . . This, you will say, was in rule, to fall in love with a female beauty; but with a house! it is out of all precedent. No, Madam, it is not without precedent in my own history. While in Paris, I was violently smitten with the Hôtel de Salm, and used to go to the Tuilleries almost daily, to look at it. . . .

If, however, Jefferson found little to admire in English architecture at least one Englishman, John Rowley, who was entertained at Monticello, had nothing but praise for that Jeffersonian masterpiece when he later wrote to his American host:

Forget, I cannot, the hospitality of your house. You live in plenty and in grace. Your white pillared rooms magnify your friendliness. Your friends call you genius. If Inigo Jones was called Vitruvius Britannicus, most meetly are you to be handed the laurels as Vitruvius Americanus.

Architecture is My Delight

Monticello is no doubt Jefferson's masterpiece but Edgemont in its simple perfection is an ideal example of what he thought the houses of Americans should be. In his *Notes on the State of Virginia*, he comments that,

Buildings are often erected by individuals, of considerable expence. To give these symmetry and taste would not increase their cost. It would only change the arrangement of the materials, the form and combination of the members. This would often cost less than the burthen of barbarous ornaments with which these buildings are sometimes charged. But the first principles of the art are unknown, and there exists scarcely a model among us sufficiently chaste to give an idea of them. . . .

In its impeccably restored state Edgemont is, as it no doubt was in its early days, "sufficiently chaste" to be the kind of model Jefferson had in mind.

"It is a unique house," says Grigg, "with a wonderful plan for adaptive use." Bathrooms and other contemporary amenities could be worked into the triangular-shaped spaces created by the octagonal drawing room without disturbing Jefferson's plan. One triangular space has been turned into a walk-in closet, the other into a bath. And with the minor addition of a few partitions one of the original bedrooms has been converted into a dressing room and bath for the master bedroom.

The interior had never been drastically changed since it was built except for the addition of the easily removable kitchen wing. The original glass was still in the windows, the original floors were intact, and even all the doors, as Southall wrote in 1935, "have brass-ring knockers instead of knobs, the locks in some instances being of solid brass." The living-room mantel had vanished but all the others were in place as were the

cornices in all the rooms on the main level. The Palladian screen between the reception hall and the drawing room, and the staircase connecting the garden level with the main level, were missing. Grigg, however, found marks on the floor for the screen and evidences of the staircase. He adapted his design for the Palladian screen from classical handbooks and matched it to the marks on the structure. The staircase is one recovered from a house in Charlottesville that was being demolished but, says Grigg, "the stair fitted the opening in the floor and may have come from the same handbook as the original." It is, in any case, inconspicuous like most of Jefferson's staircases. This has been considered a peculiar feature of his houses but he explains his reason for them in his letter about the new one-story townhouses that he admired in Paris:

. . . in the parts where there are bedrooms they have two tiers of them from 8. to 10. f. high each, with small private staircases. By these means great staircases are avoided, which are expensive and occupy a space which would make a good room in every story.

Throughout the restoration of Edgemont, Jefferson's drawings were carefully followed, and thus as Grigg puts it, the main house has been restored "pretty accurately, the rest is an adaptable reconstruction." (P 115)

It is, in any case, a typical Jefferson house in its openness, its lightness, its long vistas, and free-flowing plan. "I cannot live without books and I cannot live without light and air," as Jefferson said. (P 105)

Of all the adaptations of Palladio's Villa Rotonda, Edgemont is in many ways the most interesting because it so perfectly fits its American landscape and the simple American life that Jefferson envisioned. Jefferson, who was deeply sensitive to the relationship between a house and its natural setting, placed Edgemont on a hillside in the manner of the ancient Roman villas where "nature spread so rich a mantle under the eye," as it did at Monticello. "How sublime to look down into the workhouse of nature," Jefferson wrote to Maria Cosway from Monticello, "to see her clouds, hail, snow, rain, thunder, all fabricated at our feet! and the glorious sun, when rising as if out of a distant water, just gilding the tops of the mountains, and giving life to all nature!"

William H. Pierson, Jr. has rightly called Jefferson "a humanist, and poet concerned with the goodness of life." And Jefferson's architecture, which he called "my delight," has left us hardly less proof of his humanism, poetry, and concern for the goodness of life, than his Declaration of Independence.

The Octagon

Washington, D.C.

On January 7, 1800, Mrs. Thornton noted in her diary: "After dinner we walked to take a look at Mr. Tayloe's house, which begins to make a handsome appearance."

The single building is but an element in a complex civic or landscape design. Except in the abstraction of drawing or photography no building exists in a void; it functions as a part of a greater whole and can be seen and felt only through dynamic participation in the whole.   Lewis Mumford

The genesis of the Octagon house in Washington, D.C., ought to be of interest to Americans who are curious about their roots. It was one of the first houses to be built in the new city of Washington when there was little but a dream to herald either the city or the country. Hope and faith were the key words. Hope for an entirely new way of life and faith in its possibility.

The Octagon is a concrete symbol of that new life. Not that there weren't just as fine and perhaps even more important houses rising in the fledgling country; but in this house, the dream of a nation and the dream of a handful of men seemed to coincide in a fateful way. The fact that it was built by a southern aristocrat in what many visitors described as a crude and barren landscape is an astonishing record of the self-reliance and trust that characterized life in the early years of the new country. Thus the restoration of the Octagon adds an important dimension to our understanding of Washington's early history.

In 1902 the American Institute of Architects (AIA) purchased the century-old Octagon and used it as its headquarters until it outgrew the space. In 1968 when the AIA undertook to restore it as a house museum, there was little question as to what period it should be taken back. During the first two decades of the 19th century, the Octagon's graceful rooms had been the scene of some of the young capital's most brilliant social gatherings and important political events. In order to reconstruct that era, extensive historical research and architectural investigation of the building was carried on under the aegis of J. Everette Fauber, Jr., FAIA. Based on that research the major work involved restoring a hipped roof, which had been superimposed over the original flat roof early in the Octagon's history, making the building structurally

sound, installing year-round climate control and security systems, replacing some original partitions, restoring the basement wine cellar and kitchen, and reproducing original colors throughout the house.

It was not, however, until after the Octagon had been restored and opened to the public that a large cache of letters and other documents pertaining to its building came to light at Mount Airy, the great Virginia plantation house built in 1758 for John Tayloe II, father of the John Tayloe who built the Octagon. The Mount Airy papers include thousands of the third John Tayloe's letters, often written on the backs of jocky and breeding records, his account books, and innumerable bills that list virtually every piece of lumber in the house, every coat of paint on its walls. There are stone cutters' bills, bills for "smiths Work," for "Carpenters & Joiners Work." There are bills for "making" furniture and "putting up" furniture, for mending a stove and opening a lock. The Mount Airy papers also revealed for the first time that James Hoban (architect of the President's House) served as the Octagon's "measurer." His signature appears on many bills.

But what must be rare in the history of restoration is that although the Mount Airy papers were unknown when the Octagon was restored, they show that the restorers were about 99 percent correct in their decisions. To cite but one example, some experts believed that the kitchen area way was originally painted, but the restoration architects decided to use whitewash and the documents prove them correct.

Townhouse without a Town

In 1798 when John Tayloe III started to build the Octagon, the city hardly existed except on paper. It didn't even have the government until 1800 when the entire executive establishment was moved there from Philadelphia, and several years after that a French diplomat exclaimed with characteristic Gallic indignation, "My God! what have I done to reside in such a city?" But Colonel Tayloe, Virginia aristocrat and proprietor of large estates, had the faith and imagination to build an elegant townhouse

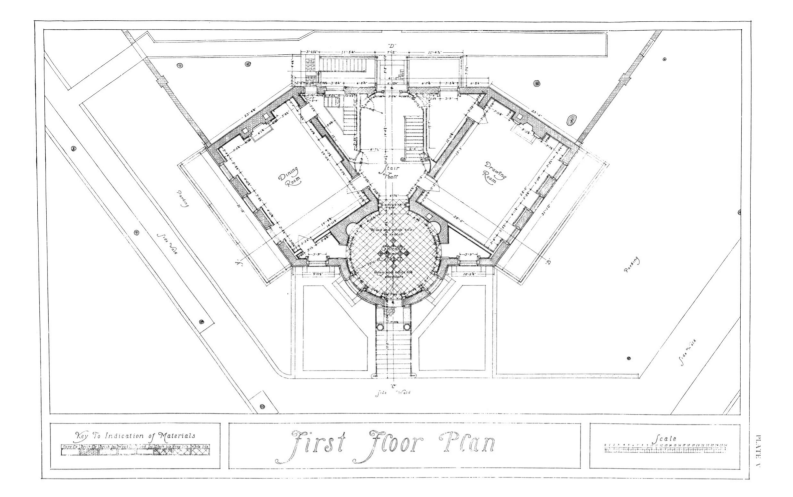

Key To Indication of Materials

First Floor Plan

Scale

PLATE V

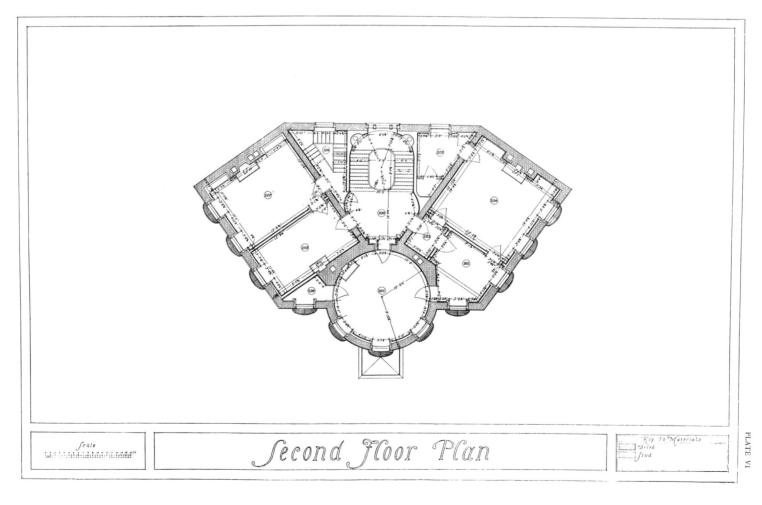

Scale

Second Floor Plan

Key To Materials

PLATE VI

Plans of the first and second floors show how functional features such as the service stair-way, pantry, and closets take advantage of the odd corners in Thornton's minutely considered plan.

where most people only saw dusty roads and empty land. A long list of visitors from poets to noblemen found little to praise in the new city. Plainly, one had to be endowed with imagination to go as far as Gouverneur Morris did when he remarked that Washington offered great advantages as a *future* residence. Even during Jefferson's administration the city was little more than a vision, judging from the condescending lines written by the English poet Thomas Moore:

> This embryo capital, where Fancy sees
> Squares in morasses, oblisks in trees;
> Which second-sighted seers, ev'n now, adorn
> With shrines unbuilt and heroes yet unborn.
> Where naught but woods and Jefferson they see,
> Where streets should run and sages *ought* to be.

And Sir Augustus John Foster, an attaché of the British legation, could only commend Washington for its "excellent snipe shooting and even partridge shooting" which, he tells us, "was to be had on each side of the main avenue and even close under the wall of the Capitol."

But Tayloe showed himself to be a man of foresight. Although he was planning to build his townhouse in the sophisticated and well-appointed city of Philadelphia, his friend George Washington convinced him of the glowing future of the new city. And thus in that wild and uninhabited landscape the Virginia aristocrat planned his house with the aid of Dr. William Thornton, the architect who had so impressed Washington and Jefferson with the drawings he submitted in the design competition for the Capitol that he was named the winner.

The Tayloes were not interested in mediocrity in anything—their houses, their wealth, their family connections, their race horses, or the number of their children. Not many American families can boast of having built two of the country's outstanding historic houses still standing—Mount Airy which ranks with the finest colonial houses in the country, and the Octagon which ranks with the finest Federal houses.

John Tayloe II of Mount Airy was one of the wealthiest men in the colonies, owned one of the few private race tracks in colonial America, and was the father of 12 children. One daughter married a descendant of "King" Carter; another married Francis Lightfoot Lee; another married William Augustine Washington, a nephew of General Washington; and still another married Edward Lloyd who presided over the famous Wye House in Maryland. His son,

John Tayloe III, married the daughter of Governor Ogle of Maryland, was the father of 15 children, and built his elegant townhouse in the virginal capital. The Tayloe family papers now in the Virginia Historical Society tell that in June 1801, as the finishing touches were being put on the Octagon, the third John Tayloe asked Charles Wingman who was about to embark for England to look for a "sporting Watch" for him,

> in order to Try my Horses against time . . . & to remind you it must not be too costly—for a Man with six Children, & the expectancy of one annually for yrs. to come;—it won't be to throw away money in Trifles. . . .

Tayloe bought the land on which the Octagon stands in 1797 only six years after Major Pierre L'Enfant had arrived in Georgetown to start laying out the new Federal city and thus inaugurating the long list of talented designers and planners who converged on that burgeoning "ten miles square" established by Washington's request on the shores of the Potomac River. Latrobe, Bulfinch, Thornton, Jefferson, Hallet, Hadfield, Hoban, are but a few of them. For no matter how disparaging visitors to the new city may have been, it provided a golden opportunity to design a house or a public building that could not fail to to attract wide attention at the time and in the future. Were they not designing with the heady inspiration of housing the makers of a dream?

The Eccentric Dr. Thornton

Dr. William Thornton, one of the most interesting pioneers in the profession, was born in the Virgin Islands of an English Quaker family. He was described by a contemporary shortly after his death as "a scholar and a gentleman—full of talent and eccentricity . . . a painter, a poet, and horse-racer—well acquainted with the mechanic arts . . . his company was a complete antidote to dullness." Although Dr. Thornton received a medical degree from the University of Edinburgh, he practiced almost every profession but that of a physician. He was an inventor and experimented with the steamboat; he wrote scholarly articles on a wide range of subjects including astronomy, philosophy, language, medicine, art, and government; he was a painter, and in his own words "Never thought of architecture, but I got some books and worked for a few days. . . ."

While this amazing self-taught architect may have been slightly exaggerating, he not only won the Capitol competition but went on to design some of the most famous houses

The two Saint-Mémin profiles of the architect, Dr. William Thornton (top), and builder, John Tayloe III (above), which hang in the dining room.

The elaborate and delicate cornice in the lovely little circular foyer (20 foot / 6m diameter) is characteristic of the lighter cornices that appeared in American houses of the Federal period. The flooring is gray and white marble, and the two original cast-iron, urn-topped coal stoves are set in arched niches flanking the stair hall—The front door with its elliptical fanlight is behind the camera. (Right) Detail of the cornice in the entrance foyer.

(Opposite page) View of the stair hall from the entrance foyer shows a "painted" settee and two matching chairs with cane seats (c. 1800), which were part of a set of 16 chairs ordered by the Tayloes for the drawing room. Vestiges of the original paint remain under the seats but any attempt to repaint them awaits the discovery of another chair in the set with its original decoration.

still standing in the Washington area—Woodlawn Plantation, Tudor Place, and the Octagon. He was, in fact, one of the group of brilliant architects working after the Revolution who developed a new architectural style. The goal of this new movement in domestic architecture, as Professor Frederick D. Nichols of the University of Virginia put it, "was to adapt geometric perfection of rectangular and circular temples of antiquity, reduce the scale, and add all the new comforts of privacy and circulation, so well exemplified in the work of Robert Adam and the French architects." In their search for pure geometrical form, Professor Nichols claims, the noted American architects of this period were "the original inventors of cubism."

The Octagon—actually a misnamed hexagon—is an excellent example of this new movement. It was Dr. Thornton's first domestic commission and it shows him to have been an adept practitioner of the new style. To begin with, Thornton designed a handsome red brick, sandstone-trimmed house which is brilliantly suited to the triangular lot created by the angled streets of L'Enfant's plan. Its dignified facade is easily recognizable as a house that could not have been built before the Federal period, with its projecting curved exterior wall, and its white plaster panels over the second story windows. But it is in the interior that the new style is most obviously new.

Federal house plans with the rich and varied organization of their spatial volumes are a direct contrast to the severe formalism of the central hall and rectangular rooms found in late colonial houses such as Cliveden (page 90). Superb examples of Federal innovation in the Octagon's plan are the gracious circular entrance hall placed on the corner, the curvilinear stair hall flanked by wings with rectangular rooms, and the elliptical stairway. Robert Adam, who was the chief inspiration for the Federal plan, wrote in the preface of his *Works* that "the parade, the convenience, and social pleasures of life being better understood, are more strictly attended to in the arrangement and disposition of apartments."

But while the Federal plan was derived from Adam's high-ceilinged neoclassic rooms linked together in a harmony of varied spaces, the Americans gave it their own interpretation to meet the needs of life in a new country dedicated to freedom and simplicity. The Federal plans were less complex, the rooms simpler and more chaste, the colors more subdued. Social pleasures, however, as in Adam's England, were an important function of the American rooms, especially in Washington where almost the only social life that existed took place in the

(Above) The elaborate Coade stone mantel in the drawing room was ordered from London in 1799. Above the fireplace is a portrait of President Madison after Gilbert Stuart. All of the first floor curtains are of white silk based on the curtains visible in an 1830s watercolor of the Octagon.

(Right) Detail of one of the pedestals of the Coade stone mantel in the drawing room indicates the fine quality of its figures.

(Opposite page) The inlaid mahogany sideboard in the dining room is set in a shallow arched recess in the wall—a characteristic feature of Federal houses. Portraits flanking the fireplace are the St.-Mémin profiles in charcoal and chalk on pink paper of Colonel John Tayloe III and Dr. William Thornton.

few houses there were. "The amusement of social life must be very limited" in such a place is how the Englishman Sir Augustus put it. "There are no clubs established and no theatres in the place except for rope dancers."

An Outpost of Culture

Guests at the Octagon included the most distinguished men of the first half of the 19th century—Clay, Calhoun, Webster, Decatur, Randolph, Adams, Lafayette, Jefferson, Madison, Monroe. Although General Washington had often watched construction of the Octagon from his horse, he died before the Tayloes moved in in 1801.

The third John Tayloe's prestigeous connections in England as well as America added to the distinction of the Octagon company. He was educated at Eton and graduated from Christ College, Cambridge, in 1791. At both Eton and Cambridge, as his son later recorded, he was associated with some of the most distinguished people in Great Britain including Wellington and George Canning who later became Prime Minister. Tayloe's son also informs us that his father was "on terms of great intimacy with the Marquis of Waterford, the Beresfords, Lord Graves, and Sir Grey Skipwith, a native of Virginia through whom he had access to the best society in England, where he acquired those Chesterfieldian manners then in vogue."

No wonder several travelers in the early days of the republic referred to the Octagon as one of the "three houses of consequence in the city." In the few drawing rooms that did exist no party was considered fashionable, as German nobleman Francis Grund saw it, "unless graced by some distinguished senator, and a few members of the *corps diplomatique*." The influence of the latter he thought much greater "on the city's moral and social habits" than on "the politics of the State." But then the finest drawing room in Washington, according to the German aristocrat, was the Senate of the United States "for it is there the young women of fashion resort for the purpose of exhibiting their attractions." In point of fashion, he added, the Capitol is "the opera-house of the city." It is frequented "during the whole Season by every lounger in the place, and by every *belle* that wishes to become the fashion." Perhaps that is why Sir Augustus found Washington "one of the most marrying places of the whole continent." And he noticed that "both parties when betrothed, use a great deal of billing and cooing, eat out of the same plate, drink out of the same glass and show off their love to the whole company."

We assume, however, that such goings-on were not part of the social doings at the Octagon but are perhaps an indication of why it was considered such a haven of culture and hospitality. As Sir Augustus put it, Tayloe lived "as to outward appearance, in the best style of any of the Americans not in office." Neither did Tayloe, judging by the Saint-Mémin portrait of him, affect the eccentricities of dress of some of the southern aristocrats who prided themselves on being an American version of Rousseau's natural man. Even Jefferson seems to have carried democracy in dress to what others thought a dangerously radical extreme. When the newly arrived British minister Mr. Merry donned his dress court uniform to pay his call, he was taken aback to find himself

Introduced to a man as the President of the United States not merely in undress but actually standing in slippers down at the heels . . . indicative of utter sloveliness and indifference to appearance, but in a state of negligence actually studied!

So much for the master of the impeccable Monticello.

Joyful Intelligence

In 1801 when the Tayloes moved into the Octagon, the nearby White House was far from finished. But 13 years later, Dolley Madison following the advice of Latrobe had reupholstered some of the formal White House furniture in a newly fashionable yellow satin, and the British found it worthwhile to burn the President's House to the ground. At the suggestion of the hospitable Colonel Tayloe who was then staying at Mount Airy, the Octagon became the Madison's temporary White House. They lived there for about a year and thus it was in the circular room above the entrance hall that the Treaty of Ghent was ratified in February 1815. Some time later Joseph Gales, an eyewitness, wrote a dramatic description of the event:

Late in the afternoon . . . came thundering down Pennsylvania Avenue a coach and four foaming steeds, in which was Mr. *Henry Carroll* (one of the Secretaries at Ghent) the bearer . . . of the Treaty of Peace concluded at Ghent between the American and British Commissioners. Cheers and congratulations followed the carriage as it sped its way . . . to the residence of the President. . . .

Soon after nightfall, Members of Congress and others . . . presented themselves at the President's house, the doors of which stood open. When the writer entered the drawing room . . . it was crowded to its full capacity, Mrs. Madison (the President being with the Cabinet) doing the honours of the occasion. And what a happy scene it was. Among the members present were gentlemen of opposite politics, but lately arrayed against one another in continual conflict and fierce debate, now with elated spirits thanking God, and with softened hearts cordially felicitating with one another upon the joyful intelligence. . . . But the most conspicuous object in the room was Mrs. Madison herself, then in the meridian of life and queenly beauty. . . .

During the rest of that winter, the irrepressible Dolley kept the Octagon's reputation for hospitality very much alive. Every Wednesday evening some 200 ladies and gentlemen paid court to her in its drawing room.

After that historic episode in the life of the Octagon, the Tayloes returned to their own house, and as his son later reported, Colonel Tayloe "maintained until his death an establishment renowned throughout the country. Here he entertained in the most general manner, all persons of distinction, whether Americans or foreigners, who visited Washington, and imparted an elevated tone to society in that city."

He died there in 1828 at the age of 58 and was buried at Mount Airy. Thornton died the same year. After Mrs. Tayloe's death in 1855, the Octagon went through a comparatively uneventful period and eventually became a tenement housing ten families.

In 1902 the American Institute of Architects purchased the Octagon from a Tayloe descendent. In 1968 it was made a Registered National Historic Landmark and its ownership was transferred to the AIA Foundation to facilitate its maintenance and operation as a museum and educational tool.

Return to Adamesque-Federal Elegance

The main objective of the restoration was to strengthen the Octagon's structure and return it as nearly as possible to the way it was in the halcyon days when the Tayloes and Madisons lived there.

Modern additions, which were revealed during the initial investigation of the structure, were removed after being identified and photographed. The major change to the exterior was to re-cover the roof with cypress shingles as it had been in the early days. Although Thornton's original roof was flat, a hipped roof had been superimposed in Tayloe's lifetime and is visible in a watercolor sketch of the house made around 1830. The hipped roof had probably been put on in 1818 when there was a large bill from building contractors for work on the house. A letter to Colonel Tayloe from Benjamin Latrobe dated March 10, 1811, says,

> My promise to call to see your roof I have performed, altho I was not admitted, and you probably have not heard that I was at your door.

This letter led to the conjecture that Latrobe might have designed the hipped roof but later documentary evidence was discovered that named George Hadfield as its designer. Thornton's flat roof of canvas and pitch still exists under the later one.

(Opposite page: top) The circular Treaty Room over the entrance hall boasts the English rent table on which President Madison ratified the Treaty of Ghent in 1815. The circular Axminster carpet was woven by Thom Moor at Moorfields, London, about 1770, from designs by Robert Adam. At the Soane Museum in London there are several of Adam's carpet designs woven to his order by Thom Moor, which bear a striking resemblance to the Treaty Room carpet.

(Bottom) The kitchen has its original beehive oven and some of the original fireplace and kitchen equipment. A bill in the recently discovered Mount Airy papers shows that there were two cranes in the kitchen fireplace instead of one as the restorers thought.

(Above) Thornton's ingenious use of the angular spaces resulting from his nonrectangular plan is to be seen in the unique triangular service stair between the drawing room and main stair hall. This was largely intact and only needs to be structurally reinforced to be used as part of the exhibit area.

The elliptical fanlight over the front door had been removed but pieces were found in the attic and replaced. First-floor fireplaces, which were thought to have been converted to accommodate coal grates, were opened. Documents in the recently discovered Mount Airy papers, however, reveal that coal was always used in the Octagon fireplaces. A bill of 1801 lists five grates, but as Robert H. Garbee, AIA, of the Fauber firm puts it, "restorers are fond of andirons and don't like the idea of coal in fireplaces." The iron Adam-style stoves in the two niches in the circular entrance hall were also original furnishings or very early additions and were possibly imported from England. Attempts have been made in the past to attribute their design to Latrobe but without success. They are, in any case, a charming and decorative part of the Federal interior, and as the architects discovered, each of the adjacent chimneys was originally built with a flue to accommodate such stoves.

The Coade stone mantel in the drawing room was ordered from Coade, London, in 1799 by Dr. Thornton but, according to the Tayloe family papers in the Virginia Historical Society, it apparently had not arrived in July 1801 when Tayloe wrote to Messrs. Lamb & Younger, Merchts. London:

In the packages of Chimney Pieces, the principal one—the mantle of the drawing room Chimney Piece (as by their draft sent) is intirely missing—therefore unless the Piece be immediately sent so as to be put up before the room is finished Coades Bill ought not to be paid, without a deduction of this Piece, which is the principal one of the whole—The Portico Pieces if not already Shipt, I wish now to be paid no farther attention to—for the Building can't wait for them—please forwd. my letter to Coade....

The enclosed letter for Coade is headed "Mr Coade—ought to be Mr. Shark." Perhaps Colonel Tayloe would have been more courteous had he known that he was addressing a lady. Mrs. Eleanor Coade had taken over her father's business in 1769. In any case he says in his letter to Coade,

Astonishing as it will appear to you, 'tis no less true, that the mantle of the drawing room Chimney piece (as p. the Sketch you sent me) has in the packing been—omitted—for 'tis in neither of the three packages sent, and my room without it cannot be finished, you will therefore please send me immediately....
The Portico Pieces, as ordered—if not already forwarded, I wish not now to be sent, for the Building can't wait for them.

An interesting account of this almost indestructible composition stone is given by Sir

John Summerson in *Georgian London* where, he tells us, Coade was as important as stucco in the "improved" London of the 1770s. Mrs. Coade's father had discovered the composition which is unknown, Summerson says, "but it was a species of terracotta, the mixing of the 'earth' being a jealously guarded secret." Since the caps and bases of the columns and pilasters of the Octagon's entrance portico are of Coade stone they must have arrived eventually and their excellent condition attests to the indestructibility of the composition.

The bare simplicity of the Octagon's painted plaster walls and delicate cornices are characteristic features of the Federal period. The walls throughout the first floor have been returned to their original colors. It is interesting, however, that under subsequent layers of paint, a darker patch of color was found beside the fireplace in every room. Garbee thinks they may have been samples which Tayloe found too dark since the original coat was a paler tint in each case.

The circular entrance hall with its gray and white marble flooring is pale yellow with warm-gray cornice and woodwork. The same colors are carried into the curvilinear stair hall behind it. The balusters and baseboard of the stairs are dark gray-green. The drawing room walls are buff-gray with a darker dado and oyster woodwork, while the dining room walls are a fairly strong green with lighter green dado and oyster trim.

The major organic changes in the original arrangement of rooms were made on the second floor during the AIA's use of the house as its headquarters. The partitions between the bedchambers in both wings were removed in order to convert the space into two large exhibition galleries. The large gallery over the dining room has been retained for exhibition purposes but the wing over the drawing room has been restored with its three original spaces—bedroom, nursery, and a small hall leading to both. The original fireplaces with their mantelpieces were restored in both wings.

The Octagon's so-called Treaty Room, located in the circular pavilion above the entrance hall, was mostly intact except for its ceiling which needed to be replaced. This delicate job was fortunately accomplished without disturbing the original ornamental cornice which, like the cornice in the entrance hall, lends the circular room much of its peculiar charm. The Treaty Room boasts the original mahogany rent table on which President Madison ratified the Treaty of Ghent while his lady was presiding over the joyful festivities in the drawing room. No doubt the president preferred it that way. When he became president he

had gallantly given up the head of his own dinner table so his loquacious, voluptuous wife could preside.

Reconstruction of the entire third floor was necessary in order to comply with building codes but, says Fauber, "while considerable cutting and patching" was needed "to replace the third floor construction and install and conceal electrical wiring, pipes and ducts of mechanical systems, the restoration of plaster and woodwork has been so carefully and sympathetically done as not to lose the patina of time and age, so important to such an aristocratic old building."

During the initial investigation of the structure the original floor and wall finishes of the old basement kitchen and wine cellar were identified and uncovered. The present flat herringbone brick paving was found under a later concrete slab floor in the wine vault and in other basement areas.

Only the furniture that was original to the Octagon or would have been appropriate in Tayloe's day was retained. Additional Federal pieces have been added, the Tayloe family has promised others. The Tayloe papers from Mount Airy show that some of the Octagon's original furniture was imported from England, some of it was made in Washington, and some in Baltimore. There is, for instance, a letter written in July 1801 to Mr. Wm. Murdock, Merch't London, in which Tayloe says,

I pray you let me hear from you when I may expect my furniture for my City house in the shipment of which I must crave your own particular care and attention.

Another letter in the Mount Airy papers is interesting because it indicates Tayloe's taste in furniture, not to mention his bluntness in matters of business. On June 1, 1801, he writes to Mr. Bagster, No 20 Picadilly, London:

Sir/Your last letter is to hand, and at my leisure, shall meet due attention, and your Debt excluding interest will be cirtainly pd you—Instead of repenting a knowledge of me, I am sure 'twould have been money in my pocket, if such a person as Jas. Bagster had not been known to me—Your furniture as sent here, is the worst I ever saw, so slight—I lament the death of Mrs. B—and in haste, am Sir,
Your Obt Servt.
John Tayloe

It is important, however, that the Octagon be furnished with the type of furniture in fashion during the Federal period no matter how slight Tayloe may have thought it, since Federal rooms and their furnishings were very much of a piece. When Adam decorated the state rooms in an English

The 20th-century A.I.A. headquarters building looms behind the elegant 18th-century Octagon.

18th-century house, he provided sets of furniture specifically designed for every room and stated the exact location for each piece. Although the Americans seldom went that far, Federal interiors were plainly enhanced by the slender lines of the Sheraton, Hepplewhite, and Chippendale furniture being turned out by the cabinetmakers of the period for they, too, were inspired by the Adamesque-Federal which has often been called America's first truly national style.

Even if Tayloe doesn't seem to have appreciated its slightness he was certainly conscious of fashion in all its manifestations and was continually asking his correspondents in England to let him know "the Fashions of everything" including the "fashionable Colors for Carriages." Neither was he unconscious of expenses as the following letter, quoted from the Tayloe family papers, to his supervisor of construction Mr. Wm. Lovering, Geo. Town Potc. of June 14, 1801, clearly shows:

> . . . I have to beg you on the receipt of this write me fully what has been done since I was up—& what still remains to be done; & the soonest Period; when you think the House—stables & inclosures of the Lott can be fully compleated, I am in daily expectancy of my furniture, & wish the House compleated with all speed to receive it particularly as I wish to inhabit it early this Fall. . . . my Object is to be done with the Building as quickly as I can—with the least Trouble & Vexation—for the Expence of it already alarms me to Death, whenever I think of it—

His alarm is not altogether surprising. Tayloe originally contracted to have his house built for $13,000 and the finished house was closer to double that amount.

A 20th-Century Controversry

The AIA used the Octagon as its national headquarters until 1948 when the office moved to a two-story building which was added onto the stables behind the garden. By 1962, the AIA had outgrown both the house and the newer structure and decided to restore the house and hold a competition for a new building to replace the stables. The new building was to "preserve, complement and enhance the historic residence." The competition program also called for "an exciting demonstration that a fresh and contemporary architecture can live in harmony with fine architecture of another period; each statement giving the other meaning and contributing to the delight of the entire building complex."

In 1964 the jury selected a design by Mitchell-Giurgola Associates which was as

brilliant a 20th-century complement to L'Enfant's city plan as Thornton's 18th-century Octagon had been. But Washington's Fine Arts Commission objected to a lightwell or "notch" at the center of the facade. The architects made many attempts to please the Commission but said that the lightwell was a design feature involving their integrity.

Eventually the job went to The Architects Collaborative (TAC). The TAC design was approved by the Fine Arts Commission, and as Ada Louise Huxtable wrote in the *New York Times,* "high-level conservative competence" had been substituted "for creative experiment"—a far cry from the bold and imaginative spirit of the Federal city's early planners.

It is not often that a historic landmark has been so directly embroiled in the architectural and planning problems of the present. Usually when a landmark gets in the way of real estate development, it is quietly gotten rid of. There can be no doubt that the Octagon solution is a better one. For now, more than a century and a half after Washington watched it being built, the Octagon is again an appropriate symbol of the optimistic new nation—a highly successful collaboration, if you will, between the hospitable Virginia aristocrat whose horses were no less successful than his enterprises and the brilliant amateur architect who, as Wayne Andrews put it, "risked his income on the race track and his principal promoting steamboats."

The beginning of Washington was a promise—the promise of a dream in which people might live in harmony with one another and with the land. L'Enfant planned the city by developing a series of spatial concepts created by radial avenues and green circles. There were wide malls and parks. There were sites for significant architectural monuments, for houses, for government buildings.

The Octagon, then, is not only important as a splendid example of Federal design and an eloquent reminder of life in the early Federal city, it is significant as an important element of the city's design. And that, of course, is one reason why the AIA is concerned with its preservation.

Even today, after suffering the results of overpopulation and bad planning that most cities have, Washington is still one of our most attractive urban centers. In it, one is aware of trees, sky, grass, the curve of a river, as is rarely apparent in our northern industrial metropolises. This may be partially explained by the fact that many of the planners and designers of the Federal city came directly from Europe—Thornton, Latrobe, Hoban, L'Enfant—or from the plantations of Virginia which in turn were patterned after the great landed estates of England where the woods had become parks and the meadowland had become lawns. "Without this cultivated example in the country," as Lewis Mumford has pointed out, "it is no wonder . . . that our pavements so quickly obliterate trees and grass; no wonder that so many towns are little more than gashes of metal and stone."

"The pioneers who turned their backs on a civilized way of life," as Mumford says, "left us with a heavy burden—not merely blasted and disorderly landscapes, but the habit of tolerating and producing blasted and disorderly landscapes." Not until we "assimilate the notion that soil and site may have uses quite apart from sale," Mumford warned more than 50 years ago, "shall we stop barbarizing and wasting them. If we are to have a fine architecture," he said, "we must begin . . . not with the building itself, but with the whole complex out of which architect, builder, and patron spring, and into which the finished building, whether it be a cottage or a skyscraper, is set." This, too, is the message that the Octagon brings from another century, if only we will heed it.

Regency England and Grecian America

Sir John Soane's Museum

Decatur House

The American houses in this section were all designed between 1818 and 1823 and they have little in common with the earlier colonial or Palladian styles. A new bold simplicity marks their exteriors, a new sense of space and light marks their interiors. They were daring and modern but they fit the American scene. It was an entirely different America—optimistic and vigorous. The cautious homespun past was left behind. It was an age in which innovation was considered a sign of progress and in which the radical ideas of Sir John Soane, the English Regency architect who remodeled his own house in London between 1811 and 1813, found fertile ground. In many ways it was a period that had been nurtured by Jefferson whose University of Virginia would not be finished until 1825.

Soane's ideas were brought to American soil chiefly by two English-trained architects, Benjamin Henry Latrobe and William Jay. Latrobe's career owed much to the patronage of Jefferson who had befriended the young English architect shortly after he arrived in 1796. And before his tragic death in 1820 his public buildings as well as his houses had given a new look to many American cities. Although Jay's work was almost entirely confined to Savannah, his impact on that little city was no less important. The elegant Regency houses that Jay designed for Savannah's cotton merchants would have been unthinkable only a few years earlier. They must have seemed like the architecture of a different civilization in that southern city of white wood houses, and the enthusiasm with which they were received shows how ready popular taste was for a change.

Soane's new ideas made their first appearance here in Latrobe's Bank of Pennsylvania (1798). It was not only unlike any bank built before the Revolution but it was the first example on American soil of the rational phase of neoclassicism that marked Soane's work. Latrobe's bank also introduced America to its first Greek Revival portico.

Soane had developed his particular style in response to a need for a change in his own country. The aim of the new architecture had actually been put into words by the French Jesuit priest Marc-Antoine Laugier who argued in his *Essai sur l'architecture* for "that which is natural and true, wherein all is reduced to simple rules and executed according to great principles." Laugier rejected useless and unnecessary ornament and tried "to distinguish between the parts which are essential to the composition of a work of architecture and those which necessity has introduced and caprice added to." Soane took Laugier's ideas and translated them into his own individual style. He also distributed Laugier's text among his students at the Royal Academy and while neither Latrobe nor Jay were among the latter, they were familiar with the Frenchman's theories as were most of the young avant-garde architects of London.

Soane, as Sir John Summerson says, "must have known intuitively that the last great chapter in the history of classicism since the Renaissance was closed. There was nothing to add. In his personal style he sought new boundaries." Both Latrobe and Jay probably witnessed some of those new boundaries before they left England. When Latrobe came to America in 1796 Soane had finished part of his influential remodeling of the Bank of England. When Jay came in 1817 it was complete. Jay, in fact, could also have seen the architect's

Scarbrough House

Robert Mills House

own house at No. 13 Lincoln's Inn Fields completed in 1813.

The work of the American architect Robert Mills, particularly in its boldness of conception, its simplicity, and its use of Greek details, also showed the influence of Soane. But here the influence was not direct; it reached Mills through his tutor Latrobe.

Soane then was not only important in bringing America its brief interlude of Regency architecture but also in establishing Greek Revival architecture both here and in his own country. While the English Regency had no large-scale influence in America, it was to influence the Greek Revival style that appeared in Mills work and was soon to have a tremendous impact on the American countryside. Labtrobe, Jay, and Mills all made use of Greek frets, arched openings, domed ceilings, and the Doric order that were favorites of Soane.

In the first half of the 19th century then, England was still an important source of American architectural inspiration. The time lag, however, was much less. What had taken months and sometimes years to reach these shores now appeared almost overnight. Latrobe was introducing Soane's ideas to America while the English architect was at the height of his career. Also through Latrobe and Jay, England was introducing America to a new professionalism. Latrobe, Mills, and Jay differed from their predecessors in important respects. They were not amateurs nor dilettantes, they were full-time technically trained architects. Latrobe and Jay were trained in England and Mills acquired his professionalism from Latrobe.

Thus all the houses in this section were designed by professionally trained architects which not only represents a new phase in American architecture but makes the restorer's job easier. An architect-designed house usually provides the restorer with the kind of evidence that earlier houses did not. Most architects have idiosyncrasies that they repeat over and over and are recognized by restorers and architectural historians. Architects are also more apt to leave drawings and other records of their work which amateurs rarely do.

But as neatly as these houses may fit into a Soanian package, they represent a wide range of restoration philosophies. Sir John Soane's Museum—a house eminently worth preserving because it is a remarkable summation of Soane's innovations and aspirations—has been preserved at the architect's own bequest with its contents almost exactly as he left it. Decatur House, important because it was designed by Latrobe and because it occupied an important place in the social, intellectual, and political life of early Washington, has been restored to reflect most of that history on its first and second floors, while the third floor and service wing have been adapted as offices for the National Trust's headquarters staff. The Scarbrough House, one of the "little palaces" Jay designed in Savannah, is not only notable as a work of its architect but as an important architectural element in the restored urban scheme. It has been restored to reflect its early appearance and to serve as a setting for activities relating to historic preservation and city planning, and its second floor has been adapted as offices for Historic Savannah Foundation, Inc. The Robert Mills House in Columbia, South Carolina, which was adapted for institution use even before its completion, has been restored to the appearance its original owner and architect intended it to have.

Sir John Soane's Museum
London, England

The exterior is recognizably Soanian in its geometric severity. The Coade stone figures were inspired by the caryatids of the Erechtheum of Athens. No. 12, the first house rebuilt by Soane for his own use, is on the left, No. 14 on the right.

I think the best reason for preserving the house of a great man is when the house has itself been an object of the man's creative work—as in the case of Sir John Soane's incomparable museum.   Sir John Summerson

Sir John Soane must have been a strange man. Professor Nikolaus Pevsner has called him "the greatest English architect of Blake's day" and the juxtaposition of these two English eccentrics is not arbitrary. Both had styles that were wholly personal and idiosyncratic. Both liked the incised line as ornament. Both were preoccupied with imposing an abstract geometry on their work. And, perhaps above all, both had a highly personal vision.

Soane's London was the London of Byron and Keats, of the flamboyant Prince Regent and Beau Brummel, of Constable and Turner, of Thomas Sheraton and Josiah Wedgwood, of Coleridge and Wordsworth. But Soane, like Blake, went his own way. He was neither part of the beau monde in that most opulent of European cities nor did he have anything in common with his fellow architect John Nash who gave London its Regent Street and Brighton its Royal Pavilion (page 159). Soane and Nash were probably the most influential architects practicing in London at the end of the 18th century and the beginning of the 19th, but they might have come out of different countries and different centuries. Both architects were part of the spirit of growing rebellion against Palladianism and what Horace Walpole liked to call the "fripperies" of Adam, but Soane's way of rebelling was strictly his own. If the poet-painter Blake and the architect Soane were outsiders in most things they were eminently English in their eccentricity. And, as Professor Henry-Russell Hitchcock has pointed out, "such intense individuality as Soane's would hardly have been fostered and supported in any other country."

Soane was born in 1753, the son of a small Berkshire builder, and apparently developed a passion for architecture at a very young age. "Devoted to Architecture from my childhood," as he himself wrote in 1835, "I have through my life pursued it with the enthusiasm of a passion."

He was ambitious almost to the exclusion of everything else. His teaching, his writing, his travels, and the circle in which he moved were all part of attaining that ambition. He became, in fact, one of the first professional architects heralding an age in which poets as well as architects were no longer gentlemen amateurs dashing off words and houses for the delectation of their privileged confreres but gainful practitioners of their arts. It is significant that Lord Burlington died the year before Soane was born and Queen Victoria came to the throne only a few months after he died. Between these two events change was in the air, and in architecture, Soane was not only an individualist but probably the age's major innovator.

Master of Surprises

Soane's individuality shows up especially in his interiors where he achieved picturesque effects that rightly earn him Pevsner's epithet as the "master of surprises in internal spaces." His own London house at No. 13 Lincoln's Inn Fields, as Pevsner says, "is full of unexpected and not easily comprehended effects of concealed lighting, concealed structure, and unexpected changes of level." But while the spatial surprises of Soane's interiors may be unlike anything else in English architecture, they have their parallel in the picturesque landscape design introduced by Pope and Burlington earlier in the 18th century. Pope's description of the composition of the picturesque garden, as Pevsner reminds us, admirably fits the architecture of Soane's interior spaces:

> Let not each beauty everywhere be spied
> When half the skill is decently to hide.
> He gains all points who pleasingly confounds,
> Surprises, varies, and conceals the bounds.

In this quote from Epistle IV "To Richard Boyle, Earl of Burlington, of the Use of Riches," Pope might have been describing Soane's own house in Lincoln's Inn Fields which seems to be a maze of subtle surprises, concealments, and confounding intricacies. And like the picturesque 18th-

The dining room as seen from the library. The ceiling in these rooms, explains Soane, "is formed in compartments, showing the construction of the floor above and is enriched with pictures by Henry Howard, R.A." The latter portray mythological subjects and were commissioned by Soane in 1834. Most of the furniture was bought by Soane for his domestic use, including the desk of Sir Robert Walpole, which was probably obtained by Soane when the Walpole House in Chelsea was demolished.

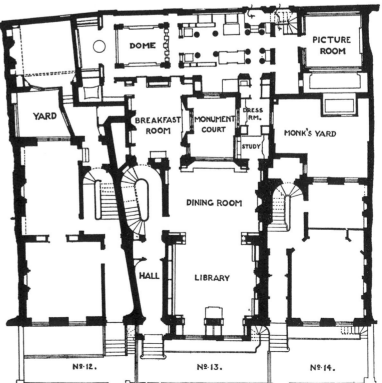

Plan of the ground floors of Numbers 12, 13, and 14 Lincoln's Inn Fields as existing about 1837. The restored library at No. 12 is the room left of the stairway.

century English garden with which Burlington surrounded his austerely classic villa (page 76), Soane's house embraces a similar contradiction in its romanticism and austerity. Inside he played with picturesque spatial combinations and light effects. Outside is all severity.

The house at No. 13 Lincoln's Inn Fields, moreover, is not only a concrete record of many of Soane's innovations but it is the best summation of the aspirations of that influential English architect whose complex character and architectural self-centeredness resulted in the creation of a unique style.

Because he himself endowed it as a museum before his death, it is almost exactly as he left it, complete with his vast collections of art and antiquities, and is certainly one of the most unusual personal memorials in existence. It has been the aim of the trustees of the Soane Museum over the years, in the words of its present curator, Sir John Summerson, "to maintain the fabric and its decoration so far as possible in the condition in which Soane left them."

Soane began his architectural career in the office of George Dance. He later moved to the office of Henry Holland who had recently formed a partnership with "Capability" Brown, one of the great 18th-century English landscape gardeners who revolutionized garden design all over Europe and America. During this period Soane undoubtedly absorbed some of Brown's theories about the picturesque garden that were to find their analogy in the picturesque effects of his interiors.

Soane attended lectures at the Royal Academy, winning the Silver Medal in 1772 and the Gold Medal in 1776. In 1778 he went to Italy and while there he created for the Bishop of Derry two designs of a "residence for a canine family," one for "ancient times," and the other for "modern times." Whether on the basis of these esoteric dog houses or on something else, the Bishop promised the young architect all sorts of opportunities and suggested that he immediately return to England. Soane rushed home only to find that the Bishop was no longer interested in him and his designs. The disappointment was extreme: "how much I had overrated the magnificent promises and splendid delusions . . .," he confessed in his *Memoirs*, "I was keenly wounded, depressed in spirits and my best energies paralysed."

This frustration apparently set Soane's promising career back for several years. But in 1788 he was elected to the Surveyorship of the Bank of England and the designs he created for the bank in the following years established his influence—an influence that

spread as far as Savannah where William Jay's work (page 139) has given that lovely city a Regency cast, and to the many cities where the work of Benjamin Henry Latrobe has left traces of the Soanian imprint on these shores (page 131). Whether Jay and Latrobe were directly influenced by Soane may be a moot point but they were certainly moved by the same spirit—the rebellion against Palladianism and the love of simplified versions of ancient classic forms. And both men must have seen the stock office that Sir John Summerson believes was "far and away, the most original architectural language in Europe at the moment."

In 1806 Soane was elected Professor of Architecture at the Royal Academy, and with his typical thoroughness, he prepared for his teaching by mastering practically the entire history of architecture. His diligence may or may not have had any effect on his students, but it greatly enriched his own architecture.

Between 1790 and 1810 Soane accomplished an extraordinary amount of work. In order to fulfill his many commissions, Dorothy Stroud, author of *The Architecture of Sir John Soane*, tells us that by "carriage or on horseback he would undertake prodigious journeys, often travelling through the night so as to get to town by early morning for some other appointment." His architectural students "were expected to emulate this rigorous example by working from seven to seven in the summer, or eight to eight in the winter, six days a week." On rare occasions Soane would spend a day coarse fishing in the country or an evening at the theater with Mrs. Soane. After 1800, Miss Stroud says, the Soanes would often entertain their guests with "Gothic scenes and intellectual banquets."

In 1792, the banner year in which Soane designed the Bank of England stock office, he rebuilt the first house in Lincoln's Inn Fields, No. 12, for his own occupation. Between No. 12 and No. 13, the adjoining house, there is an angled party wall that runs back from the street at a tangent supposedly following an ancient boundary between two fields. This curious angle gave Soane a chance to exercise his ingenuity in the plan. This he did by creating a wedge-shaped staircase wider at one end than the other. He later repeated the wedge shape in reverse when he designed No. 13.

Not long after moving into No. 12 Soane's expanding collections of art and antiquities outgrew the space. In 1808 he got permission from the owner of No. 13 to create an extension along the back of both houses. Thus he built the part of his museum now known as the Dome which took the

form of an open well surrounded by arched passages at the basement and ground-floor levels. This annex was extended behind No. 14 in 1824 and later it was made accessible to No. 13.

It was in 1812, however, that Soane's ever-expanding collections outgrew the first extension and he persuaded the occupant of the larger premises at No. 13 to exchange houses with him. The architect completely rebuilt No. 13 for his personal use and his overflowing acquisitions and in October 1813 the Soanes "drank tea in [the] new study."

By this time Soane's collections included thousands of classical and medieval architectural fragments, coins, casts, Greek and Roman bronzes—everything, in fact, from a desk that belonged to Sir Robert Walpole to an Egyptian sarcophagus, from drawings by Piranesi and Soane's own models for the Bank of England to *The Rake's Progress* by Hogarth. These and much more are displayed, often with surrealistic effect, in the Monk's Parlor, the Crypt, the Dome, the Monument Court, among other areas constructed by Soane for the purpose. A Picture Room added in 1824 is a splendid example of Soane's ingenuity. Designed so that it accommodates enough pictures to fill a gallery more than three times its size, this very small room (about 12 feet square/1 square meter) has three walls consisting of hinged planes, inside which more pictures are hung. Also in 1824 Soane installed his prized sarcophagus of Seti I (1303–1290 B.C.) in the Sepulchral Chamber and gave a three-day party in its honor.

Thus the romantic classicism of No. 13 Lincoln's Inn Fields not only embodies what Soane called "the poetry of architecture," it is also an example *par excellence* of the acquisitive traits of the early 19th century.

The Poetry of Architecture Preserved

Soane had the foresight to obtain an act of Parliament to preserve his collections intact so they could be permanently accessible to "Amateurs and Students in Painting, Sculpture and Architecture" after he died. Those collections include some 4,000 architectural volumes and more than 32,000 architectural drawings ranging from plans of Elizabethan houses to drawings by Sir William Chambers and Robert Adam.

So great were his collections, however, that shortly after his death in 1837 some of his furniture was sold and during the ensuing years some objects were put into storage. In 1919 the South Drawing Room at the front of the house above the library was turned into a study room by adding fixed

(Top) The breakfast room, with its shallow dome and indirect lighting, its vista across the Monument Court, and its cleverly placed mirrors, is characteristic of Soane's dramatic imagination. (Above) The Dome presents one of the most surrealistic vistas in the Museum with its great variety of antiquities displayed beneath a miniaturized dome over an open circular well surrounded by arched passages at two levels. A marble bust of Soane stands on a lion-headed pedestal and was done by Sir Francis Chantrey.

bookcases and chests for drawings, as well as laying a new floor. This was done to make the collections more accessible but it drastically changed the appearance of the room as Soane knew it.

Fortunately in 1968 No. 12 Lincoln's Inn Fields, Soane's first house, became vacant and the Trustees of the Soane Museum were able to acquire the house and restore it as a place in which to display parts of the collection no longer on view and to provide space for those who wanted to examine the drawings. The acquisition of No. 12 thus made it possible to return the drawing room at No. 13 to its original appearance. For many years the No. 12 house had been used for law offices necessitating the subdivision of the original rooms. During the restoration (by Edward Duley of William Holford and Partners) all the later partitions and alterations were removed with the exception of a few details that were considered worth preserving as industrial archaeology.

One intriguing discovery made during the restoration resulted in uncovering the famous "starfish" ceiling in the library of No. 12. This ceiling had long been known from a watercolor of Soane and his family having breakfast there, and in the hope that it might still exist under subsequent layers of paint, several exploratory scrapings were made. Enough traces of the original ceiling were found to make it feasible to strip the later layers of paint (there were 16) off the entire ceiling. There was not sufficient money left to retouch the "starfish" ceiling but it is complete enough as it is and a fine example of one of the characteristic features of Soane's style. He used a variation of the "starfish" ceiling in many of his designs and Summerson believes Soane derived it from an engraving by Santo Bartoli of the ceiling of an Etruscan tomb at Corneto. It is, in any case, a charming indication of Soane's proclivity for avoiding flat ceilings.

The watercolor of the library at No. 12 was also used as a guide to restoring as much of the original furniture to the room as possible. Two bookcases on the right wall have been returned to their original place but, unfortunately, those on the opposite wall have disappeared. The pictures have been rehung, and the panels of the doors have been edged black as in the painting.

The adjoining room in the front of No. 12 is now being used for the display of Soane's collection of architectural models—models of his own buildings as well as of the temples of Paestum and other antiquities. Above this room is the Students' Room where Soane's extensive collection of architectural drawings can be studied. The doors and shutters in the new Students' Room were stripped of paint and left that way, even though they had always been painted,

because of the quality of the wood and the precision of the joincry.

Those Fanciful Effects

Except for the staircase and the "starfish" ceiling, No. 12 Lincoln's Inn Fields does not have anything like the fascination of the interiors at No. 13. In No. 13 one finds the most interesting expression of Soane's dramatic imagination and what he called "the poetry of architecture." The highly original domed and skylit spaces, the dramatic effects of light and shade, of groupings and vistas, are superb examples of the Soanian style as is the exterior of No. 13 with its geometric austerity, its bold simple massing and incised lines. Although Soane designed the houses on either side of the museum, Nos. 12 and 14, he apologizes in his description of No. 13 for the lack of perfect symmetry in the group, which, he says, resulted from the fact that the sites came into his hands at different periods—No. 12 in 1792 and No. 14. in 1824.

The ground floor of No. 13 is entered through a hallway which is painted to imitate porphyry. Straight ahead is the wedge-shaped staircase with an iron balustrade in a typical Soanian design. The dining room and library on the right of the hallway is really one room separated by two projecting piers formed into bookcases. These rooms are almost exactly as Soane left them and it is here that one begins to understand what Ian Nairn means when he says that after a visit to the Soane Museum "four walls and a ceiling can never look the same again." Soane tried in these unique rooms to create a sense of illusion and mystery within the confines of an ordinary house, and he succeeded to an amazing extent. The use of segmental and semicircular arches, Gothic pendants, mirrors placed in the recesses over the bookshelves creating the illusion that the ceiling is repeated in another room, the Pompeian colors—all combine to produce a rich and intriguing background for the books and works of art. In his description of the house, Soane explains that from the large dining-room window "the Monument Court, with its architectural pasticcio, and assemblage of ancient and modern art, and particularly the frieze of Grecian sculpture are seen to great advantage." Soane's "pasticcio"—a precarious tower of ancient and modern fragments—was removed in 1896 because it became dangerous. On the window sill is an arrangement of pots and vases, the effect of which, in Soane's words, "is considerably heightened by the looking-glass in the splayed jambs of the window." The pots and vases also serve to blur the division between room and court.

The breakfast parlor behind the stairway is probably the most characteristic example of Soane's personal style in the house and therefore his own description of it here is:

In the centre rises a spherical ceiling, springing from four segmental arches, supported by the same number of pilasters, forming a rich canopy. The spandrels of the dome and the soffits of the arches were decorated with a number of mirrors. In the dome is an octangular lantern-light, enriched with eight Scriptural subjects in painted glass. At the north and south ends of the room are skylights, which diffuse strong lights over the several architectural and other works decorating the walls. The view from this room into the Monument Court and into the Museum, the mirrors in the ceiling, and the looking-glasses, combined with the variety of outline and general arrangement in the design and decoration of this limited space, present a succession of those fanciful effects which constitute the poetry of architecture.

And, as Ian Nairn puts it, "God knows what the breakfasts must have been like."

It is in the breakfast room that Soane's disposition of planes in such a way as to draw the eye through one after another, from one vista to another, is most masterful. Here, too, one is again reminded of the appropriateness of Pope's description of the 18th-century picturesque garden:

He gains all points who pleasingly confounds
Surprises, varies, and conceals the bounds.

Soane's breakfast room also seems to answer what Uvedale Price called the "two most fruitful sources of human pleasure" in his *Essay on the Picturesque* (1794):

the first, that great and universal source of pleasure, variety—the power of which is independent of beauty, but without which even beauty itself soon ceases to please; the second intricacy—a quality which, though distinct from variety, is so connected and blended with it, that the one can hardly exist without the other. According to the idea I have formed of it, intricacy in landscape might be defined as that disposition of objects which by a partial and uncertain concealment, excites and nourishes curiosity—the most active principle of pleasure.

Although Soane apparently did not know Uvedale Price, he owned an annotated copy of his book and, as mentioned before, he knew "Capability" Brown—two of the 18th-century's most influential proponents of the picturesque elements of garden design. It is, moreover, fascinating to realize how closely Soane's interiors follow those

(Top) Watercolor of Soane and his family having breakfast in the library at No. 12 Lincoln's Inn Fields, the house designed by Soane in 1792 and recently incorporated into the Museum. (Above) The library at No. 12 after the restoration of its "starfish" ceiling and most of its original furniture.

The South Drawing Room at No. 13 as it was restored when the Students' Room was moved to No. 12.

Watercolor of the South Drawing Room at No. 13 painted in 1825 by C. J. Richardson.

18th-century precepts of the picturesque while being totally Soanian in originality.

It is Ian Nairn, however, who puts Soane's breakfast room in 20th-century terms by calling it,

> probably the deepest penetration of space and of man's position in space, and hence in the world, that any architect has ever created. You might infer the second part from Soane's other buildings, but the first part, the human understanding of the nature of eating breakfast, can only be caught here. If man does not blow himself up, he might in the end act at all times and on all levels with the complete understanding of this room.

The breakfast room was entirely redecorated in 1951 on the basis of remains of the original oak graining found under successive repaintings of the walls and the dome. The pale oak graining of the dome was carefully imitated panel by panel as the old work was covered up.

One of the happy results of moving the Students' Room to No. 12 during the 1969–70 restoration of that house was that it made it possible to return the South Drawing Room, which is above the library, to the way Soane knew it.

Again a watercolor made in 1825 by C.J. Richardson was an aid to restoring much of the original furniture as was an inventory made in 1837. Also thanks to the watercolor and a fragment of the room's original paint found behind a bookcase, the color scheme—a strong yellow edged with green—has been restored.

The accuracy with which the South Drawing Room has regained its original character can be judged by Soane's own description of it in 1834:

> The ceiling is formed in domical compartments and flat surfaces enriched with a variety of architectural decorations. . . . According to the original constuction, this room was lighted from the south by three large windows opening into a loggia, commanding views of the gardens of Lincoln's Inn Fields . . . this loggia has since [in 1832] been enclosed, and now forms a gallery extending the whole length of the room. . . . The boxings in which the shutters were formerly placed are filled with bookcases, containing a variety of general and miscellaneous literature.

Even the English writer Marcus Binney has admitted that "as one stands in this room one can but conclude how fortunate it is that for once pressures for improvement and change have meant that atmosphere has not been extinguished but rather rekindled." Such is the aim of all historic res-

toration but the British are usually wary of changing anything in a historic house. They are skeptical of the house museum as it is known in the United States, which they believe, not without reason, is often sterile—devoid of the eccentricities that give a house its particular character. The English philosophy in general is to keep a house lived in if possible and to retain its sense of life in any case even if it means, as it sometimes does, "a discreet intermingling of homely rubbish with works of art" in order to provide "a salutary, and not contemptible relief to the visitor in search of atmosphere," as James Lees-Milne puts it.

The British distrust of house museums, however, does not prevent that country's poet laureate John Betjeman from saying in his *First and Last Loves*: "There is only one London museum of an antiquarian sort which really moves me, and that is Sir John Soane's in Lincoln's Inn Fields. And this is interesting not only because of its wonderful plan and exquisite furniture and pictures, but also because it was Sir John's private house."

As might be expected, that complex, lonely, self-centered architect who was fanatical in the pursuit of his career, did not get along very well with his two sons, nor with people in general. He was not easy to understand except perhaps by a few perceptive people such as the young George Wightwick who was employed by Soane as a secretary in 1826 and 1827 and has left us a marvelous word-picture of the "dear old tyrant" who he describes as,

> distinguished looking: taller than common; and so thin as to appear taller; his age at this time about seventy-three. He was dressed entirely in black; his waistcoat being of velvet, and he wore knee-breeches with silk stockings. . . . He was ill when I saw him, and sorely worn with perplexity and vexation; and therefore I ought to say, that at *that* time, it can be scarcely said that he had any front face. In profile his countenance was extensive; but looking at it "edgeways" it would have been "to any thick sight" something of the invisible. A brown wig carried the elevation of his head to the utmost attainable height; so that, altogether his physiognomy was suggestive of the picture which is presented on the back of a spoon held vertically. His eyes, now sadly failing in their sight, looked red and small beneath their full lids; but, through their weakened orbs, the fire of his spirit would often show itself in proof of its unimpaired vigour.

Soane's portrait painted in 1828 by Sir Thomas Lawrence tells us the same story.

There could be no more fitting memorial

for Soane the man and Soane the architect than his own house at No. 13 Lincoln's Inn Fields. Its careful preservation through the years allows us more than a glimpse of that strange, eccentric man, it gives us an appreciation of his dramatic imagination, his remarkable experimentations with light and space—truly the "master of surprises in internal spaces." It expresses the spirit of Soane's curious vision. But unlike Blake, who was never really appreciated during his lifetime, Soane was. He became a member of the Royal Academy of Arts in 1802 and was knighted in 1831 and his influence was extensive—at least until the architects of the Victorian age became smugly satisfied with their imitations of the past.

The portrait of Sir John Soane by Sir Thomas Lawrence, painted in 1828, hangs above the fireplace in the dining room—"almost the last picture painted by that distinguished artist," as Soane put it.

Decatur House

Washington, D.C.

The east facade as seen from the President's (now Lafayette) Square. The elegant townhouse designed by Latrobe has been restored as both a house museum and headquarters for the National Trust for Historic Preservation.

There is nothing that more divides civilized from semi-savage man than to be conscious of our forefathers as they really were, and bit by bit to reconstruct the mosaic of the long-forgotten past. . . . Our imagination craves to behold our ancestors as they really were, going about their daily pleasure.

G. M. Trevelyan

Old houses are the keepers of legends, the fragments of a nation's history, its mysteries and its myths, but few houses still stand in America to tell more brilliant tales of the past than the Decatur House on Washington's Lafayette Square. A long list of distinguished tenants, which reads like a who's who in American history, has lived behind its elegantly restrained brick facade. Its gracious rooms have been the center of social and diplomatic life ever since a ball was given there in 1820 for the most important bride of the season. She was President Monroe's youngest daughter Maria Hester, whose marriage to Samuel Laurence Gouverneur was the first to take place in the executive mansion. The ball was given in her honor by Commodore and Mrs. Stephen Decatur in their new house on the President's Square, so called by L'Enfant in his plan for the city.

Mrs. Truxtun Beale, the last private owner of Decatur House, bequeathed it to the National Trust in 1956, and the Trust restored it to reflect the assimilation of time and tenants that made it such a gay and illustrious residence during its first 138 years. On the basis of research the first-floor rooms have been restored to interpret Stephen Decatur's era through wall colors and coverings as well as some of the furnishings that belonged to the Decaturs. The second-floor rooms reflect subsequent eras of the building's life. Thus the first two floors of Decatur House recreate the succession of generations, tastes, and styles that have become an organic part of it, while the third floor, the basement, and the service wing have been adapted as offices for the National Trust's headquarters staff. Decatur House, then, remains an active part of the Washington scene.

Although no single document or group of documents can give a complete picture of a furnished house at any one moment throughout the years, as former National Trust curator John Pearce puts it, "the information available to the Trust on the furnishings of Decatur House was fuller than for most historic museums." There were inventories of the house made during several periods, many estate bills, documents that provided information about other important Washington houses of the time, along with newspaper accounts, and the diaries of such interested and accurate observers of 19th-century life on the President's Square as Benjamin Ogle Tayloe (son of the Octagon's builder) who recorded much of the drama and gossip of the Square during the first half of the 19th century.

Commodore Decatur, the 37-year-old naval hero acclaimed for his daring exploits in the War of 1812 and for suppressing the Barbary Pirates in the Mediterranean, came to Washington in January 1816 to serve on the Board of the Navy Commissioners. He used the prize money from his feats on the high seas to purchase a small lot on the President's Square, diagonally across from the front of the President's House. Decatur then enlisted Benjamin Henry Latrobe, the most able architect on the American scene, to design a house for him. Rarely have two such colorful personalities collaborated on the design of a private house—the brilliant naval hero and the British-trained "genius of the Capitol."

Latrobe was born in England of Moravian parents. His father was born in Dublin, and his mother who was the granddaughter of a German baron was born in Bethlehem, Pennsylvania. Latrobe had studied in Germany and traveled widely in France and Italy before returning to England where he was apprenticed first to John Smeaton, the engineer, and later to Samuel Pepys Cockerell, one of the most successful architects of his day. As head draftsman in Cockerell's office, Latrobe worked on such important projects as the Admiralty Buildings in London, and was on his way to establishing his reputation in England when his young wife died. Partly because of his wife's death and partly because he had an inheritance to

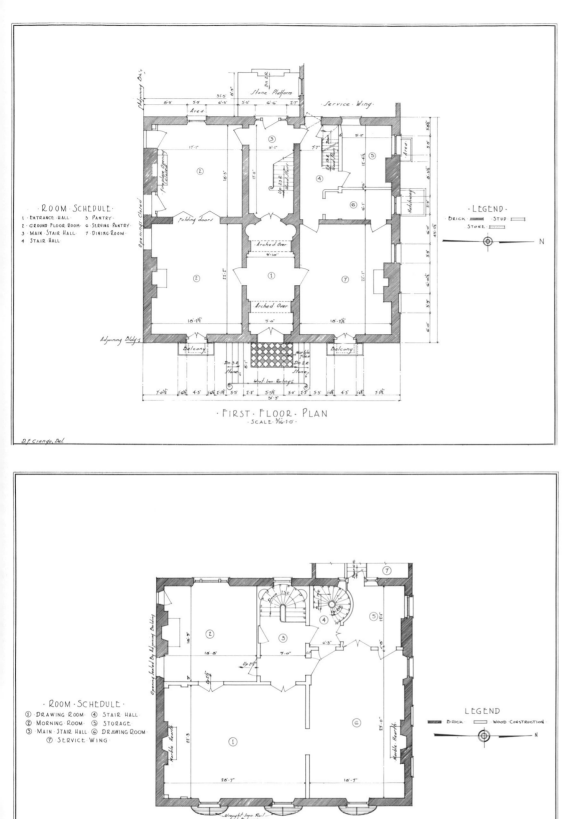

· R O O M · S C H E D U L E ·
1 · ENTRANCE · HALL ·   5 · PANTRY ·
2 · GROUND · FLOOR · ROOM ·   6 · SERVING · PANTRY ·
3 · MAIN · STAIR · HALL ·   7 · DINING · ROOM ·
4 · STAIR · HALL ·

· LEGEND ·
BRICK ▨ STUD ▭
STONE ▭

N

· FIRST · FLOOR · PLAN ·
· SCALE · 3/16" · 1'-0" ·

D. F. Ciango, Del.

· R O O M · S C H E D U L E ·
① · DRAWING · ROOM ·   ④ · STAIR · HALL ·
② · MORNING · ROOM ·   ⑤ · STORAGE ·
③ · MAIN · STAIR · HALL ·   ⑥ · DRAWING · ROOM ·
⑦ · SERVICE · WING ·

LEGEND
BRICK ▨ WOOD CONSTRUCTION ▭
N

· SECOND · FLOOR · PLAN ·
· SCALE · 3/16" · 1'-0" ·

D. F. CIANGO, DEL.

First and second floor plans made before the Victorianisms were removed from the front facade.

claim in Pennsylvania, Latrobe set sail for America. Had he remained in England, as Wayne Andrews suggests, he would certainly have challenged Soane and Nash, the architectural leaders of the coming generation. In America there was no one to match either his imagination or his experience, and as Andrews puts it, "it would be impossible to exaggerate the blessings of his example in our midst."

Latrobe arrived in Norfolk in 1796 and was soon recognized by Jefferson as the most accomplished architect on this side of the Atlantic. During the rest of his life he fulfilled a variety of commissions in every part of the country. He designed churches, theaters, college buildings, lighthouses, residences, waterworks, tombstones, furniture. He created the first Greek Revival structure in America for his 1798 Bank of Pennsylvania in Philadelphia. He designed Grecian furniture for Dolley Madison in the White House. A new Greece, he prophesized in Philadelphia in 1811, is developing "in the woods of America." But that new Greece didn't develop until after Latrobe's death in 1820.

In Washington, Latrobe gave the expanding capital much of its style. Many of the finest early houses were of his design. He gave the Capitol and the White House their polished forms. He collaborated with Jefferson on many buildings, perhaps most successfully on the porticos of the White House. Latrobe, in fact, might have taken part of the credit for himself when he wrote to Jefferson in 1807:

> It is no flattery to say that you have planted the arts in your country. The works already in this city [Washington] are the monuments of your judgment and of your zeal and of your taste.

Stephen Decatur joined the Navy in 1798 and soon rose to fame in the Tripolitan wars where his daring in setting fire to the captured frigate *Philadelphia* was hailed as the "boldest act of the age" by no less an authority than the British admiral Lord Nelson. During the War of 1812, Decatur captured the British frigate *Macedonian*, another bold feat which won him wide acclaim. In a letter Latrobe wrote from Washington on December 9, 1812, to his son in New Orleans, he describes a Naval Ball given for "Captns Hull & Morris." About two hours before the ball, he writes,

> handbills arrived from New York, announcing . . . Com. Decatur had captured the Macedonian. . . . It was immediately resolved to illuminate the city, & the Pennsylvania Avenue & the scattered houses on the hills, cut, I assure you, a most singular & splendid dash of

scattered fires. The company assembled, all the secretaries & wives. . . . Doubt was then thrown on the truth. . . . People were ashamed to have wasted their candles. . . . The dancing, however went on. . . . About 9 o'clock, young A. Hamilton arrived at the door with the colors of the Macedonian . . . the applause was absolutely boisterous. . . . The colors were taken up and spread over the heads of Captns. Hull, Morris, Stewart & other Naval men, including the Secretary, & marched like a canopy round the room, & at last spread at the feet of Mr. Madison. . . . Nothing could be more effecting, at the same time dramatic, as the scene.

On March 8, 1806, the intrepid Decatur married Susan Wheeler, daughter of a prominent Norfolk merchant, who had been courted by Napoleon's brother Jerome. Both Decatur and his wife must have had great personal charm judging from contemporary accounts, and they made their house on the President's Square a favorite rendezvous among the select cosmopolitan society of early 19th-century Washington. "Commodore and Mrs. Decatur lived comparatively in splendor," reported Benjamin Ogle Tayloe, "and were much courted for their different high qualities,—Decatur, the Bayard of the Navy, for his renown; his wife for her accomplishments and intellectual attractions."

Historic Hospitality on the President's Square

The unadorned brick facade of the townhouse Latrobe designed for Decatur seems to affirm the architect's creed: "It is not the ornament, it is the *use* that I want." But the delicate perfection of its interior detail, the graciousness and beautiful proportions of its rooms—while admirably fitting it for its long career as the setting for some of Washington's most brilliant social gatherings—seem to belie the heavy connotation of the word *use*.

Although, as Talbot Hamlin points out, Latrobe's love of niches and hemicycles, like his feeling for surface, might be traced in part to the pervasive style of Robert Adam, he belonged to a different school, the work of which was characterized by simplicity, geometric power, and rationalism. It achieved its greatest triumph in Sir John Soane's work (see page 122).

In 1818 the working drawings for the Decatur House were finished and sent to two contractors for bids. Latrobe forwarded their proposals unopened to Decatur with a note saying he thought they would indicate a cost of about $11,000. He also suggested that if Decatur expected to rent the house at

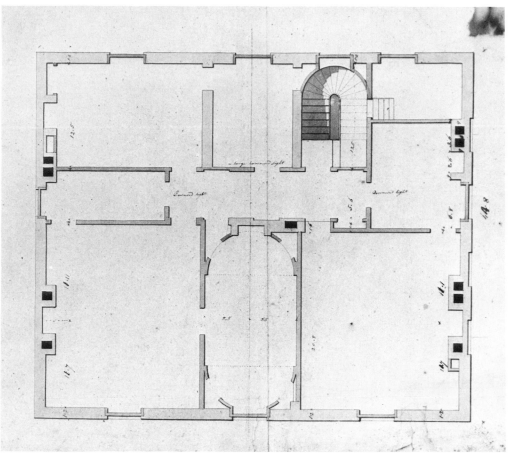

Latrobe's drawing in ink and wash (c. 1818) for the third floor of Decatur House.

some time to a foreign minister he ought to add a lightly built one-story addition at the back for a servant's hall. The bids, Latrobe further explained, did not include papering or the marble mantels for the principal rooms. The mantels, Latrobe thought, could be "better procured from Italy."

The house was built with the addition suggested by Latrobe and on January 16, 1819, Decatur writes, "I have just moved into my new house." Today that house is one of the few remaining of the many private houses designed by Latrobe. It is also remarkable that the atmosphere of one of the country's most important public squares comes partly from three works linked with Latrobe—Decatur House, St. John's Church, and the front colonnade of the White House.

The Decaturs only occupied their house for 14 months when their tenancy came to an abrupt end with Stephen Decatur's fatal duel with Commodore James Barron in March 1820, just two days after the ball they had given for the bride. "Commodore Decatur's death was a striking and melancholy event," writes Margaret Bayard Smith in *The First Forty Years of Washington Society:*

This week had been destined to be the gayest of the season, and parties for ev-

ery night in the week were fixed for the bride, not one of which took place, for the moment Decatur fell, nothing else was thought of. Mrs. Decatur has left the city, house, carriages, &c &c, are to be sold, and from all this gaiety and splendor she retires to solitude and melancholy. No one but her friend Mrs. Harper, who was in the house, ever saw her, and even to her, she seldom spoke a single word. More impressively than any words, did these events preach the vanity of honors and pleasures of rank and wealth.

And John Quincy Adams, who attended the burial, notes in his *Diary:*

There were said to be ten thousand persons assembled. . . . A very short prayer was made at the vault by Dr. Hunter, and a volley of musketry from a detachment of the Marine Corps closed the ceremony of the earthly remains of a spirit as kindly, as generous, and as dauntless as breathed in this nation, or on this earth.

Fame, Beauty, and a Rabble of Beards

What was Washington like when Commodore Decatur and his wife moved into their new house on The President's Square? Margaret Bayard Smith, describing the young city to her sister, says

(Top) The front doorway as it was reconstructed in 1944. Architectural historian Paul F. Norton has suggested that the doorway arch was incorrectly restored. "It needs visual vertical supports, like a pilaster, at the impost of the arch. Neither on the interior of the vestibule, nor in any other building does Latrobe disturb the peaceful resting of arches on some reasonable visual support." (Above) View of the entrance hall looking toward the stair hall. The double stair hall (see floor plan) is a typical Latrobe feature.

... Washington possesses a peculiar interest and to an active, reflective, and ambitious mind, has more attractions than any other place in America. This interest is daily increasing, and with the importance and expansion of our nation, this is the theatre on which its most interesting interests are discuss'd, by its ablest sons, in which its greatest characters are called to act, it is every year, more and more the resort of strangers from every part of the union, and all foreigners of distinction who visit these states, likewise visit this city. There are here peculiar facilities for forming acquaintances, for a stranger cannot be long here, before it is generally known. The house of representatives is the lounging place of both sexes, where acquaintance is as easily made as at public amusements. And the drawing-room,—that centre of attraction,—affords opportunity of seeing all these whom fashion, fame, beauty, wealth or talents, have rendr'd celebrated....

Latrobe had a different impression. "Mrs. Madison gives drawing rooms every Wednesday," he writes to a friend in 1809. "The first one was very numerously attended by none but respectable people. The second, La, la. The last by a perfect rabble in beards and boots."

It should also be remembered that neither oil lamps nor bathtubs were yet in common use. At a ball on Washington's birthday in 1817, the guests were reported to have danced to the light of 2,000 candles, and Mr. Franklin's theory on the beneficial effects of the tub bath was still controversial. Although Latrobe had designed a bathroom complete with water closet and bath for the Markoe house in Philadelphia in 1808, it was considered an extravagant novelty. An advertisement appearing in Washington's *Daily National Intelligencer* on January 3, 1817, also shows us the premium put on baths:

> Dr. Jennings' Celebrated Patent Portable Warm & Hot Baths are now offered for sale by David Ott in Washington City, and John Ott in Georgetown.... Travelling gentlemen can carry them in their saddlebags, Portmanteau, or Pocket, and be ready at all times to meet and remove disease in its forming stage.

Nevertheless Washington in the early 19th century was, as Mrs. Trollope notes in her *Domestic Manners of the Americans*, "rising gradually into life and splendour... a spectacle of high historic interest."

Foreign Ministers... Polished Scholars

It is that "spectacle of high historic interest," that the restoration of Decatur House attempts to bring to life for present-day Americans. "We tried to reproduce the style of life around the Square and in residential and diplomatic Washington during the Federal period," says John Pearce. The first floor rooms were restored as nearly as possible to the way they were when the Decaturs lived there—to convey something of the "brilliant life of Federal Washington." The second floor was restored to reflect the "solid Washington" of the Victorian era as it was after its purchase in 1871 by Mary Edwards Beale and her husband General Edward Fitzgerald Beale whose gallant conduct in the Battle of San Pasqual, California, during the Mexican War, was in the heroic Decatur tradition. It was Mrs. Truxtun Beale, a widow of Edward's son, who bequeathed Decatur House to the National Trust in 1956. Mrs. Beale, the 20th-century's "queenly chatelaine" of Decatur House, as newspaper columnist Arthur Krock described her, lived there for more than 50 years. In 1944 she retained Thomas Tileston Waterman as architect to remove the Victorian brownstone trim with which Edward Beale had embellished the front door and windows of Latrobe's beautifully restrained facade. Edward Beale's Victorianisms, in fact, completely disguised the classical clarity of the Latrobe facade as if behind a mask. The stylish new Victorian furniture, great gas chandeliers, rich hangings, and new inlaid floors of the 1880s were gradually modified as time and generations went on. But in the 1930s, says John Pearce, "Mrs. Truxtun Beale, perhaps first inspired by the Historic American Buildings Survey study and photographing of the house, embarked on a series of changes deliberately seeking to recapture the original Latrobe character of the architecture and Decatur character of furnishings, particularly on the first floor." It is this philosophy that the Trust has continued.

Between the Decaturs and the Beales, the tenants in this storied house on The President's Square included the French Legation, the Russian Legation, the British minister, three secretaries of state, and a vice president, among other colorful and cultured personalities.

After Decatur's death, the house was closed for months. Then in 1820 it became the residence of His Excellency, Baron Hyde de Neuville, French Minister to the U.S. "This was the period of the best society in Washington," according to Benjamin Ogle Tayloe, the self-appointed historian of the President's Square. "Gentlemen of high character and high breeding abounded in both Houses of Congress, and many of the foreign ministers were distinguished for noble birth, talent, learning and elegant manners." He adds that "the Baron Hyde de

(Top) The "Bedchamber" which is to the right of the entrance hall features the bed that Decatur was born in. A portrait of Decatur hangs over the mantel. (Above) The Victorian era of Decatur House is reflected in the second floor rooms where furnishings are a typically Victorian mixture from various periods including Belter chairs, early 19th-century paintings, Chinese export porcelain, 18th-century Philadelphia chairs, even a Portuguese table. This view of the north drawing room shows the California seal which the Beales had incorporated in the parquet floor to honor their native state. The decorative ceiling and flooring were added in the 1870s.

Stephen Decatur's desk was listed in the inventory of 1820 as "1 mahogany cabinet with sliding mirror," appraised at $55.

(Opposite page) This charming drawing by Baroness Hyde de Neuville was probably done from the doorway of Decatur House in 1821 when her husband was French Minister to the U.S. and they lived in the House on the President's Square. It depicts the White House in the center flanked by the State, War, Navy, and Treasury buildings.

Neuville admirably represented the French aristocracy of the old regime."

In 1822 Decatur House became the residence of Baron de Tuyl, as the Russian Minister was called. The Baron thought that "Washington, with its venison, wild turkey, canvasback ducks, oysters and terrapin, furnishes better viands than Paris and," he adds, "needs only cooks."

Secretary of State Henry Clay and his family moved into Decatur House in 1827 and shortly afterwards Clay writes to E. Everett: "We have made a most agreeable change of residence since you left the City, by getting into Mrs. Decatur's house, which is the best private dwelling in the City." The Clays remained there until Jackson made Martin Van Buren his Secretary of State in 1829 and gave Decatur House its next tenant. It was during Van Buren's tenancy that a signaling device was installed in an attic window of Decatur House and another in the White House so that the President and Secretary could exchange messages across the President's Square—a kind of 19th-century hot line.

Edward Livingston succeeded Van Buren as Secretary of State and as master of Decatur House. Jackson called Livingston a "polished scholar, an able writer, and a most excellent man." Beaumont, Tocqueville's traveling companion during his American tour, notes an evening he passed

at the home of the Secretary of State, Mr. Edward Livingston, the most celebrated writer in America. He is a man of about sixty years who is very kindly and speaks French wonderfully well. He is almost French in his ways because he . . . has spent most of life in Louisiana. His *soirée* was charming. They play *bad* music, because none other is made in America; but the concert didn't last long and soon they began to dance. I mingled my square dances and waltzes with most interesting conversations with Mr. Livingston on the penitentiary system and especially on capital punishment. . . . That society, furthermore, has no peculiar character; it's absolutely a European *salon*, and the reason is simple; all the members of the diplomatic corps gathered in Washington set the tone; French is the common language, and you would believe yourself in a Parisian *salon*.

In 1834 Sir Charles Richard Vaughan, British Minister in the U.S., succeeded the Livingstons at Decatur House. When Harriet Martineau visited America in 1835, she found Washington

unlike any other that ever was seen, straggling out hither and thither, with a

small house or two a quarter of a mile from any other, so that in making calls . . . we had to cross ditches and stiles, and walk alternatively on grass and pavements, and strike across a field to reach a street. . . . Then there was the society, singularly compounded from the largest variety of elements; foreign Ambassadors, the American government, members of Congress, from Clay and Webster down to Davy Crockett. . .; flippant young belles, pious wives dutifully attending their husbands, and groaning over the frivolities of the place; grave judges, saucy travelers, pert newspaper reporters, melancholy Indian chiefs, and timid New England ladies, trembling on the verge of the vortex; all this was wholly unlike anything that is to be seen in any other city in the world; for all these are mixed up together in daily intercourse like the higher circles of a little village.

But the Society, my God!

In 1836 that observant southern gentleman Benjamin Ogle Tayloe notes that when Sir Charles Vaughan left Decatur House, "it passed into the possession of mine host of the *National*, Mr. John Gadsby." As proprietor of famous hotels and taverns, the Gadsby tenure introduced a new element to Decatur House not to mention the President's Square. The French Minister, the Chevalier Adolphe de Bacourt, tells us of an evening party he attended when Gadsby was in residence:

He is an old wretch who has made a fortune in the slave trade, which does not prevent Washington society from rushing to his house, and I should make my government very unpopular if I refused to associate with this kind of people. This gentleman's house is the most beautiful in the city, very well furnished, and perfect in the distribution of the rooms, but the society, my God!

George Mifflin Dallas, James K. Polk's vice president, leased Decatur House in 1844 from Gadsby's widow and then a series of tenants occupied it until shortly after the Civil War when it was purchased by General Beale and his wife. Around this time new flooring was laid in the second floor drawing room—inlaid with the seal of their native state of California. "When the renovation of the house was completed," writes General Beale's daughter-in-law Marie Beale in *Decatur House and Its Inhabitants*, "he furnished it in the early General Grant taste of the period."

Putting the Pieces Together

One of the cardinal rules in reconstructing and furnishing a historic house, as John Pearce puts it, is to erase one's own taste reactions and have a reason for everything that is done. If we have a fact, that fact must be adhered to no matter how strange it may seem to us. It is as if we thought of Decatur House as a lens in which is gathered every bit of information that might have something to do with the house—the individuals who lived there, the community, the fashions and events of the time. The more we understand the rest of the pattern, the better we can re-create the house as it was, and that includes the mood. "There was something slightly melancholy—elegiac—about Federal Washington," adds Pearce, "in spite of its brilliance."

Extensive architectural and archaeological investigations of the property, research of all sorts of written and verbal documentations pertaining to the House on the President's Square were used to reconstruct the Decatur era. A lot about contemporary tastes, fashions, and thoughts were gleaned from notes and advertisements which appeared in the Washington *Daily National Intelligencer* in 1817 and 1818. Other aids included wills, inventories, bills, estate sales lists, letters, diaries. "We never have as much information as we would like," says Pearce. "We are delighted if the inventory says *carpeting*, delighted if it says *Wilton*, but why doesn't it say *red*, or *green*, or mention a pattern if there was one? . . . We say we are trying to show rooms as they were—interpret life as it was—but when the people are not there, we can't possibly show life as it was. How can we take furniture and interiors and make them talk about people?"

Listed in the Decatur inventory was "1 mahogany cabinet with sliding mirror." This gives little information about the actual object which turned out to be Stephen Decatur's desk—a mahogany Louis XVI fall-front secretary—in which Decatur, it was learned from a document, had placed some court-martial papers. Those papers might have been Barron's, at whose trial Decatur served. When Decatur was brought home dying after his duel with Barron, did he perhaps glance at that desk, and if so, what were his feelings, his thoughts? That is what Pearce means when he asks how can we make furniture and interiors talk about prople.

The Brilliant Life of Federal Washington

The lovely vestibule and front hall of Decatur House, as Talbot Hamlin has noted, show how brilliantly Latrobe could work even in spaces relatively confined. To restore this area, the paint was scraped down to the original coat which was then reproduced—French-gray walls and ocher woodwork. Ceilings are all white. Although it looked as if the moldings might have been another color, the scraping did not indicate it and there was justification in the fact that the ceilings of Lathrobe's houses were often all white.

To the left of the front door are two rooms—the dining parlor and Decatur's office. On the right is a "Bed Chamber" as it is called in the Decatur inventory of 1820. The bed is the one in which Decatur was born and is on loan from a descendant of Decatur's sister. Since no description of the original wallpapers has been found it was necessary to discover what wallpaper patterns were being used in such houses around 1814. The 19th-century reproduction wallpaper patterns selected for the first floor rooms were based on the findings of that research. Efforts to locate as much as possible of the original furniture and other objects listed in the inventory is a continuing process. "Within the Decatur household," as John Pearce says, "the actual items of furniture illustrate the range we might expect in an eclectic, transient, Washington house of the early 19th century"—from an American bed of about 1770 through a handsome Directoire secretary to very stylish andirons of late Empire or Restoration style.

And so the house on the President's Square has taken a new lease on life—as an eloquent and dignified reminder of an important part of our past. For almost 150 years, Decatur House enjoyed an intimate connection with the mainstream of American history. And that history is reflected in its furnishings from the first phase of the Classical Revival through the Victorian period. In recent history, Decatur House proved to be "the anchor that preserved the Square," as Gordon Gray, former chairman of the board of the National Trust, put it. He was referring to the plan devised by architect John Carl Warnecke at the request of President Kennedy to save the Square's facade of historic houses. They had been marked for destruction to make room for huge Federal buildings. Warnecke's solution was to set the new structures back and screen them with the older houses. This has since been carried out and the President's Square, at least at eye level and with a little imagination, once again evokes the brilliant life so faithfully chronicled by Benjamin Ogle Tayloe when he was a resident of the Square between 1829 and his death in 1868.

Scarbrough House

Savannah, Georgia

(Top left) Before restoration with vastly disfiguring third floor addition. A monumental garden gateway is on the right. (Left) The south porch before restoration. It is constructed entirely of cast iron, including the floor of diamond-patterned grating.

The past is never dead. It isn't even past.
William Faulkner

"There are," wrote Timothy Healy, an English clergyman who visited Georgia in 1885–86, "far vaster and wealthier cities with much more commerce and culture than this city, but for architectural simplicity and natural beauty, for the indescribable charm about its streets and buildings, its parks and squares . . . there is but one Savannah. Without a rival, without an equal, it stands unique."

The clergyman's compliments still apply to the little southern city that owes something to its planner James Oglethorpe and something to the Regency houses of the young English-trained architect William Jay. Jay was only in this country a brief seven years (1817–24), but he left an impression on Savannah that is apparent to this day. Although he was certainly one of the most original architects practicing in America during the first decades of the 19th century, Jay has never been widely recognized. One wonders why. Is it because most of his work was limited to Savannah or because his practice was so brief? Or might it have been because he was one of those rare individuals who don't take themselves too seriously? A short but telling notation in his father's autobiography suggests that this may be so. Besides possessing "professional talent and cleverness," wrote the elder William Jay, he "had a large share of wit and humor, qualities always dangerous and commonly injurious to the possessor. . . . His comic powers drew him into company not the most friendly to youthful improvement." It is not surprising that the Reverend William Jay, who was the famous nonconformist clergyman and pastor of the Argyle Independent Chapel in Bath for 62 years, should have been more concerned for his son's moral and spiritual development than for his architectural prowess, but the wit and humor he mentions were not lost in the architecture. There can be no wit without imagination, of which Jay's Savannah houses reveal more than a fair share. They show the young architect to have possessed the "deft, intuitive coordination of thought

and imagination, that Sir John Summerson has called poetic."

But if Jay didn't take himself seriously, the Savannah of 1817 did. He was only 21 when he arrived in this country but he was well equipped to design houses for the cultured society of that flourishing southern city. He was born in Bath, the elegant 18th-century spa with its widely praised Palladian architecture and its gracious crescents, and he served his apprenticeship in Regency London at a time of high taste and prosperity. It was the London of John Nash's recently completed Regent Street and Regent's Park. It was the London of Sir John Soane's Bank of England and his own house at No. 13 Lincoln's Inn Fields (page 000), both of which were probably known by Jay. Although there is no evidence of Jay having studied with Soane, he was profoundly influenced by his work. It is also possible that he heard Soane's advice to his students at the Royal Academy:

> We must be intimately acquainted with not only what the ancients have done, but endeavour to learn from their work what they would have done. We shall, therefore, become artists, nor mere copyists; we shall avoid servile imitation and what is equally dangerous, improper application.

Little is known of Jay's work in London except that he was apprenticed to David R. Roper, an architect and surveyor, and that several of his designs were exhibited at the Royal Academy in 1809, 1810, and 1812. By 1815 he had opened his own office, but the only building in London that can be definitely attributed to him is Albion Chapel in Mooregate, which was described by James Elmes in his *Metropolitan Improvements of London in the Nineteenth Century* as the work of a "a young architect by the name of Jay." Elmes called the chapel "a neat and unaffected building." Its domed roof "gives it somewhat the air of a theatre but it possesses a character of original thinking in its design that is highly pleasing."

While the work of Soane seems to have had the most discernible influence on Jay's architecture, there is no doubt that the daz-

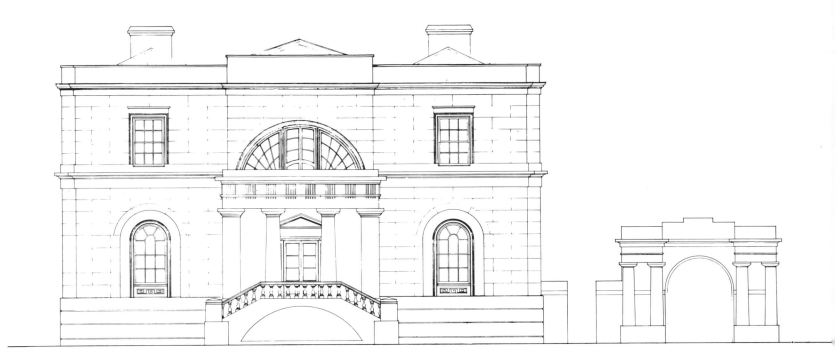

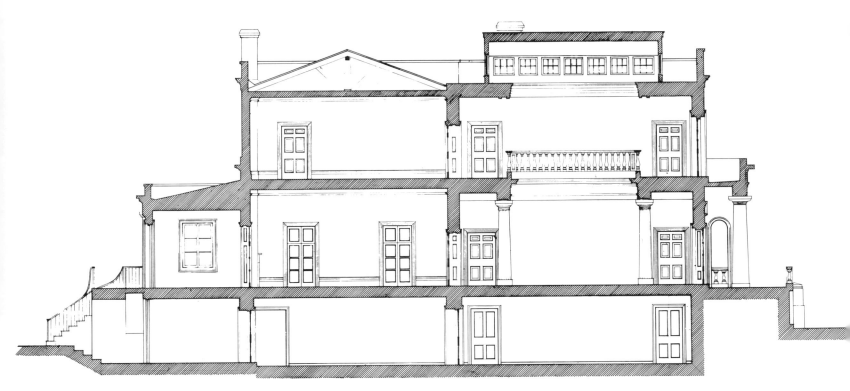

(Top) East elevation after restoration—a
two-story structure set on a high basement
and crowned with a parapet which conceals
the low-pitched roofs. Subtle scoring of the
stucco simulates large ashlar block masonry
at the first and second floors; the basement
level is further articulated with bold but
simple molded horizontal plaster bands.
"Profoundly influenced by British architect
Sir John Soane's mastery of bold, unadorned
architectural form and the impact of natural
light on such form," as restoration architect
John Milner puts it, "Jay created this highly
significant structure as one of his series of
monumental residences in Savannah."
(Center) Section after restoration shows the
reconstructed atrium. The massive Tuscan-
style portico on the right is the only major
element projecting from the exterior. (Bottom) First floor plan.

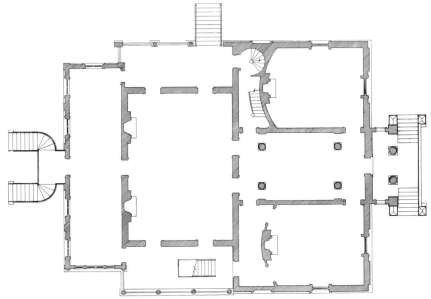

zling city of Bath in which he spent his most formative years played a subtle part in his development. That beautiful and spacious 18th-century city could not have helped leaving its impression on someone as sensitive and imaginative as the young Jay.

In 1817 the young British architect came to Savannah where the ctoon merchants were quick to ply him with commissions. The time and place were right and Jay's genius flourished for however brief a time.

Too Beautiful to be Occupied by Yankees

No one visiting Savannah today could be surprised that the beautiful Georgian city of Bath and the Regency architects of London had a place in its background. Savannah, like Bath, seems to have been designed as a city in which people of culture might live. James Oglethorpe's imaginative city plan—a series of green squares around which the town revolves—has accommodated Savannah's many changes from primitive settlement to an established community with extraordinary grace. Not only is there this remarkable spatial experience, as John Cornforth writes in *Country Life* (January 2, 1975), "but the architectural concept is underlined, held together and softened, by generous planting throughout the city. Rows and avenues, mostly of ilex, some with beards of moss, and interspersed with oleander and palm, pace out its pattern, providing welcome shade . . . as well as acting as camouflage for the inevitable gaps and eyesores that seem to creep into every town." It is, he adds, "this combination of planning, planting, and architectural history that gives Savannah its particular flavour."

It is hard to believe that Savannah was not always admired but in 1778 it was disparaged as "A small Town, situated on the top of a Sand-Hill" with "few good houses," and when Washington visited it in 1791, he had more to say about the beauty of the women than that of the city. But it wasn't long after the Revolution that a perceptive visitor from Virginia, John Pope, was predicting that Savannah would be "a place of Opulance" as long as "Commerce spread her canvass to the Wind." In 1794 Eli Whitney patented his cotton gin and commerce did indeed "spread her canvass to the Wind." Like all possessors of new wealth, Savannah's cotton tycoons wanted new houses in which to show off their affluence. But until Jay arrived in 1817 there was no one to give them the elegant architecture they thought befit their importance. Jay did just that. The Englishman J.S. Buckingham who visited Savannah in the 1830s and recorded his impressions in *The Slave States of America* (1842) tells us that:

The greater number of the dwelling houses are built of wood, and painted white; but there are many handsome and commodious brick buildings occupied as private residences, and a few mansions, built by an English architect, Mr. Jay—son of the celebrated divine of that name in Bath—which are of beautiful architecture, of sumptuous interior, and combine as much of elegance and luxury as are to be found in any private dwellings in the country. . . .

In fact after Jay's Regency architecture had given the cotton tycoons what they wanted, visitors couldn't say enough about the charms of Savannah and they invariably mentioned his houses. "With this little city I was exceedingly pleased," writes the Irish actor Tyrone Power in the 1830s. He particularly mentions

> several very ambitious-looking dwellings, built by a European architect for wealthy merchants during the palmy days of trade; these are of stone or some composition, showily designed and very large, but ill-adapted, I should imagine for summer residences in this climate. . . .

Savannah had been transformed into a "Southern Paradise," as one delighted resident put it, with stuccoed houses as "yellow as my letter, with elegant columns and balstades, with Drawing Rooms full of Golden Eagles holding up Damask coloured curtains."

"Talk of Philadelphia, and New-York, and Boston, and Richmond, and New-Haven—Savannah outstrips them all, both in artificial and natural beauty," raved William Alexander Caruthers in his book *The Kentuckian in New-York* (1834). "It seems the residence of the prince of the world and his nobility!"

But perhaps the supreme compliment accorded Savannah was that of General Jeremiah P. Gilmer, Confederate Army Engineer, who rhapsodized in 1862, "The place is too beautiful to be occupied by Yankees—may Heaven spare this affliction." And even a Yankee can see his point.

An Assemblage of Villas

Jay must have felt at home in the Savannah of 1817. It was predominantly English and reflected English ideas and customs, although Buckingham tells us that the "youths of both Sexes appear to be brought up in less subjugation to parental authority than in England," which may account for Jay's father's reference to his son's doubtful company. Buckingham goes on to say that Savannah's

young ladies . . . have much greater liberty allowed them in the disposal of their time . . . than girls of the same age in England. The consequence is great precosity of manners in both sexes, and often very early marriage. . . . There are, however, few elopements, or seductions and domestic infidelity is very rare.

Nevertheless to this day Savannah is often called one of the most English towns in the U.S. and part of that Englishness can be attributed to Jay's Regency houses.

His first commission—the beautifully preserved Owens-Thomas House—introduced Regency ideas to Savannah, but the full influence of the English Regency of Soane appeared in the two-story coffee-colored stucco house he designed for the prominent Savannah merchant William Scarbrough, who was one of the promoters of the company which launched the first trans-Atlantic steamship, the S.S. Savannah. The Scarbrough House may not have been Jay's first Savannah house but it is certainly an important member of that splendid group of townhouses that were the architect's legacy to the city and may have inspired Frederika Bremer's charming tribute. "There cannot be in the whole world a more beautiful city than Savannah," she writes in *The Houses of the New World; Impressions of America* (1854), "an assemblage of villas, come-together for company."

The Scarbrough House with its bold architectural form, unadorned except for a powerful Tuscan-style portico leading into a central atrium that rises the full height of the house, shows Jay's affinity with the English Regency of Soane. The two-story entrance hall or atrium, which Professor Frederick D. Nichols has called "one of the grandest spatial compositions in American architecture," is surrounded by a balcony on the second floor supported by four Tuscan columns, and surmounted by a large lantern with barrel-vaulted ceiling and perimeter windows. A stairway of simple design once penetrated the atrium to provide access between the first and second floors. Two parlors, each with a curving fireplace wall, flank the entrance hall. Directly behind it is the ballroom, a spacious area with a pair of fireplaces on the garden side. The restrained architectural decoration is limited to simple plaster cornices on the first floor and heavily molded projecting door and window architraves throughout.

It is not surprising that soon after the Scarbrough House was completed in 1819, it acquired a reputation for "the most splendid entertainments," brilliant balls, and "kingly feasts." When President Monroe visited Savannah in May of that year, he was Scarbrough's guest. On May 6, 1819,

Scarbrough writes to his wife:

> My dearest Julia:
> . . . It was understood the President was not to be here till Monday next; but a messenger . . . reports he is to be here tomorrow or Saturday at the furthest. . . . Our house is quite in readiness for him. It is most tastefully and elegantly decorated and furnished—and seems to bring to the recollection of all who have lately visited it—the House of the Lord Governor in the neighborhood of Chester and Liverpool. Mr. Jay is fixing up a temporary Pavilion of great extent on the Church Square opposite to Andrew Low offices for the Ball and Supper Rooms. It is lined with red Baize or flannel with festoons and pilasters in white muslin. It is also most tastefully and elegantly done—and by candle light will look most superbly. The President must be pleased with Savannah; as in the whole course of his extended tour, he may be recd. at costly and splendid rate; but no where with such pure and genuine taste,—Jay will begin to attain the prominence, which low jealousy and perverted judgement would not before award him.

President Monroe duly arrived with his Secretary of War, John C. Calhoun, and according to contemporary accounts, he mounted an elegant charger and rode "to the new house of William Scarbrough Esq. which was fitted up in a superb style for his reception."

But in spite of all the "splendid entertainments" and illustrious guests, the Scarbrough House's dazzling beginning was soon to start its downward path to near squalor. During the three or four decades following its construction, it went through a series of alterations and additions—some of which had a major effect on Jay's original design. In 1878 it became a public school resulting in further minor alterations and deterioration. But even in its derelict and distorted state there was an air of dignity about the Scarbrough House that marked it as the fashionable and sumptuous residence it once had been. In 1965 it was taken over by Historic Savannah Foundation, the organization that might well be called the angel of the "tranquil old city, wide-streeted, tree-planted" that Thackeray admired in 1855.

By 1955 many of Savannah's once handsome townhouses had either been abandoned or had deteriorated into shabby tenements. Its once-lovely squares had become overgrown with weeds or taken over as parking lots. Then, at the instigation of a few imaginative citizens, a gigantic restoration program was begun under the aegis of the newly formed Historic Savannah Foundation. Had those Savannahians not been so sensitive to the personality of their city, it might be just another urban blight today. Besides restoring hundreds of important old houses and keeping so many of them lived in, the Foundation has rebeautified the city's ever-present green squares.

In 1972, while the Scarbrough House was still awaiting restoration, the idea was conceived to make it a pilot project for the Bicentennial. Toward that end the Foundation commissioned the National Heritage Corporation of West Chester, Pennsylvania, to make a study of the house which subsequently resulted in its restoration.

Early Elegance—Modern Function

In an effort to determine the chronology of the building's evolution and assist in establishing the most appropriate period to which to restore the house, says John D. Milner, AIA, who heads the National Heritage Corporation, extensive architectural investigations were undertaken. This research was further complemented by limited archaeological survey and analysis. Physical evidence, explains Milner, "indicated that in the 1830s a one-story long gallery was constructed across the rear of the ballroom and a side porch added to either side of the ballroom. Several years later, a full third floor was added to the front portion of the building. At some time during these alterations, the original staircase was removed from the atrium and a small stair was installed in the passage-way behind the north parlor."

In developing an overall philosophy for restoration of the house two major factors were considered. The primary consideration was, as Milner puts it, "respect for the architectural significance of Jay's original design, not only to Savannah but also to the nation." The second consideration, however, was that "the restored building must also serve the objectives and needs of the owner, Historic Savannah Foundation, who has made a commitment to preservation and restoration of the structure as a major historical and cultural asset for the city of Savannah."

Early in the planning stages, it had been decided not to restore it as a house museum since Savannah was already endowed with an impressive number of such facilities. Nevertheless the Foundation wanted to encourage public usage of the building for cultural purposes. Thus it was decided that the first floor should be essentially a public space for the presentation and interpretation of the furnishings and decorative arts of early 19th-century Savannah and that the ballroom and long gallery be used for meetings, seminars, receptions, and temporary exhibitions pertaining to historic preservation, city planning, architectural and horticultural research. Offices for Historic Savannah Foundation and other nonprofit service oriented organizations would be on the second floor and in the basement.

Restoration of the building to reflect Jay's original design, Milner explains, would not only have involved removal of the third floor, the long gallery and the side porches, but also reconstruction of the atrium stairway and other missing original features. And, he adds, "while such an approach would be academically interesting it would not only require a certain amount of conjecture in architectural detail, but also would limit the options for effectively utilizing the building to fulfill contemporary needs." It was therefore "decided to restore the house to the earliest period for which there was adequate physical evidence." Clear evidence existed for the configuration of the original roof and atrium lantern which made it feasible to remove the third floor. Such evidence, however, "does not exist for the appearance of the rear of the building prior to construction of the long gallery or for the original configuration of the atrium stair." The decision was thus made to restore the Scarbrough House to "its appearance immediately following completion of the long gallery and prior to the addition of the third floor."

The architects' initial examination of the structure, for example, revealed that the 1819 parapet walls behind which the roof was concealed had been retained to serve as the base for the newer third-floor construction. Although the cap stones of the walls were removed, several had been reused as subhearths for two third floor fireplaces. The form of the low sloping roof in the rear was determined by original joists that were still there as was the framing for the atrium lantern.

A description of the original atrium appeared in the Savannah *Morning News* of May 23, 1897, although no further documentation has yet been found to vouch for the vivid picture the writer paints:

> In the old days there was an arcade on each floor of the house the same size all the way to the roof, and directly above the arcades on the roof was a beautiful skylight, or dome upon which there was an enchanting painting by an artist of degree. The painting represented nothing but the heavens, and gave the effect to the up-turned eye below of the natural sky. The stranger within the gates of the hospitable man of this estate was almost invariably deceived by this painting and thought when looking overhead, he

was seeing the skies naked and bare to the eye, until upon close inspection he realized the mistake.

Since a visible skylight would have dispelled the impression created by the painted ceiling, it is likely that the painted sky was lighted indirectly. Indirectly lighted surfaces were employed by Soane in the Bank of England as well as in his own house at No. 13 Lincoln's Inn Fields, and Jay himself had already used indirect lighting in the Owens-Thomas House dining room.

We know from Jay's own words that he believed in restrained fenestration. In an article he wrote for the *Savannah Georgian*, January 22, 1820, he expressed his feeling about windows:

> . . . another circumstance of considerable importance is, to avoid so many openings, they are neither useful nor ornamental, in buildings devoted to commerce they are unnecessary, and in buildings for civil purposes they are better avoided. In the finest specimens of architecture you cannot find them, they distract the eye, and destroy that repose which is so essential in architecture, and which is so often exemplified in a disunion of color.

The Scarbrough House windows are simple openings—round-headed on the first floor, rectangular on the second, a large fan shape over the portico—with a minimum of adornment.

Professor Nichols has made an interesting comparison between the great fan window of the Scarbrough portico and the one Latrobe proposed to Jefferson to be used on Pavilion IX at the University of Virginia. "This romantic conception combined with classical forms—Romantic Classicism—was introduced into America by Latrobe," says Nichols. "The motif," he adds, "may also have been remembered by Jefferson who had seen it in France at the Pavilion de Louveciennes by Ledoux." The Scarbrough House fan, according to Nichols, "is derived from Ledoux who used it at the Hotel Guimard, Paris, 1772."

In accordance with current preservation philosophy—*don't do anything that can't be undone*—the architects have transformed the second floor into seemingly thoroughly modern offices. The new partitions that help create this appearance, however, can easily be removed leaving the original architectural fabric intact. Some of the partitions even cover the original windows without disturbing them.

The first floor of the Scarbrough House—with its more lofty ceilings and marked simplicity of interior finish—is particularly characteristic of Jay. During the initial investigation of the house and grounds, traces of the molded cast plaster anthemion ornament that had been used as a free-standing cornice in all the first floor rooms except the atrium were found and served as the pattern for reproductions. One of the ballroom mantels was still intact but the other had been removed and had to be reproduced. Fragments of it were found during the archaeological investigation as was the original handrail of the portico's Coade stone balustrade.

A Model of Architectural Good Manners

Like Jay's other existing Savannah houses, the Scarbrough House shows him to have been, as Nichols says, "one of the most important architects practicing anywhere in America in the early period of the 19th century. No one else had his feeling for plain surfaces, the simple elegance of which was pointed up with incised lines and the finish of which presaged the machine age; his feeling for curves and movement . . . his use of materials . . . his understanding of the power of the Doric order . . . or his conviction that architecture is based on the creative use of space, indicated in his imaginative plans." With the Scarbrough House, as Nichols says, "Jay's gift for building space is realized."

After a devastating fire of 1820, Jay tried to persuade Savannah's merchants to build fireproof stores and houses, but commercial prosperity was at a low ebb not to recover until 1840. Lack of commissions forced Jay to go to Charleston to look for clients and in 1824 he returned to England. Had he waited for the recovery, Jay's elegant houses probably would have graced other cities and Jay's name would have been as well known as that of Latrobe, Mills, Bulfinch, and other more widely recognized architects working in America at that time.

He was, in any case, spared seeing those "ambitious dwellings," as Tyrone Power notes during Savannah's depression years, "mostly deserted, or let for boardinghouses, and have that decayed look which is so melancholy, and nowhere arrives sooner than in this climate."

A house, as architectural historian James D. Van Trump has written, should not be "the architect's oration, nor his monumental treatise, nor his novel in three volumes, but his private letter to the world." Jay's private letter to the world, then, is to be read in the four existing houses which he designed for that graceful and elegant society. Their stuccoed facades make a generous contribution to what Carl Feiss has called "the special patina of the city, with its textures, of bricks, slate, cobble and ballast stones," its moss-fringed trees and green squares.

Born and bred in the Georgian city of Bath which his aptly been called the model of architectural good manners, it is not surprising that Jay should have taken to Savannah, and Savannah to him, for that little garden city of the south is surely America's model of architectural good manners.

A handsome Ionic portico raised on a brick arcade projects from the front facade of the Ainsley Hall mansion. The windows flanking the portico are set in recessed brick arches.

Robert Mills House

Columbia, South Carolina

> *. . . architecture, in fact, is only building "writ large."*
> W.R. Lethaby

"Every new proof of your talents, your excellent disposition, & of the respect you acquire wherever you are known, gives me the truest pleasure," Benjamin Henry Latrobe wrote to his former student Robert Mills in 1806. And the restored Robert Mills House in Columbia, South Carolina, is one proof of those talents. It was designed by Mills for his friend Ainsley Hall, Columbia merchant and businessman, who had emigrated from England around 1800 and accumulated enough wealth by 1823 to commission the architect to design "a fine house" for his wife Sarah. Sarah's "fine house," however, was to suffer a strange fate. Hall died in 1823 while he was vacationing in Virginia and although his widow completed the construction of the house, it was apparently never finished as the elegant residence Hall and Mills envisioned.

In 1839 the still unlived-in mansion was purchased by the Presbyterian Synod of South Carolina and Georgia and Sarah's "fine house" was used as the central building of the Columbia Theological Seminary for almost a century. The Columbia Bible College took over the property in 1940 but the mansion became vacant in 1960. In 1962 it was about to be torn down when the South Carolina chapter of the American Institute of Architects led a fight to save the building that resulted in the formation of Historic Columbia Foundation. The architects struggled in vain, however, to raise sufficient funds to buy the four-acre property until a group of local women headed by Mrs. James F. Dreher took over. In a whirlwind campaign enough money was solicited to take possession of the house and grounds just as the wreckers were tearing up the clay tile floors in the basement.

Albert Simons, FAIA, of Charleston, who is an authority on the architecture of the southeast and has worked on the restoration of several Mills' buildings, was commissioned by the Foundation to restore the Ainsley Hall mansion with H. Reid Hearn, AIA, of Columbia as associate. The purpose of the restoration was to remove later remodeling and to finish the interior in the manner that Mills would have done had Ainsley Hall lived to complete the house with the same elegance with which it was started.

Sarah's "fine house" was never lived in as the residence it was designed to be. In fact it represents a reversal of the present trend of adapting historic houses for modern uses. It found an adaptive use before it was completely finished and not until nearly a century and a half later did it achieve the appearance that its builder and architect meant it to have.

Little is known of Ainsley Hall except the inscription on his tombstone:

> Enterprise and perseverance gave him success in trade and combined with enlightened views and a liberal spirit, enabled him to contribute largely to the prosperity of the Town of Columbia while an enlarged but discriminating benevolence rendered the ample fortune his industry had accumulated, the unceasing Source of Relief to the Distressed. . . .

And since Mills was more intimately associated with the structure than the man under the tombstone, it was decided to restore the mansion and surrounding park as a memorial to its architect.

Such a gesture would have pleased but surprised Mills who was far better known for his public buildings than he was for his domestic architecture and particularly for his great Washington column in Baltimore and the beautifully simple obelisk to the first president in Washington. Mrs. Trollope was not the only one to be impressed by Mills' "noble column erected to the memory of Washington" when she visited Baltimore in the 1830s. And the later obelisk in Washington—"the greatest and proudest work of modern times" as a contemporary journalist put it—has never ceased being described in superlatives.

Latrobe apparently didn't think much of Mills' houses which is perhaps why there are so few of them. There is a letter written by Latrobe in which he criticizes certain features of the house Mills designed for John

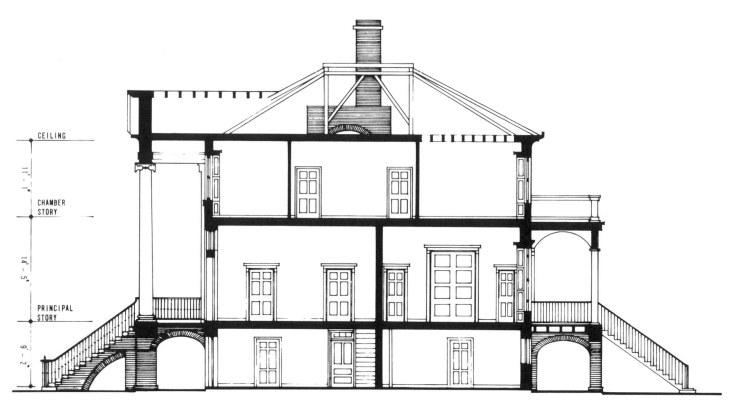

Section. The large door shown on the principal story is the curved door between the drawing and music rooms.

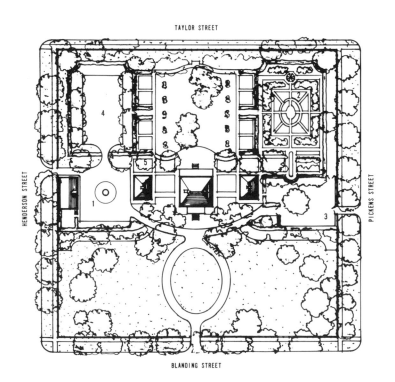

Proposed development of the site showing the main house and two flankers in the center, the carriage house on the left, and screened parking in the upper left-hand corner.

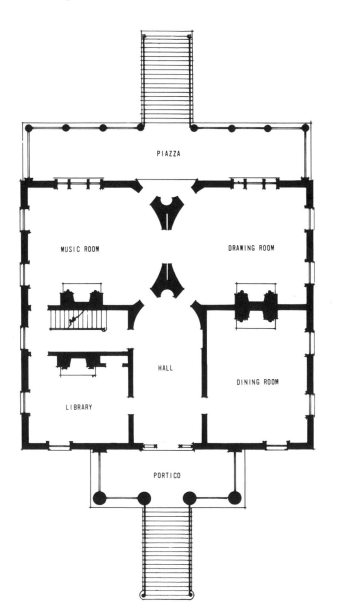

Plan of the principal story.

Wickham in Richmond in 1812, particularly the front hall and staircase which he considered in the worst taste of Charles IX of France. Mills' talents, in any case, were more suited to monumental public buildings. His imagination, as Talbot Hamlin points out, worked best on a larger scale.

The success of the handsome brick residence that Mills designed for Ainsley Hall might well be attributed to its affinity with his public buildings. It shares their monumentality, simplicity, and solidity of construction. It reveals such characteristics of the architect's public work as a portico set on a basement arcade, round-headed single windows, and flat-headed triple windows. Such triple windows, incidentally, appeared in Soane's *Plans* of 1788 and were widely used by Latrobe in his domestic designs. The stylish front facade of the Mills' house with its Ionic portico raised on a brick arcade is not unlike the facade of his famous fireproof Record Office in Charleston. And like the Record Office, the front facade of the house for Ainsley Hall is handsome but not what one calls pretty.

The rear facade with its seven-bay arcaded porch is quite different in feeling. Here the monumental austerity of the front has been toned down by the rhythmic filigree of the "South Colonnade" as it is called in the Carpentry Agreement. Both facades, however, are typical of Mills.

America's First Professionally Trained Native Architect

Robert Mills was born in Charleston of a Scottish father and a mother who was descended from a provincial governor of the colony. He had a classical education at Charleston College after which he worked as a draftsman for the Irish-born James Hoban who won the competition for the design of the President's House. At 20 Mills met Thomas Jefferson who took him to Monticello to continue his architectural studies. In his *Notes on the State of Virginia*, Jeffer-

son had expressed the wish that "some young subject of natural tastes would practice a reformation in this most elegant and useful art," and he undoubtedly thought of Mills as that subject. In 1804, on Jefferson's advice, Mills became apprenticed to the English-trained architect Benjamin Henry Latrobe with whom he completed his education as an architect and engineer.

When Mills was planning to marry in 1808 he decided to leave Latrobe and open his own office in Philadelphia. But before he did, he wrote to Jefferson to ask his advice. Jefferson answered on June 23, 1808:

Dear Sir:
I have duly received your two favors of the 13th and the 16th. In the former you mention your design of now offering yourself for business in Philadelphia as an architect. This you may certainly do with confidence, after so many years devoted to the theory and practice of the art—and under the best direction in the

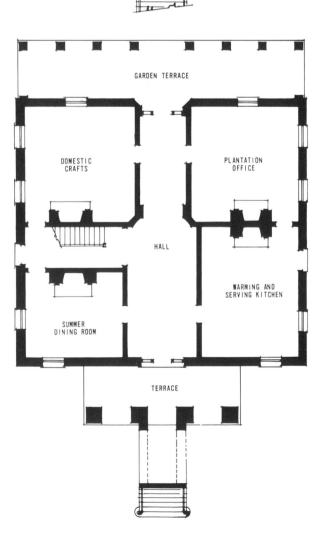

Plan of the ground floor.

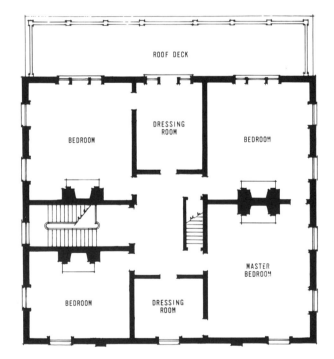

Plan of the chamber story.

A seven-bay arcaded porch extends across the garden facade. The center bay is slightly wider to emphasize the unusual entry.

The hall is elegantly curved at one end to accommodate the tangent curves of the drawing room and music room. A statuary niche separates the doors leading into the music room on the left and the drawing room on the right.

United States, as far as I am a judge. I may safely affirm that the various excellent drawings which I have seen of yours, which prove you to be familiar with the principles of the art, and the years you have been a principal aid of Mr. Latrobe, must have given you satisfactory experience in the practical part. But when, in compliance with your request that I look abroad among my acquaintances in Philadelphia for one who could be useful to you, I find them to consist of Literati and officers of government, no one of whom will probably ever have occasion for services in your line. I have, therefore, thought it better that you should show this letter whenever and to whomever you may have occasion, as it contains my testimony of the grounds on which you may justly claim employ—I salute you with esteem and attachment.

Thomas Jefferson

With such an endorsement from the designer of Monticello and President of the United States one wonders why the young architect wasn't besieged with commissions to build houses. That, however, was not the case. In 1817 Mills moved to Baltimore where he was appointed chief engineer for the city, and in 1820, he returned to his native state where he succeeded William Jay on the Board of Public Works of South Carolina and was appointed engineer and architect of the state. During Mills' ten years in South Carolina he designed many buildings—churches, hospitals, court houses, prisons, as well as the fireproof Record Office in Charleston and the house for his friend Ainsley Hall in Columbia.

Mills could hardly have had better training as the "first *native born American* to enter the study of architecture," as he termed himself. Jefferson was not only the originator of the classic school in America but he had first-hand knowledge of contemporary French and English architecture. Latrobe brought the Greek Revival from the Regency England of Soane to America. As Fiske Kimball points out, Mills' three tutors—Hoban, Jefferson, and Latrobe—represent "three phases of architectural progression in styles; the Palladian, the Roman, and the Greek; in practice, the builder-architect, the amateur, and the professional." It was from Latrobe that Mills received the kind of professional experience he could not have received from anyone else in this country. But all through Mills' writings there are indications that Jefferson's ideals held a prominent place in his thoughts.

The house he designed for Ainsley Hall shows him to have been a student worthy of both his eminent teachers while lacking the particular genius of either one—Jefferson's charming originality or Latrobe's restless brilliance. But Mills, like both his tutors, was striving for a typically American architecture. He warned his fellow architects not to "forget the original models of their country, neither its customs nor the manners of their people . . . study your country's tastes and requirements and make classic ground *here* for your art!" Such an idea would have particularly appealed to Jefferson who longed for a monumental architectural expression of the American genius to raise America to the level of, if not above, European countries. But Mills' soundness of construction, his mastery of essentials, and excellence of execution were learned from Latrobe as was his sense for monumental mass.

The plan of the Ainsley Hall house is perhaps especially indicative of the Mills' legacy from his teachers. The combination of curved and rectangular spaces on the principal floor owes something to both Jefferson and Latrobe, but as Albert Simons points out, the Mills' plan actually seems to be a variation of two plans by Latrobe—one for Senator Pope's house in Lexington, Kentucky, and one for the proposed Commandant's House for the Pittsburgh arsenal. The Mills' plan is particularly close to Latrobe's plan for the Commandant's House which has two rooms meeting in curved walls that create one end of the hall on the entrance side and a vestibule on the opposite side. Instead of a vestibule, however, the Mills' house has an unusual entry in the form of a concave recess with two doors flanking a niche with a half-dome effect above. The similarity with the Latrobe plans, as Simons says, is significant in demonstrating the lasting influence of Mills' tutelage under Latrobe.

But treating the principal story as the dominant feature of the house is a legacy from Jefferson who introduced this Roman idea at Monticello. The rooms of entertainment on the principal floor are separated from the bedroom floor above and the services on the ground floor below. The Mills' house plan is one of the clearest and simplest statements of this Jeffersonian ideal, as noted by the late Meyric Rogers, former curator of the Garvan Collection at Yale, who helped in the interior restoration of the house. Concealed stairways, another Jefferson innovation inspired by the neoclassic houses he had seen in Paris, also appear in the Mills' house. Here, however, the stairway is hidden from the hall by a door which serves as an aid to climate control, a problem thet greatly interested Mills.

While Mills seems to have been closer to Jefferson than he was to Latrobe, he appreciated both his tutors. He called Latrobe "one of the first architects in any country," and he was continually marveling at Jefferson's amazing knowledge of architecture.

The Ainsley Hall house also seems to have benefited from some of the building technology of the architect's own fireproof Record Office which was being constructed at the same time. It, too, is fire resistant thus allowing Mills to supplement the main kitchen in an outbuilding with a warming kitchen on the ground floor. Mills' ingenuity and concern with practical matters are evident throughout the house. The space between the ceiling of the ground floor and the flooring of the main story is filled with cedar shavings, which serve as insulation and also act as an insect repellent.

But while the house designed for Ainsley Hall reveals some of Mills' architectural characteristics, it also reveals Mills himself. Talbot Hamlin has called his forms "frequently over-heavy, blocky, even stodgy," and that is the impression one has of the man. His writings show a practical but over-serious nature lacking Jefferson's humor or Latrobe's imagination. The latter once referred to the younger architect as "the pious Robert Mills." All this, however, is not to say he didn't create masterpieces. "The vast obelisk in Washington, long the highest of human structures," as Fiske Kimball puts it, "was the conception, in which the simplicity and grandeur of the forms are matched with the character of the subject. In a day when Greece was, to the modern world, a new discovery, there was no questioning of the validity of its forms which furnished the language of Robert Mills. We find his words a little stereotyped, a little arid, but very sober, very competent, very dignified—contributing to that austere tradition that forms the basis of the simplicity even of our modern style." Mills believed that "the character, the personality of a structure . . . should appear before beauty of line or ornamentation." And the austerity implicit in such a statement belongs to the man as well as his work.

Mills' architecture was also an expression of its culture. During the 1820s and 30s there was tremendous belief in the superiority of all things American. It was an "era of good feelings" as the people themselves called it. There was a striving for artistic expression. Cultural progress was considered as important as material prosperity. To those who lived through the nationalistic America of the 1820s, it seemed to be the land of all possibilities. The American dream was indeed a fact. "We have entered a new era in the history of the world," is the way Mills put it, "it is our destiny to lead, not to be led. Our vast country is before us and our motto Excelsior."

The restored Robert Mills House recalls this era of American pride and American promise as well as its architect.

Columns of the Doric Order . . . a Privy with a Pediment Front

Although the Mills' house has been one of the architect's least known works, its authorship and construction are thoroughly documented in a series of contracts and material lists found in the South Caroliniana Library at the University of South Carolina. This data provided invaluable information for restoring the main house and reconstructing the flankers and carriage house. The architects also studied drawings of other Mills' buildings in the Library of Congress as well as the extensive building records kept by the Theological Seminary. One photograph in the Seminary records, for example, showed a railing around the top, flat part of the roof. But while the restoration architects included details for the weathertight installation of a reconstructed railing in their working drawings, funds have not been appropriated for its execution.

Among the building documents in the South Caroliniana Library is a *Schedule and description of the carpenters work referred to in the agreement entered into between Ainsley Hall and Charles Beck, Carpenter,* and witnessed by Robert Mills. This includes details of construction for the main house, the smokehouse, and even the privy which was to have "four holes" and a roof to "shew a pediment front." Although Mills' drawings have never been found, the specifications proved invaluable in the restoration. For the principal story, for instance, they include such detailed instructions as

> The stairs to be neatly & handsomely finished with a continuous rail of mahogany, & a scroll—balusters of curled maple of mahogany: nosings moulded & mitered: risers dovetailed into step—plain brackets.—Circular stud partitions between the South rooms & straight d° all braced in the Parlor agreeable to drawing. . . . Handsome mantles to the fire places, if ordered, with the necessary hearth borders. The South Colonnade or Piazza to extend the whole front—The Columns to be of the Doric order, ceiling to be panneled. . . .

After measured drawings had been made of the house, says restoration-architect Albert Simons, "the beauty of the original plan showed unmistakably clear in spite of later accretions." During its theological period the house underwent several structural changes. The service stairs between the basement and first floor were removed, and

the long porch, or "South Colonnade," was covered by a sloping tin roof which necessitated changing an original second-floor door into a window. Removal of the pitched roof revealed a flat wooden deck underneath it, as well as brick walls that still retained their original red color wash that had almost faded from the rest of the building. Mills' use of the red wash, explains Simons, "was undoubtedly to make this building resemble the red brick houses he had become accustomed to in Philadelphia and Baltimore." Many early 19th-century Charleston buildings constructed of native brown brick, Simons points out, "were given a red color wash to make them look like those in the nation's early capital, Philadelphia."

Simons was surprised to find "completely commonplace" wooden mantels in the otherwise elegant music and drawing rooms, which meet in two tangent segmental arches on the south side of the principal floor. He explains the disparity between the elegant spatial effectiveness of these rooms and the banality of their mantels by pointing out that the inferior mantels were only intended to be temporary until more ornate marble ones could be imported from Europe. But the spatial refinement of these rooms, as Simons puts it, "called for enrichment," and so the architects designed plaster cornices and centerpieces for the ceilings based on similar work in the Mills-designed Valentine Museum in Richmond and the DeBruhl House in Columbia.

When the architectural work was nearing completion, Meyric Rogers joined the architects to work on the interior decoration. The principal rooms were painted in the deep tones of color inherited from the English Regency which lent "vivacity to the austere simplicity of the architecture." Rogers' own explanation was that he selected colors that tend to reinforce the plan of the principal floor with its "sense of organization and expansion from the central hall." The yellow hall, he says, "is central to the blues and greens of the salons facing the south, and the soft plums and reds used in the flanking north rooms to the east and west." The wood mantels on the principal floor were replaced with marble mantels of classic design. It was decided to furnish the house mainly with pieces of the Regency period—a logical choice based on the fact that Ainsley Hall was an Englishman and kept in close touch with his native country.

As though in Reverential Prayer

Originally there were flankers on either side of the main house. Ainsley Hall's widow lived in one of them because of a law suit over the property brought by Hall's brother. The Seminary, however, had de-

molished both flankers and erected larger buildings on their site and those, in turn, were demolished. Excavations were made by the Archaeology Department of the University of South Carolina to determine the location and size of the original flankers. But the foundations of the later buildings had destroyed those of the originals. A few small and inconclusive fragments, however, did indicate the distance of the original structures from the main house.

Another clue to the appearance of the original flankers was found in a letter written by an early theological seminarian who had been housed in the upper story of one of them. The ceiling height was so low, he writes, that when he stood up he had to bow his head "in reverential prayer." The ceilings of the reconstructed flankers were kept low although not quite so low as described by the student.

The new flankers, explains Simons, "were extremely useful in providing space for necessary ancillary services and keeping the main building entirely unencumbered by the heating and cooling equipment, toilets, snack lounge, kitchen, reception hostesses, and clerical staff."

In 1937, the original carriage house was moved to the campus of Winthrop College where it was converted into a chapel. The architects made measured drawings of it in order to reproduce it on its original site. They also studied surviving carriage houses and stables in Charleston. Many of the latter, says Simons, "showed considerable architectural character in the interior woodwork of the stall divisions." But, he explains, while the exterior of the Ainsley Hall carriage house was recreated according to the data gathered, the interior had to be reduced to the "starkest economy" because of limited funds.

The Greek Mania

Latrobe and then his disciple Mills were among the earliest American architects to take up the theme of Greek Revival forms that dominated the American scene between 1825 and 1833. (William Jay, of course, used Greek motifs in his Savannah houses but his influence was limited.) By December 1834 the New York correspondent of *The Architectural Magazine* of London felt called upon to report:

> The Greek mania here is at its height, as you infer from the fact that everything is a Greek temple from the privies in the back court, through the various grades of prison, theatre, church, custom-house, and state-house.

Nor was he exaggerating. "A friend of mine," says Aristabulus Bragg in James

Fenimore Cooper's *Home as Found* (1828), "has just built a brewery on the model of the Temple of the Winds."

Mills recognized his part in the movement when he mentions "the mite" he contributed "in this important work, and has acted as a pioneer in the undertaking." It is clear, though, that in advocating Greek forms Mills had no thought of copying Greek buildings. In an essay on *The Progress of Architecture in Virginia*, he says:

> I have always deprecated the servile copying of the buildings of antiquity; we have the same principles and materials to work upon that the ancients had, and we should adapt these materials to the habits and customs of our people as they did to theirs. There is no objection to the use of orders in columns as established by the ancients, for the proportions of these are founded upon nature and where we are applying them to the same purpose as their architects did we should follow their proportions rigidly. I have regretted to see American architects and artists taking European, Asiatic and Egyptian examples for their models. We have the same natural models, which the ancients had when they formed their buildings, their statues, etc., and shall we go to the copy and not to the original for our models?

Mills was not only a pioneer in the Greek Revival movement, he was, as he often liked to remind us, America's first professionally trained native architect—"altogether American in his views." He was, moreover, an optimistic American who believed in himself and his country. He wrote in an autobiographical fragment that:

> The increasing prosperity of the Union, the wealth and good taste of our citizens are every day aiding the cause of the fine arts, and we may anticipate the time when the United States will rival the most enlightened country of the Old World, if not in splendor, yet in the magnitude, utility, and good taste of its public works.

Mills did his part to make this prediction come true. His handsome buildings were constructed to last, and so they have. Many of them are still in use, if not for their original purpose, as successful adaptations. His Old Patent Office in Washinton, now doing admirable service as the National Portrait Gallery, is but one example.

Mills took himself and his architecture seriously. In his autobigraphical fragment, he says that "Utility and economy will be found to have entered into most of the studies of the author, and little sacrificed to dis-play." The "principle assumed and acted upon was that beauty is founded upon order, and that convenience and utility were constituent parts." In private dwellings, he adds, "it is of special importance that convenience, utility, and economy should be associated, and the author was generally successful in developing these."

The stylish and substantial house designed for Ainsley Hall, with its straightforward plan of four rooms to a floor, its separation of social, private, and service functions, and the orderly and harmonious flow of the principle rooms, shows how at one were Mills' words and his deeds.

Doorway from the front hall into the stair hall.

The Romantic Era

The Royal Pavilion

The Shadows-on-the-Teche

I f the Regency architecture of John Soane found its American counterpart in the work of Benjamin Henry Latrobe and William Jay, it might be said that John Nash's Royal Pavilion at Brighton was the forerunner of the Romantic trauma that America underwent a quarter of a century later when Gothic castles and Italianate villas made their unlikely appearance on American soil.

It is not by chance that this section opens with the romantic dream of a prince and ends with the romantic dream of a real estate promoter for, as Kenneth Clark says in *The Gothic Revival*, once romanticism sets in it begins to touch every department of life and art; and in literature, above all, causes a violent fermentation. "An intoxicating cup of poetry, coming after the barleywater of the Augustans, blinds our eyes to other features of Romanticism; the taste for Gothic seems an insignificant example of a movement essentially literary, and one hardly to be understood without a quantity of literary allusions."

The romantic movement in America was no less literary in origin, no less intoxicating in its diversity. But if Coleridge is the Pavilion's poet, and Edgar Allan Poe is the poet of America's Gothic Revival, perhaps P.T. Barnum should be called the poet of the elephant hotel in Margate, New Jersey.

For the most part, however, America's 19th-century romantics depended on the authors of other countries to provide them with the kind of fantasy they craved. The romances of Sir Walter Scott particularly seem to have fired the 19th-century American imagination along with importations of Indian, Chinese, and Persian classics. In all else, however, Americans were imbued with limitless confidence in themselves and their country. Their confidence broke out in all sorts of shapes from huge landscape paintings to rococo étagères for their living rooms, from Gothic and Italianate villas to elephant hotels. It was only that their authors (with the possible exception of Poe) didn't tell them about realms distant enough or mythical enough to counteract the vigorous but rather materialistic present. It was, as Emerson noted, "a country of beginning, of projects, of vast designs and expectations. It has no past; all has an onward and prospective look." But while accepting the expectations, Americans revolted against the industrialism of the present and longed for a past. And romanticism, of course, is always an escape from the world of now into the dream of an exotic country or an idealized past.

Americans had their own historians like Francis Parkman, their own transcendentalists like Emerson, their own speechmakers like Daniel Webster, their own naturalists like Thoreau. They had gold in California and clipper ships racing around Cape Horn. But these were too present, too real. They had their own poets and storytellers too. There was Melville's *Moby Dick*, Whittier's *Voices of Freedom*, Harriet Beecher Stowe's *Uncle Tom's Cabin*, Longfellow's *Hiawatha*, and Hawthorne's *House of Seven Gables* to name but a few. But apparently none of these were heady enough to inspire the building of exotic villas. Even Hawthorne lamented that America had "no shadow, no antiquity, no mystery, no picturesque and gloomy wrong. . . ."

As if to prove that truth is not only stranger than fiction but more varied and interesting, American architecture attempted to evoke memories of distant lands, past exploits, and cultures far removed from a present that may seem romantic to us but was merely prosaic to them. They looked to the golden ages of mythology, to the Indies, to the Middle Ages, to Tuscany, for inspiration for their new-world castles and villas. It wasn't until toward the end of the century that William Dean Howells came to realize "that we have only to study American life with the naked eye in order to find it infinitely various and entertaining. The trouble has always been that we have looked at it through somebody else's confounded telescope."

But then, as the Queen said to Alice, "living backwards always makes one a little giddy at first" and she added, "there's one great advantage in it, that one's memory works both ways." When Alice protested that her memory "only works one way. I can't remember things before they happen," the Queen called it "a poor sort of memory that only works backwards." Those 19th-century Americans looked backward for their art and architecture but forward in almost every other respect.

It was the American landscape gardener Andrew Jackson Downing who told many 19th-century romantics what they wanted to hear when he wrote that "picturesque villas—country houses with high roofs, steep gables, unsymmetrical and capricious forms," were for "men whose aspirations never leave them at rest—men whose ambition and energy will give them no peace within the mere bounds of rationality." It is for such, Downing added, "that the architect may safely introduce the tower and the campanile—any and every feature that indicates originality, boldness, energy, and variety of character. To find a really original man living in an original and characteristic house, is as satisfactory as to find an eagle's nest built on the top of a mountain crag—while to find a pretentious, shallow man in such a habitation, is no better than to find the jackdaw in the eagle's nest." Downing, however, had little to say for "those who copy foreign houses and imitate foreign manners, *for the mere sake of the imitation*, in a country so full of good and noble suggestions for social and domestic life as our own." But, he adds, we will not "shut our eyes to the fact which no observer of men will dispute, that in every age and country are born some persons who belong rather to the past than the present—men to whom memory is dearer than hope—the bygone ages fuller of meaning than those in the future. These are the natural conservatives whom Providence has wisely distributed, even in the most democratic governments, to steady the otherwise impetuous and unsteady onward movements of those who, in their love of progress, would obliterate the past, even in its hold on the feelings and imaginations of our race."

Since it is unlikely that Downing or anyone else would classify the builder of Lyndhurst as a "natural conservative," we must assume he wasn't referring to a nostalgia for the Gothic past. And he does admit that there is "both history and poetry in the use of foreign styles of architecture as may be adapted to our life, when they are thus lovingly and fittingly used by those to

Fountain Elms

whom they are fraught with beautiful memories and associations." Among a variety of suitable styles described by Downing were Norman, Romanesque, Pointed, Rural Gothic, and Italianate. For the last, he says, there is "a strong and growing partiality among us." Many of the romantics of Downing's day—still searching for an architecture that would symbolize America as Jefferson had thought classic architecture would—seem to have decided that the Italianate villa was the answer.

The interiors of the storied castles and villas of America's Romantic era were no less exotic than their exteriors and often strike us much as Henry James describes his first visit to the Louvre in *A Small Boy and Others:*

> I shall never forget how—speaking, that is, for my own sense—they filled those vast halls with the influence rather of some complicated sound, diffused and reverberant, than of such visibilities as one could directly deal with. To distinguish among these, in the charged and coloured and confounding air was difficult. . . .

Nineteenth-century romanticism in the deep south, of which the restored Shadows-on-the-Teche is a splendid example, was less a separate manifestation than a continuing thing. Louisiana's lush landscape—its bayous, swamps, moss-draped trees, and magnolias—is not only romantic enough in itself but creates an ideal setting for the white-pillared, galleried houses that are a peculiar product of that southern state. They were built for the climate and for comfort as well as for show. Although Louisianians traveled and were familiar with Greek Revival styles, they didn't copy them except perhaps in a few classic details such as the orders of their columns. Their houses were their own—an indigenous style with wide verandas and white columns.

In the last analysis a house, like the books on the shelves and the pictures on the walls, as Robert Furneaux Jordan says, "is an outward and visible statement about its owner—but that owner, in some sense or other, is also a child of his time. The house, therefore, although 'private' is, no less than other buildings, a social phenomenon . . . perhaps more than any."

All the restored houses in this section tell us something of the tenor of their time and place as well as the dreams of those who built them. From a princely fantasy such as the Royal Pavilion at Brighton to a commercial fantasy such as Rafferty's elephant "house" in New Jersey is a long way but both are unmistakable creations of a romanticism that would be unimaginable to a classicist. But it may be, as Clifford Musgrave says, that "no great civilization has been without its vision of an ideal land, of a Golden Age," and he suggests that many of our modern discontents may "arise because we no longer seek inspiration from some ideal realm of the imagination."

The Royal Pavilion at Brighton has been restored to its appearance when the Prince Regent and John Nash had finally evoked the romanticism they were after. The Shadows-on-the-Teche has been restored to its original appearance but also to reflect the continuing generations who lived there and helped to enhance its special romantic aura. Fountain Elms, with the first floor restored to its original period, is a fine example of the Italianate style that

Lyndhurst

Lucy, the Margate Elephant

Downing and many other 19th-century Americans came to believe was one of the best vehicles for expressing American aspiration. Lyndhurst—a superb example of Gothic Revival which is all the more valid because it is in the Hudson River Valley, spiritual center of the style, and because it was designed by Alexander Jackson Davis, the style's outstanding architect—has been restored as a reconciliation of its three important eras. And finally, Lucy, the Margate Elephant, certainly one of the 19th century's most distinguished architectural follies, has been given a new lease on life with the impeccable restoration of her Gothic Revival interior and larger-than-life exterior. Lucy, like the other American houses in this section, tells us something about the ingenuity of 19th-century building techniques and perhaps something of the materialism that was at the source of many a 19th-century fantasy.

The Royal Pavilion

Brighton, England

View of the Pavilion's entrance from its roof.

. . . the Pavilion may still remind us that the vision of a golden age is necessary to mankind.
                                    Clifford Musgrave

The Royal Pavilion at Brighton defies description. Many have tried, but the Pavilion itself outdoes all attempts except perhaps the Reverend Sydney Smith's irreverent remark that "the Dome of St. Paul's must have come down to Brighton and pupped!" But an architectural fantasy which could easily have been the inspiration for Coleridge's dream of Xanadu deserves more reverence than that. Although princes and poets are capable of flights of fancy which we lesser mortals cannot afford to indulge in, there can be little doubt that the greatest monument to such a royal flight is the wondrously poetic pavilion creating exotic chiaroscuros against the Brighton sky.

The Pavilion was conceived as a royal pleasure palace by two of the most romantic personages that a romantic age could boast of—His Royal Highness, the Prince Regent, later George IV, who has been called "the most temperamental as well as the most spendthrift patron in Europe," and his architect John Nash who has been described by his biographer, Sir John Summerson, as a bounder of "irrepressible good humor, mischievous wit, and quite extraordinary knowledge." Summerson also points to such pertinent characteristics as Nash's love of the theater, his "fatal ebullient optimism," his tendency to pour his own and other people's money "into schemes of brilliant design but doubtful structural validity."

That these two spendthrift exhibitionists got together is one of those coincidences that seem to point to a mysterious logic at work in the universe. But, coincidence or not, the partnership was responsible for giving us one of the world's most celebrated architectural frivolities and a very plausible setting for one of the world's most romantic royal liaisons.

Fortunately for us, the Pavilion was preserved from destruction by the townspeople of Brighton who had become so fond of the royal extravaganza in their midst that,

when Queen Victoria dismantled it and took all its furnishings and decorations to Buckingham Palace and Windsor Castle, they petitioned the Crown to be allowed to purchase it in 1850 for £50,000.

In 1863 Queen Victoria returned some of the large decorations and chandeliers, but most of the original furnishings have been returned in recent years by Queen Elizabeth II. Since the 1940s, a program has been in progress to restore the Pavilion to its appearance when it was completed in 1822.

It was not difficult to decide on a period to which to restore the Royal Pavilion. In spite of the many phases it went through from "respectable farmhouse" to classical villa and eventually as it appears today—resting "on its lawns by the sea as though it had drifted down in a night of Oriental enchantment"—there was a moment in 1822 when the Pavilion was a finally completed creation. Nash and the chief decorators, Robert Jones and the firm of Crace, had fully achieved the transformation. The appearance of the Pavilion at this date is recorded in the colored aquatints and engravings that make up Nash's "Views of the Royal Pavilion" published in 1826. These exquisite aquatints, which convey the poetic atmosphere as well as the details of the Pavilion far better than any photograph could, have been an invaluable aid in the restoration. Among Nash's views are some showing an early phase of the final period that would have been possible to reconstruct. But the integrity of the ultimate scheme—the product of years of collaboration among George IV, Nash, and the decorators—has been the imperative behind the work of restoration since 1946.

A Prince and his Pleasure Pavilion

The exotic story of the "Marine Pavilion" properly begins in 1785 when the riotous Prince of Wales, son of George III, brought his lady love Mrs. Fitzherbert to Brighton. The 23-year-old Prince of Wales, probably one of the most difficult princes in all royaldom, maddened his father and enchanted his mistresses. When he was 15, his tutor, Archbishop Hurd, was asked how he thought the Prince would turn out. The

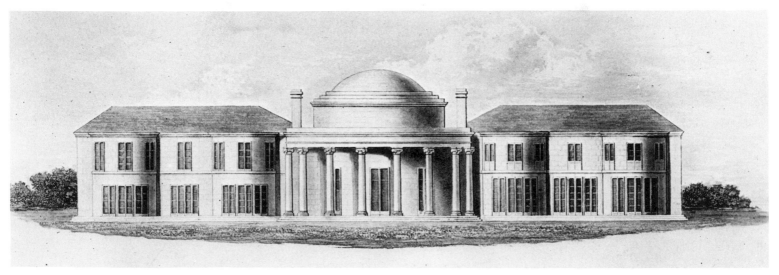

(Top) *The romanticism and influence of the East—such strong elements in Regency paint-ing and literature—found architectural expression in the Royal Pavilion. (Above) Henry Holland's 1787 Pavilion forms the core of the present building.*

Archbishop replied that he would be "either the most polished gentleman or the most accomplished blackguard in Europe. Possibly both."

The Prince and Mrs. Fitzherbert were secretly married in 1785 but since no one knew of the Prince's marriage to the Roman Catholic lady who entertained for him, gossip was rife. It seems that even Marie Antoinette sent for the British Ambassador to come to Versailles to ask his advice about the propriety of allowing the Princess de Lamballe to go to Brighton. "I cannot judge the propriety or impropriety of her being in a place with the P. of Wales and Mrs. F_____," the Ambassador wrote to the Duchess of Devonshire.

In 1786 the Prince leased and later bought the "respectable farmhouse" that was to suffer such a strange transformation. The first Pavilion, which replaced the farmhouse, was built for the Prince by his architect Henry Holland—an elegant classical villa in what Holland called his "Graeco-Roman style." But this was only the beginning of a series of refurnishings, refurbishings, and rebuildings which was eventually to result in the Royal Pavilion as we see it today. It was never redesigned as a whole, points out Sir John Summerson who warns that to attempt to judge the building as a unity is to miss the point. He compares it to a random autobiography which is "good in parts; tiresome and clumsy in others." It was not a public building, he reminds us, but the owner's private toy "and the Prince was under no obligation to please anyone but himself. His architect was merely the instrument of his whims."

Holland's classical Pavilion was completed in 1787 but it wasn't long before the Prince's passion for building needed further expression. In 1803 he decided to have a room built in which to hang some Chinese wallpaper he had received as a gift and which, in turn, suggested the addition of an extraordinary Chinese passage-room of painted glass. And thus began the oriental fantasy that was eventually to make the Pavilion interiors the most outstanding examples of *chinoiserie* to be seen in Europe.

About 1805, the famous landscape gardener Humphrey Repton was sent for to make suggestions. Repton had been working on the grounds at Sezincote in Gloucestershire, Sir Charles Cockerell's villa in the India style, and he was certain that architecture and gardening were "on the eve of some great future change . . . in consequence of our having lately become acquainted with the scenery and buildings in the inner provinces of India." Repton drew up plans for Indianizing the Pavilion and its grounds, which pleased the Prince, but they

were never carried out. Nothing was done until shortly after 1811 when the Prince of Wales became Prince Regent and Nash began the alterations which were to evolve into the present fairy-tale palace with its Indian exterior and Chinese interior. The latter, says Clifford Musgrave, former Director of the Royal Pavilion, "raised the Chinese taste in decoration to heights of magnificence never before attained."

Besides the ingenious addition of the great bulbous domes and tall minarets which transformed the roofline of Holland's classic villa, Nash added the banqueting room at one end of the old building and the music room at the other. He also created the gallery or corridor that runs between them. The final improvements were the addition of the King's private suite in 1819 and the famous underground passage in 1822. But Musgrave warns romanticists who are inclined to make interesting conjectures about the passage that "the Royal owner of the Pavilion was in his sixtieth year and suffering acutely from gout." It seems more likely, says Musgrave, that the passage was provided as a convenient means of reaching the stables rather than "to aid nocturnal rambles." In any case, he says, the existence of a passage from the Pavilion to Mrs. Fitzherbert's house cannot be confirmed. Mrs. Fitzherbert rarely spent a night in the Pavilion although she dined there and always did the honors as the Prince's wife. Thomas Creevey, the diarist, described his first invitation to the Pavilion:

> Mrs. Fitzherbert . . . sat on one side of the Prince, and the Duke of Clarence on the other. In the course of the evening the Prince took me up to the card-table where Mrs. Fitzherbert was playing.

The Pavilion was almost finished in 1820 when, on the death of his father, the Prince succeeded to the throne as George IV. The year 1821, when the Pavilion was completed and the King was crowned, "marks the height of its importance as an historical building," says Musgrave, "where many of the most distinguished persons in Europe had been received, and to which the news of the victories of Talavera and Trafalgar had first been brought." The interior decorative schemes had entered their second Chinese phase and were more restrained than the earlier Oriental rooms with their barbaric colors and exuberant designs. The 1821 decor had been in the hands of the King's decorators, Frederick Crace and Son, assisted by Robert Jones. Jones worked with Crace between 1817 and 1823 and seems to have been largely responsible for the Pavilion's final decorative phase. Crace's original watercolor designs for the decoration of these

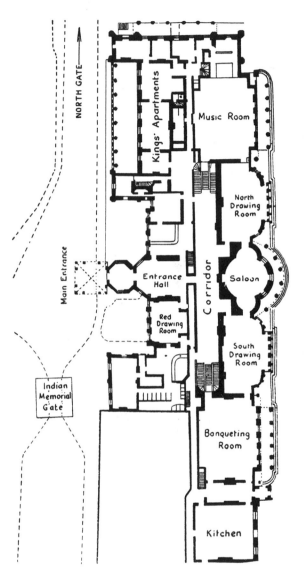

Ground floor plan.

The music room is, as Musgrave has described it, a room wherein the romantic fairyland of China is imprisoned as in a great lacquer cabinet or red, yellow, and gold. Under the domed ceiling of gilded shells is a huge tapestry carpet woven at Aubusson for one of Catherine the Great's palaces in Russia.

This watercolor design by Frederick Crace for the west wall of the music room was executed in 1822 with slight variations.

rooms are in the collection of New York's Cooper-Hewitt Museum and have proved helpful in restoring the decorative details of the Pavilion.

Carpenter and Courtier

John Nash, the creator of this exotic seaside fantasy, was certainly a lover of large undertakings and large financial speculations. He dreamed of a London that would outdo Napoleon's Paris and many believe his major achievement was as the author of London's Regent Street and Regent's Park. Summerson thinks he grasped the essentials of town planning as nobody else had done and attributes his success to the fact that "he was not only an architect, but a man of the world, a Londoner who had known his town in poverty and wealth, failure and success; as a carpenter and courtier...." Summerson makes an apt comparison between Nash and his contemporary Beau Brummell and finds Nash the lesser artist. When "Brummell brought in starched neck-cloths, Nash brought in stuccoed facades" but Nash, he says, "never reached the quintessential tact and absolute mastery of style which Brummell achieved in dress. His dandyism was of a less reticent order."

Some have attributed Nash's success to his friendship with the Prince. The architect, it has been said, obliged the Prince by marrying one of his mistresses thereby acquiring his unexplained fortune. In later years, Summerson tells us, the Nashes' drawing-room was full of royal portraits, and some exquisite chairs which came from the Regent. He also mentions more personal gifts which a "puritan hand consigned . . . to destruction." In any case, Nash and the Prince were obviously allies whether or not their alliance was contrived by circumstances, and certainly Nash's talents and enthusiasms jibed with those of the Prince. He was able to capture the poetic subtlety of the Prince's oriental imagining remarkably.

It is difficult to realize that Nash and Soane were exact contemporaries for they were also exact opposites in their persons and their work. Soane was almost antisocial, but he was an architect of genius who used the classical tradition to evolve a highly personal style. Nash was an exhibitionist who designed in a wide array of styles from Tudor and Italianate to Gothic and Oriental. He had more in common with the later eclectics than with his contemporary Soane. So here in the early years of the 19th century, as Pevsner puts it, "the fancy dress ball of architecture is in full swing."

Of Horses, Houses, and Women

The Prince was continually redesigning and furnishing a whole series of his own resi-

(Top) The saloon forms the center of the state apartments. The present chandeliers have been reconstructed with early parts. The domed ceiling represents a clouded sky with a golden star in the center and silvered fish between its rays. The Chinese carpet repeats the shape of the dome. (Above) The banqueting room has been called the most brilliantly magnificent of the state apartments. When the chandeliers were originally illuminated by gas in 1818 the Prince Regent and his architect John Nash met to see them lit for the first time. Most of the furniture was designed by Robert Jones, Nash, or Crace.

The restored south drawing room boasts some of the most important Regency furniture in existence, including the famous suite of Dolphin furniture which was presented to Greenwich Hospital for Seafarers in 1813 in memory of Admiral Lord Nelson. Cabinets on the left wall were designed for the Pavilion in 1822 by Robert Jones.

The great kitchen has been restored almost exactly as it appears in this illustration of it from Nash's Views of the Royal Pavilion. The columns are formed of cast-iron tubes topped with palm leaves of copper.

dences and palaces as well as houses in London and Brighton for Mrs. Fitzherbert. In 1801 a Brighton historian felt called upon to comment:

> The improvement which His Royal Highness has made and is still projecting and the elegant house which Porden, an architect of uncommon merit, is raising for Mrs. Fitzherbert will, I trust, check the listless torpor, and selfless apathy which has too long prevailed at Brighton, and reflect a certain taste and liberality on the sordid natives of this lawless waste.

Anita Leslie says in her book about Mrs. Fitzherbert that the Prince trained his taste "starting with horses, silver, food, and wine; later he became a connoisseur of pictures and furniture." And, in spite of his gross appetites, he was "as fastidious over women as over furniture."

A first-hand account of his habits and tastes soon after he became King is to be found in an entry of November 14, 1820, in Mrs. Arbuthnot's journal:

> The King had talked of going to Hanover, but the Duke of Wellington says there is not much chance of that unless we allow him to take his eating and drinking money, his money for buhl furniture and for buying horses, which we could not think of doing.

From the beginning, Brighton's fantastic gazebo-by-the-sea has incited strong reactions. Shortly after it was completed, ever-increasing numbers of London's smart set drove their carriages down for the sea air and a glimpse of the minarets and domes outlined against the summer sky. On December 28, 1819, Mrs. Fitzherbert writes to Creevey:

> You would scarcely know Brighton.... When I tell you that 52 public coaches go from hence to London every day and bring people down for six shillings you will not be surprised at the sort of company we have besides which the Royal Palace attracts numbers who are puzzled to know what to make of the appearance of the building which it is impossible for me, or indeed anyone else to describe ...!

Anita Leslie puts it another way. The banqueting hall and music room, she says, with their "cyclamin pink wallpapers," their "chandeliers that glistened with writhing, roaring dragons," were enough to reduce some of the Prince Regent's guests "to tongue-tied embarrassment or stuttering eulogy."

And from the vantage point of the present there is Summerson's more objec-

(Top) The design of the carpet in the restored Corridor was based on the original as it appears in Nash's Views. *Above the Corridor's central space is the restored painted glass skylight surrounded by a canopy hung wth bells. The water-lily-shaped chandelier, the smaller Chinese lanterns, and the three marble fireplaces are original and were returned from Buckingham Palace in 1898. The design of the wallcovering was reproduced from original remnants. (Above) The Corridor as seen in Nash's* Views.

(Top) Reproduction of the Music Room chimneypiece. The original is at Buckingham Palace. (Above) In the process of restoring the Music Room.

tive opinion that the Pavilion's "intrinsic beauty is small; surprise and novelty were the great things about it, and the thrill of such ephemeral virtues is not easily recaptured." And Clifford Musgrave, who is probably more familiar with this fabulous plaything of a sybaritic prince than anyone else, speaks of the "breath of magic that belongs to the Pavilion, revealing it as surely as any of the poems of Keats, Coleridge, or Shelley, as an expression of the Romantic movement of the early 19th century with its passion for the Orient and its love of strange beauty."

Magic Regained

That "breath of magic" so long dimmed has gradually been reemerging since the 1940s when Musgrave instigated the process of scholarly restoration that still continues.

During the 19th century the interiors had undergone much overpainting ind insensitive redecoration almost obliterating their imaginative splendor of 1822 when, in Musgrave's words, the Chinese taste had "attained to a vast exotic grandeur that made it confederate with the ultimate kingdoms of the romantic imagination."

Much of that splendor has been regained through careful research and the work of gifted craftsmen. Wall decorations have been faithfully restored, silkscreen copies have been made of original papers, skies have been repainted on ceilings, graining has been uncovered on doors and casements, chandeliers have been restored, much of the original furniture has been returned, and as one member of the restoration staff put it, the Pavilion boasts "the assemblage, from nothing, of the finest and most sumptuous collection of Regency furniture in the country."

Nash began with the alterations of the 162-foot, or 48.6m, long corridor with imitation-bamboo (actually cast iron) staircases at either end. The corridor went through several changes between 1815 and 1820 but its lovely wall decoration—pale blue foliage on a delicate peach ground—remained unchanged until 1877 when an irreverent Victorian artist covered it with somber green and apricot paint. It has now been returned to its original appearance by Roy Bradley, the Pavilion's decorative artist who has been responsible for restoring much of the splendor to the Pavilion's walls and ornamentation. The corridor's original wall decoration was found under moldings where its colors had been protected from fading and thus provided an accurate guide for their restoration. A carpet was especially woven for the corridor in a design based on the original as it appears in Nash's "Views."

The banqueting and music rooms (at either end of the corridor) were added to Holland's original building by Nash in 1817 and completed in 1820. Restoration of the fabulous banqueting room is almost complete. Its great mural paintings of Chinese figures, its chandeliers in the shape of waterlilies, and its domed ceiling painted like a huge palm tree with a dragon among the leaves, once again reveal it as a setting for the magnificent parties described by one guest as "realizing the ideas of entertainments . . . in the Arabian Nights." Its 45-foot, or 13.5m, high domed ceiling has been cleaned and restored. The wallpaper has been reprinted from the original blocks, the mural paintings have been cleaned and their frames gilded. Although some of the original wall paintings by Robert Jones were removed in 1863, replacements were executed in a style that Musgrave calls "similar and hardly inferior to the originals."

One can easily imagine Coleridge's Kubla Khan holding forth in the Pavilion's restored music room with its nine waterlily-shaped chandeliers; its great wall decorations of Chinese landscapes painted in scarlet, yellow, and gold; its dragon-twined pillars; and its carved imitation bamboo ceilings at the ends of the room, which are not unlike the "roofs of bamboo-cane" in the Palace of the great Khan described in Marco Polo's account of his travels. Major work has been done to strengthen and clean the great domed ceiling made of carved and gilded shells which is supported on an octagonal gallery with eight elliptical windows of painted glass. Darkened varnish and crimson overpainting have been removed from the wall decorations to reveal their original effect of brilliant lacquer. A faithful reproduction has been made of the original chimneypiece (now at Buckingham Palace) in white scagliola and gilded plaster. A comparison with the aquatint in Nash's "Views" shows the restored music room to be the exotic setting for the King's celebrated musical parties that it originally was.

The saloon, one of the most elegant rooms in the Pavilion, was the principal apartment in Holland's classic 1787 design. Chinese wallpaper was introduced in 1802 and later removed. When some of it was returned from Buckingham Palace, it was restored to the wall panels. The surrounding wallpaper was reproduced from the original blocks, and the original mahogany dado decorated in silver and gold on flake white has been restored to replace the painted plaster dado which had served since Victorian times. Under the clouded sky of its domed ceiling, the saloon is seen today almost exactly as Robert Jones and Nash planned it—an opulent environment for the pursuit of royal pleasures, albeit not as dramatic as the music and banqueting rooms.

The north and south drawing rooms with their ceilings supported on palm-tree columns were also part of Holland's original Pavilion. Both have been restored to their 1821 appearance. In 1948 some pieces of linen decorated with gray paint and gold leaf were found in the Pavilion and recognized as the 1820–21 decorative scheme for the north drawing room. This scheme was restored by Roy Bradley who used the original medium of gold leaf for the designs on a gray ground.

The restoration of the Royal Pavilion is a continuing process but enough has been accomplished to reveal it as no less a monument to the romantic era than Keats' *La Belle Dame sans Merci* or Coleridge's *Kubla Khan*. The latter, incidentally, was published in 1816 while the Pavilion's decorations were being executed. This is no coincidence. Romanticism is poetic, as Geoffrey Scott points out in *The Architecture of Humanism*. It derives its inspiration from literature, and while *Kubla Khan* might be called the most romantic poem of a romantic age, the Royal Pavilion is certainly its most romantic building. Nikolaus Pevsner has called it "the most lavish member of the delightful and crazy tribe of the Follies;" John Gloag speaks of it as an ornate experiment "of the heady and exuberant kind;" Summerson passes it off as the plaything of its royal owner; and Peter Fleetwood-Hesketh considers it the most "conspicuous mark" left by any architect upon the closing decades of the Georgian era. Yes, but more than any of these, the Royal Pavilion is high romantic theater.

George IV by Sir Thomas Lawrence.

The Shadows-on-the-Teche

New Iberia, Louisiana

The dining room is the only elegant room on the first floor. The blue and white tile floor is original but at some point it had been taken up an replaced with a wood floor. In 1921 the marble was found in the basement and relaid in the'loggia. During the 1961 restoration it was returned to the dining room where it had originally been.

Rice, tobacco, cotton—out of these three elements alone the South created a great symphonic pageant of human activity.

Henry Miller

There is something poetic about the Louisiana bayou country—the semitropical lushness of the landscape with its immense oaks and mysterious mosses, winding bayous, and white-pillared plantation houses. One can easily imagine ghosts wandering in the shadowed gardens—ghosts of such charming antebellum belles as one described by an early diarist as "very beautiful and graceful with a suggestion of pensiveness about her . . . always in a soft, trailing white gown, full of romantic fancies, and always accompanied by a great dog, the gift of a lover, an absent one, about whom there was some mystery."

For many, The Shadows-on-the-Teche in New Iberia is the most beautiful and bewitching of all the early plantation houses. Certainly Weeks Hall, the last member of the original family to live there, was captured by its magic. "I have never considered myself anything but a trustee of something fine which chance had put in my hands to preserve," he wrote in 1940. "Fine things are without value, in that they belong only to those rare people who appreciate them beyond price. It is to those people that I should like to entrust this place." Thus shortly before his death in 1958 Hall bequeathed The Shadows to the National Trust for Historic Preservation.

The Shadows might be said to have led two distinct lives—one from 1834 until the Civil War and the second from 1922 until Hall's death. It was built by Weeks Hall's great grandfather David Weeks in 1830 as the townhouse of an almost feudal family. The Classic Revival was in full sway at the time and architectural adaptations were appearing throughout Louisiana which made allowances for the local climate, the culture, and materials. Banks of clay on the bayous provided the bricks, and the huge cypress trees growing in the swamps provided the wood. "Here are structures," as Clarence J. Laughlin puts it in *Ghosts Along the Mississippi*, "actually designed so purely and directly in terms of the intrinsic character of cypress wood and the plastic capacities of plastered brick . . . that the design seems to have grown, inevitably and profoundly, from their substance."

These houses, too, are endowed with a special quality derived from the culture which brought them into being, a culture which was elegant, sophisticated, romantic, and largely self-sufficient. Each plantation had its own slaves, its own doctor, its own pastor, its own cemetery. While the lives of these people may seem circumscribed to us, actually they lived more spaciously than we do. They lived closer to the earth. The seasons moved through them. They knew how to entertain themselves. They lived outwardly and openly.

The Shadows, with its back to the Bayou Teche, is a soft pink brick with eight classic columns rising from the level of its garden to support the roof. Designed to catch the breezes in Louisiana's humid climate, the ceilings are high, and most of the main rooms are on the second floor. Outside stairways lead from the downstairs loggias to the second-floor galleries. The only interior stairway is the stair at the rear of the house. The chaste simplicity of its architecture, the elegant detail of its interior woodwork, the fine furniture, silver, and family portraits handed down by successive generations of a family of planters make The Shadows stand out even in that country of architectural gems. But, as Henry Miller wrote of The Shadows in his *Air-Conditioned Nightmare*, "to speak in architectural language of a house that is as organically alive, sensuous, and mellow as a great tree is to kill its charm."

Of Legends and Legacies

One might expect a country that inspired Longfellow's *Evangeline* to have legend-making qualities, but it would be difficult to think of any part of the fiction-loving south more continuously productive of legends than the Teche country in general and The Shadows in particular. The legends of its recent past—between 1922 and 1958 when Weeks Hall lived there—may well prove the most fascinating to future generations.

Entrance facade. This soft salmon-pink brick-galleried house blends the French and Spanish architectural influences that highlight the Louisiana scene of the antebellum era. Probably the most interesting detail of the house, in the words of restoration architect Richard Koch, "is that the exterior cornice is Roman and not Greek or Federal as in many other houses of this date."

When he returned home in 1922 from studying art in Paris, The Shadows began its second life. Weeks Hall was, according to his friend Harnett Kane, "a man of high taste, of superb gusto and a deep love of his scene—and also of his house . . . one of the two or three major lights of the Creole country." A southern eccentric in the true sense, he was not only in the habit of sharing his midnight coffee with his dog, but as Henry Miller noted, there was "an unholy sort of bond between them." He was also addicted to telephoning friends all over the world in the small hours of the morning. During the last years of his life, however, he devoted his entire energy to ensuring a future for his beloved Shadows. He curtailed his long-distance phone calls and lived chiefly on peanut butter and bourbon in order to leave a large enough endowment for its preservation. He was overjoyed when, shortly before his death in 1958, the National Trust accepted his bequest of The Shadows will all its accumulated furnishings and treasures of each generation. There were some 40,000 documents in the house including bills, journals, receipts, inventories, diaries, letters, and so on.

Because The Shadows was the home of one family from 1834 until 1958 it was first of all necessary for the National Trust to decide to what stage in its history it should be restored. The antebellum period was se-

lected since no major changes had been made in the house after 1865. The influence of Weeks Hall on The Shadows and on Louisiana as a well-known artist and intellectual has fortunately not been neglected. His studio has been arranged as it was during his lifetime with the addition of a display of his works on the wall. His presence, however, is felt throughout the house and garden where he is buried along with other members of his family. The garden as it appears today is largely the creation of Weeks Hall. "I have lived on the place attending to it and building it," he wrote before his death in 1958. "Nothing in life has meant, or will mean, more to me than this garden on a summer morning before sunrise. At all hours, no place is more tranquil nor more ageless. Its inherent charm to me has been in its placid seclusion from a changing world, and, in that, will be its value to others. This quality must be preserved."

Probably no other restoration has been better documented. It was possible to verify the colors of wallpapers and fabrics in particular rooms through descriptions in family records. There were bills and receipts showing when and where certain pieces of furniture were purchased. Family pleasures, travels, reading habits, the planting of certain trees and shrubs could be traced through letters and journals.

Like any house lived in by one family

over a period of years, the restored Shadows fittingly boasts a varied collection of furnishings including Chippendale and Hepplewhite styles of the late 18th century, Sheraton of the early 19th, and the later American Empire style. Some are Weeks' heirlooms, some were purchased by Weeks Hall, and others were added by the National Trust. Esthetically, says Robert G. Steward, former director of the department of properties for the National Trust, "The Shadows is the best building I have ever worked on," and from someone who worked on the restoration of Independence Hall, this is no faint praise.

Weeks Hall himself recorded so much information about his research and the restoration that was done for him in 1922 by New Orleans architects Armstrong & Koch that many facts were immediately available. Richard Koch, FAIA, also kept a detailed record of replacements and modern improvements made during the 20s restoration. In 1961 Koch & Wilson, as the firm was subsequently called, handled the restoration for the National Trust which thus had the benefit of Richard Koch's personal knowledge of the house.

In Weeks Hall's painstaking records of the changes made under his aegis, he writes: "This place has for over one hundred years, been the home of my family. It has remained intact in arrangement, structure,

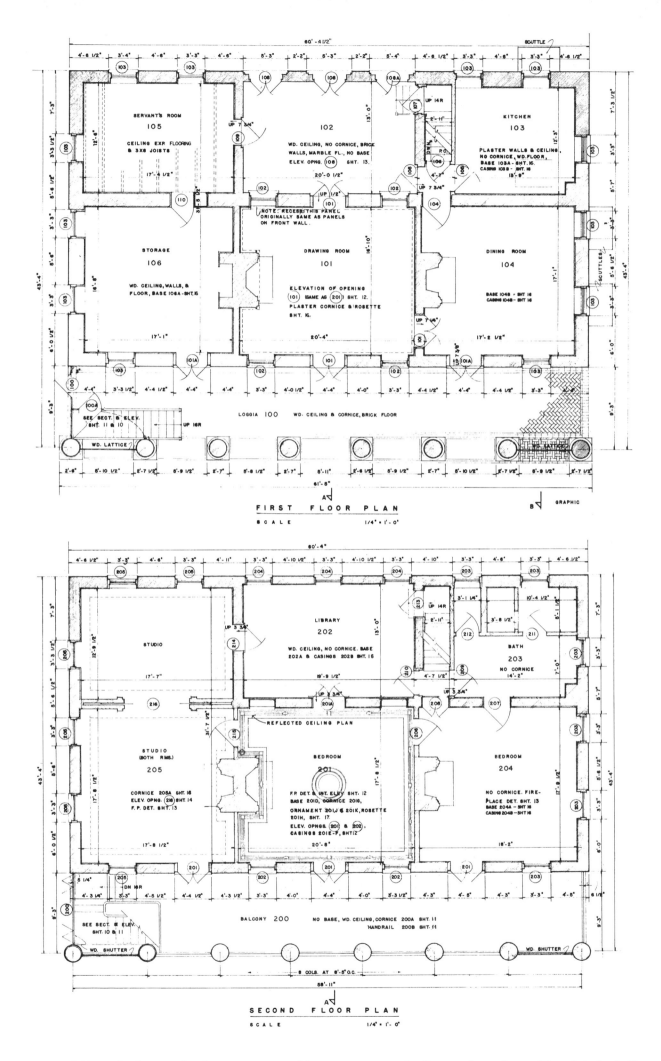

The plan follows the favorite Creole arrangement of three rooms across the front and two deep with no interior halls.

(Top) The entrance through a wide porch with outside stairways at both ends leads to the second floor gallery. The tapered Tuscan columns are made of brick encased in stucco. A door flanked by two windows opens into the dining room which has a duplicate door with flanking windows opening on the rear loggia. "Almost all the window blinds are cypress 1830 originals with the marks of strap-iron hinges showing in paint," noted Weeks Hall. (Above) The loggia has three open arches on the bayou side of the house. All the first floor rooms have access to the loggia from which the "slave stairway" (the only enclosed stairway in the house) rises to the upper gallery.

and detail, to an extent which is at least unsurpassed by any other similar residential building of its contemporary period in the state." Later on he writes: "For almost twenty years I watched the public's reaction to this place. I know it as few people are privileged to know it. Except to those who know gardens, the interest is entirely in seeing how the people in these houses lived . . . ninety-five per cent of the tourists coming into this place care nothing whatsoever about anything but seeing the inside of the house. . . ."

Antebellum Days

The Weeks family moved into their new house in the spring of 1834. Andrew Jackson was President and Lincoln, at 25, had just entered the State Legislature in Illinois. A few days after the Weeks moved in, David Weeks took the steamboat Lancaster on the Bayou Teche on the first step of his journey to New Haven, Connecticut, where he went in a vain attempt to regain his health. There the original master of The Shadows died and never saw his mansion again.

His widow Mary Conrad Weeks lived on there, taking over the responsibilities of The Shadows and educating their six children until she married Judge John Moore in 1841. A widower who had been prominent in Louisiana public life, Judge Moore was elected to Congress that year.

In July 1834, while her husband was still alive, Mary Weeks wrote to him in New Haven: ". . . our old furniture distributed about the rooms looks better than you would think. We have got from New Orleans one dozen thirteen-dollar chairs that I have put in the dining room—the chairs and bedsteads from Franklin are all that we have bought. . . . Think not that poverty has such horrors as you think. Your health is the worst we have to contend with. I would take a basket and pick cotton every day if it would do you any good."

A receipt to David Weeks from E. Develu of New Orleans, dated July 11, 1834, for "1 dozen Windsor chairs—$13.00" are undoubtedly those Mary Weeks refers to.

David Weeks also sent furnishings from New Haven. A letter from her brother Alfred Conrad to Mary Weeks dated July 27, 1834, says: "Your husband is well enough this morning to requisition me to say that by the vessel to sail next month he will send you carpeting enough for four rooms . . . together with what articles of furniture you cannot do without." A bookcase, now in the sitting room, was sent by David Weeks in 1834 among other pieces still in the house.

Prosperity, however, was more usual than poverty at The Shadows. The family, like other plantation families, created a rich

The parlor on the second floor boasts the only marble mantel in the house. The wallpaper with its handpainted border was selected because bills were found in the house for such paper and it is in scale with the Greek Revival cornice. The portrait over the mantel is of Frances Weeks Magill Prewitt, eldest daughter of David Weeks, The Shadows' builder. The red damask draperies, horsehair couch (not shown), and mantel reflect the styles of the 1850s.

This view of a second floor bedroom shows the original "graining" that was reproduced on the doors. Original paint colors were reproduced throughout the house.

(Top) Watercolor of The Shadows done in 1861 by Adrian Persac, an itinerant artist who painted many Louisiana plantation houses between 1857 and 1872. Figures in the foreground are prints from Godey's Lady's Book pasted on by the artist. (Above) Persac's watercolor of The Shadows from the bayou. Both views hang in the restored dining room.

existence for themselves in those exuberant antebellum days. There were great balls, soirées on the bayou bank, trips to New Orleans to the opera and masquerades, and vacations at Last Island, White Sulphur, Newport, and other fashionable resorts. The art of living was truly cultivated. They read, they played the piano, they gardened, they did needlework, and they entertained. They also followed the fashions and innovations of the day. An advertisement appearing in the Louisiana *Courier for the Country* of June 29, 1883, titled "Revolution in the Art of Washing," extols the virtues of Appleton's Patent Washing Machines and refers to a list of persons who had purchased them which included David Weeks. And in 1825, Alfred Conrad writes to his sister Mary Conrad Weeks from New Orleans where her husband, David Weeks, had been visiting: ". . . Your husband has requested Brother to get Mrs. N. to choose you a Bonnet, and I am to display my taste in the choice of a Sett of China. I am afraid I cannot please you. . . ." It is also safe to assume that such newspaper ads as one appearing in the early 1850s calling attention to a brand-new patented hoop skirt, did not escape the notice of the ladies of the family. It was guaranteed to give satisfaction "in all crowded churches, assemblies, carriages, cars, in the home or on promenade," a truly remarkable garment which can "never offend the modesty, as the single-hoop skirt sometimes does."

Mary Conrad Weeks was an avid reader and enthusiastic pleasure gardener. She was continually writing to members of her family asking for books, exchanging shrubs and cuttings. "I have nothing to read," she writes her brother Alfred, "and the weather is so gloomy it gives me the *horribles*. Try Mr. Bronson, Miss Parrot or some of our novel reading friends." Again in 1853 when she was Mrs. Moore, she writes: "I have a number of Godey's Lady's Book from you for which I thank you many times. I wish you not forget *Uncle Tom's Cabin*. I have seen so much of it in the papers . . . in dark bad weather when I cannot go in the garden time hangs heavy on my hands." Many of the books she read are still in the house and much of what The Shadows' first mistress planted still thrives in its lovely garden where she herself is buried.

The Shadows' children, like most plantation children, were tutored at home. The two eldest Weeks sons went to the University of Virginia, and after they were expelled, to William and Mary. They entertained Charles Dickens on one of his American visits, and in 1841 Alfred writes to his sister Harriet from the University of Virginia: "I am becoming very fond of the University. I associate a great deal with the

ladies, a great deal too much for my own good, I am going to stop visiting ladies altogether. . . ."

Malaria and Mardi Gras

It was altogether a life of extremes. High pleasures intermingled with hard work and sickness. There are continual references in letters and diaries to malaria, yellow fever, and cholera, and newspaper ads frequently appeared in the Louisiana papers for such products as a "beautiful beverage" for curing "all invalids at this season," especially those suffering from "billious, yellow, congestive, or typhoid fever."

But on the whole it was an opulent life in an opulent landscape. The great sugar and cotton crops produced plenty of money and, failing that, a best-seller published in New Orleans in 1858 called *The Bliss of Marriage, Or, How to Get a Rich Wife* suggests that a Louisiana gentleman had other ways to supplement his income.

The Shadows, like the rest of the plantations in the Teche country, continued to flourish until the Civil War when the Union Army marched into New Iberia and established headquarters there. A contemporary report of the conduct of the troops has this to say: "Mrs. Moore, a lady far advanced in years, belonging to a family distinguished in the annals of the nation, accustomed not only to the convenience, but the elegancies of life, was driven with the ladies of her family to the upper apartments where she was subjected to every privation. . . . She died—imprisoned in her own dwelling, deprived of the comforts she would have bestowed upon the humblest of servants. . . ."

Last of the Southern Gentlemen

The Shadows drifted into a kind of apathy after the war. The disintegration of the slave system, the later collapse of the cotton and sugar markets helped bring about a decline in the whole culture of the Louisiana plantations. Poverty came to The Shadows. It remained in the Weeks family, however, and was lived in intermittently by one member of the family or another. But it didn't really thrive again until Weeks Hall returned from Paris in 1922 and, as one of his friends put it, "literally became captured by the past." He spent the rest of his life restoring The Shadows and its garden.

Throughout the 1920s and 30s such celebrities as Edmund Wilson, Stark Young, H.L. Mencken, Henry Miller, Max Ernst, Abe Rattner, the Lunts, Cecil B. de Mille, Lyle Saxon, and Mae West enjoyed the revived hospitality of The Shadows and all of them were struck by the remarkable personality of its host. Some described Weeks Hall as "last of the Southern gentlemen," to

others he was a *grand seigneur* with a Puck's sense of humor, or as a newspaper columnist wrote in 1954, ". . . he is an institution of culture, wit, and the science of living."

Many of the celebrities who were entertained at The Shadows during this period signed their names on one of the doors of the house. When Weeks Hall discovered they had been removed by a cleaning man he was seriously considering taking the door with him on a world tour so that his then far-flung guests could restore their names. Not without misgiving he gave up the idea when someone suggested it might be easier to invite the original signers back to The Shadows. Most of the signatures were later reinstated and the signed door remains in the house.

Of Weeks Hall, Henry Miller writes in *The Air-Conditioned Nightmare*,

he was an artist to his finger-tips. . . . Already, in certain domains, he had amassed the knowledge of a savant . . . he saw the relatedness of things. Naturally he could not be content in executing a masterful painting. . . . In a sense it might be said of him that he had already completed his great work. He had transformed the house and ground, through his passion for creation, into one of the most distinctive pieces of art which America can boast of. He was living and breathing in his own masterpiece, not knowing it, not realizing the extent and sufficiency of it. . . . I felt his presence all through the house, flooding it like some powerful magic fluid. He had created that which in turn would recreate him. . . . I hoped that he would remain, that as the last link in the ancestral chain he would close the circle and by realizing the significance of his act expand the circle and circumferance of his life to infinite dimension.

Weeks Hall in the 1920s with his famous English setter "Lady Shadow's Ghost," known as Spot.

Fountain Elms

Utica, New York

Few modern designs can match the Gothic archwork wallpaper in the front hall. The tile floor, marble statues, and ornate furnishings made a grandiose gesture.

God has predestinated, mankind expects, great things from our race; and great things we feel in our souls.   Herman Melville

The mid-19th-century villa Fountain Elms, expertly restored by the Munson-Williams-Proctor Institute in Utica, New York, presents a faithful impression of the best of contemporary taste in an ebullient age when the ladies were fully draped and so were their drawing rooms. A handsome house dating from 1850, it was designed in the then fashionable Italianate villa style by William L. Woollett of Albany for James Watson Williams and his young wife as a gift from her father Alfred Munson. Richard B.K. McLanathan, former director of the Munson-Williams-Proctor Institute, who supervised the restoration, points out that it is necessary to reduce imagination to a minimum if one is to restore such a house with any accuracy. "Imagination," he adds, "is only used in right interpretation—in combining the parts." Period rooms done in this country in the 1920s, as McLanathan says, "are like forgeries. The prejudices of the people who did them are obvious."

Thus to recapture the atmosphere of the Williams' Italianate villa of 1850, it was first of all necessary to find out what kind of man Williams was—his habits, tastes, and personality. The stylistic tastes of the period were too varied to be of much immediate help.

Le Style c'est L'homme

As leading citizens of Utica the Munsons and Williams were to be counted among that self-respecting upper-middle-class gentility—the "best people," as Henry James put it, who still frowned on vulgar ostentation. Williams' extensive library provided an excellent clue to the type of man he was. Many books on Italian archaeology and architecture, Frederick Law Olmsted's books, all the volumes of the English *Journal of Design and Manufacturers*, and everything written by that influential mid-19th-century tastemaker Andrew Jackson Downing showed Williams' tastes to be wholly in tune with the fashionable roman-

tic tenor of his time. He maintained an active interest in the arts throughout his life. He knew Washington Irving and James Fenimore Cooper, among other learned and literary gentlemen of that Golden Day.

In the confident pre-Civil war year of 1850 when Fountain Elms was begun, Emerson published his *Representative Men* and Hawthorne his *Scarlet Letter*. California joined the Union, and Queen Victoria gave birth to her seventh child. Darwin was still refining his theories for the *Origin of Species* which would not be published until 1859, and no one had yet heard of *Alice's Adventures in Wonderland* (1865). Neither had Bell patented his telephone (1876), nor Edison his incandescent electric lamp (1879). The great California Gold Rush had gotten underway the previous year, and the London Crystal Palace exhibition was to make international headlines the following year. Williams, incidentally, owned the catalogs of both the London Crystal Palace exhibition and the one in New York in 1853.

High ideas, mechanical improvements, melodramatic plays, sentimental novels, high-flown phrases, the pleasures of home were all components of the Victorian idiom, and what they did not like they called immoral. But while they may have spoken of breasts as bosoms and legs as limbs, it is a mistake to think the Victorians lacked imagination. We have acquired the habit of labeling their ideas prudish and their tastes poor, but if you can forget the clichés, such a house as Fountain Elms with its daring combinations of patterns and colors suggests that a boldness and vitality permeated the lives of the early Victorians which, with all our talk about space and sex, is not often equaled in our own day. Although America certainly borrowed more inspiration from France than England for its exuberant and fanciful furnishings, there may be good reason for calling it the Victorian age. Queen Victoria herself was an exuberant woman who once remarked "My nature is too passionate, my emotions are too fervent." Who, moreover, remembers Millard Fillmore, inaugurated President of the U.S. in 1850 or Franklin Pierce who succeeded him in 1853? Victorian is a far more deserving

The restored facade calls to mind a mid-19th-century admirer's comment about the villa styles of his time: "The trees cover the architectural beauty, making it more rare, more bewitching and enticing than if it appeared exposed."

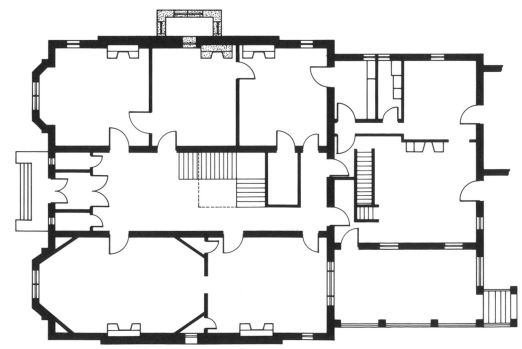

Composite first floor plan taken from drawings by Williams and Woollett and the actual building. The parlor is to the right of the front door and the dining room is behind it. The library is to the left of the front door, the nursey and bedroom are behind it.

epithet for the flamboyant originality that flourished in America at least until the Civil War.

Williams and his young wife moved into Fountain Elms on February 12, 1852. Their two daughters grew up there and later married two brothers, Thomas Redfield Proctor and Frederick Towne Proctor, and the Frederick Proctors lived at Fountain Elms until 1935 when it was inherited by the Munson-Williams-Proctor Institute.

Amid the Serenity of Sylvan Scenes

Like thousands of his contemporary Americans, Williams was influenced by the landscape architect Andrew Jackson Downing from Newburgh, New York, of whom Russell Lynes wrote in *The Tastemakers*, "No one had a greater influence on the taste of Americans a century ago than he, and no one had a more profound impact on the looks of the countryside."

In *The Architecture of Country Houses* published in 1850 (of which Williams owned a well-used copy), Downing tells us that a villa.

is the most refined home in America—the home of its most leisurely and educated class of citizen. Nature and art both lend it their happiest influence. Amid the serenity and peace of sylvan scenes, surrounded by the perennial freshness of nature, enriched without and within by objects of universal beauty and interest— objects that touch the heart and awaken the understanding—it is in such houses that we should look for the happiest social and moral development of our people.

Downing also extols a "growing partiality among us for the Italian Style," which he calls "remarkable for expressing the elegant culture and variety of accomplishment of the . . . man of the world." Such was the Williams' Italianate villa in the 1850s and such it has become again.

Many changes had been made in the house since 1850. A small two-story wing was added on one side and several additions were made to the ell in back. Partitions had been removed in the interior to make the drawing and dining rooms into one room, the original ground floor bedroom became the dining room, and all the fireplaces were changed. It was decided not to remove the additions since the Institute needed the space, but to restore the hall and four major rooms on the ground floor as nearly as possible to the way James Watson Williams and his wife Helen Elizabeth had known them. Thus Fountain Elms is partly a house museum and partly adapted for exhibitions, meetings, and other Institute activities.

The drawing room, says Victorian tastemaker Andres Jackson Downing, should always exhibit more beauty and elegance than any apartment in the house. The elaborate marble fireplace in this elegant drawing room is flanked by a pair of rosewood side tables by Baudouine which were bought by Williams in 1852. The center table and carved rosewood chairs are the work of the popular 19th-century cabinetmaker John Henry Belter.

From family papers, bills, letters, inventories, and original architectural drawings, it was possible to reconstruct the interior of the original house as well as its furnishings with a good deal of certainty. Many of the bills for the construction of the house had been preserved and since Williams often combined his business trips to New York with shopping for furniture, there are many letters written to his wife describing pieces he had seen. Apparently one of his first purchases was a worktable that he bought shortly before their wedding in 1846. He describes it in a letter to his fiancée, as quoted by Barbara Franco in "New York City Furniture Bought for Fountain Elms by James Watson Williams," *Antiques*, September 1973, from the James Watson Williams Papers, Oneida Historical Society:

After looking into various places for a gift for you, I have selected at Baudouine's, a work table which I am sure must please you; no lacquer-work, nor papier mache, nor tinsel of any sort; but a neat, well-made, and convenient table of the most approved French pattern. You saw it, and I tried, in vain, to remember whether it pleased you or not. If I could have been sure of your sanction, I should have been delighted; but let it please you, my dear girl, for your sake. It is a writing desk also; and already I fancy you seated at it, penning me one of your

delightful, sensible letters. It will go with any sort of furniture; and particularly well with black walnut, should you decide on that.

Williams' description exactly fits a table from the Williams and Proctor family collection which is now in the bedroom. There is also a bill from Charles A. Baudouine of July 11, 1846, for "1 work Table (Boxed) $60.00."

Letters referring to other pieces of furniture apparently purchased in New York for Fountain Elms during the 1850s mention a parlor set and étagères, among others. "I do not see any étagères for the parlor which in all respects satisfy me, price included," he wrote in 1854, and on the following day he was still "at a loss about a rosewood étagère."

Thus the restorers knew at least the general type of furnishings that decorated Fountain Elms in the 1850s. They knew, too, the basic colors of the rooms, including the fact that the dining room was red, but for the rest a Victorian frame of mind, a knowledge of the people who lived there, and the fashionable tastes of the time and place were indispensable. In addition to the furniture inherited from the family, other pieces, either of regional origin or ownership, were collected over a three-year period by McLanathan with the assistance of Robert R. Palmiter who had been in the antiques business in central New York State for many years. Palmiter estimated he traveled some 60,000 miles locating appropriate items for Fountain Elms. To give authenticity to such a restoration it is of course necessary to realize that the original occupants did not have everything all from one period. Some might have been inherited, and most families then as now used a combination of old and new furniture and accessories. In the 1850s, for instance, Empire styles were often used in conjunction with the newer so-called Victorian pieces, and even Downing warns his readers against "the blunder of confounding fashion with *taste*; of supposing that whatever the cabinet-makers and upholsterers turn out as the latest fashions must necessarily be the only things worth having."

Fitness and Truthfulness

Early in the project all sorts of scraps of wallpaper and fabric of the period were collected from junk dealers in the area. After studying these for some time, McLanathan and his staff acquired a feeling for the kinds of materials and colors used. The designs and colors of these fragments along with other documentary evidence (principally from the Cooper-Hewitt Museum in New York and the Victoria and Albert Museum in London) were later used to reproduce the wallpapers, drapery and upholstery fabrics for the restoration. The dining room draperies of heavy red silk damask were purchased from the Joseph Bonaparte house in Bordentown, New Jersey, and represent the only original fabric in Fountain Elms. It is well to remember, however, that the original occupants of historic houses did not live with faded fabrics and dingy carpets. And we can assume that Downing would consider reproductions more fitting since "fitness and truthfulness" was one of his favorite phrases. Palmiter did find some sage-green lambrequins of the period which, although faded, seemed perfect until moth cocoons were discovered in them. They were accurately reproduced except cotton and wool was used instead of the pure wool of the originals, and thus they appear to us as they did in the 1850s.

Actual woodwork in Westminster Abbey inspired the Gothic design for the entrance hall wallpaper. It was taken, in characteristic Victorian fashion, from the background in a photograph depicting Victoria and Albert receiving guests in the Abbey.

The original carpets were imported from England and purchased from A.T. Stewart and Company in New York. With the help of London's Victoria and Albert Museum, the successor to a firm in Durham, England, which had exported carpets to America in the 1850s, was located. They were able to weave and dye carpets for Fountain Elms according to mid-19th-century specifications.

Grave and Simple . . . Lively or Brilliant

The Victorians believed in giving each room its own decorative quality. Downing informs us that,

> A person of correct architectural taste will confer on each apartment by expression of purpose, a kind of individuality. Thus in a complete cottage-villa, the hall will be grave and simple in character, a few plain seats its principal furniture; the library sober and dignified . . . ; the drawing room lively or brilliant. . . .

After passing the elegant terra-cotta fountain in front of Fountain Elms—a typical front-yard accessory of the era which, in this case, was designed by Williams who acted as his own superintending architect—one enters the front hall with its Gothic wallpaper in rich reds and browns. Downing states that halls, entries, and passages should be "of a cool and sober tone of color—gray, stone color, or drab." The hall flooring at Fountain Elms is of Dutch and New York State tiles in brown, black, and wheat color. Although there was no documentary evidence for the original hall flooring, such tiles were frequently used, and after the design had been selected an almost identical pattern was discovered in a signed and dated pavement in front of an 1850s house in nearby Cazenovia. Downing also mentions a preference for "tiles of marble or pottery to carpet or oil-cloth" for hall floors.

To the right of the hall is the drawing room done in the "French taste," a fashion of which Downing says, "Its lightness, elegance, and grace renders it especially the favorite of ladies." The furniture, he advised, should be rich and delicate in design, "and the colors of the walls decidedly light, so that brilliancy of effect is not lost in the evening." Elegantly carved rosewood table, chairs, and étagère are by New York's most popular 19th-century cabinetmaker John Henry Belter whose furniture adorned many central New York houses. Yellow moiré silk covers the walls, the chairs are upholstered in olive-green brocade with gold roses, and the carpet is purple, green, and gold. The drawing room's elaborate white marble fireplace, like all the fireplaces in restored Fountain Elms, came out of a central New York house of the period.

The dining room is, as Downing says it should be, "rich and warm in its colouring" with furniture that is "substantial without being clumsy, but simpler in decoration

This monumental rosewood étagère is in the drawing room. "In the centre is a handsome mirror, on the side of which are shelves for articles of virtu—*bouquets of flowers, scientific curiosities, or whatever else of this kind the owner may indulge his taste in," writes Downing of a similar étagère shown in his book as "suitable for the drawing room of a villa."*

Lusty Victorian appetites survived the dining room's bold patterns and sentimental por-
traits. Here, says Downing, more of contrast and stronger colors may be introduced than in
the drawing room.

than that of the drawing room." The old red Italian brocade draperies are combined with rich red flock wallpaper in a Renaissance pattern. The original black and gold Empire chairs have seats of cut-velvet and the carpet is green with a red and gold design.

The library on the other side of the hall has striped purple flock wallpaper, green velvet draperies with gold tassels, and a brown-and-black carpet. For "rooms of importance," says Downing, flock papers are in "the best taste." A pair of tall mahogany bookcases containing Williams' library were made in the 1840s for the Gothic summer cottage on Nicholas Biddle's Pennsylvania estate Andalusia.

Beyond the library is the master bedroom—truly a vision of Victorian romanticism. The wallpaper, inspired by a French paper of the 1830s, combines garlands of roses and lilacs with classic motifs in a metallic gold on a gray ground. A massive mahogany-veneered bed is ingeniously draped in green silk, the carpet is slate blue, gold, and black, and the chairs are upholstered in red velvet and purple taffeta.

Downing tells his readers that "the most powerful source of pleasure in all interiors, next to style, is colour," and the restorers of Fountain Elms have done a masterful job in conveying what he must have meant. Unfortunately black-and-white photographs conceal the exciting effects of the daring Victorian color schemes.

In view of the flamboyance of Fountain Elms' furnishings, it may come as a shock to learn that Williams' tastes were restrained, at least for his day. He plainly states his preference for simplicity when his house was being planned (quoted by Barbara Franco in "New York City Furniture Bought for Fountain Elms by James Watson Williams," *Antiques*, September 1973, from the Fountain Elms Papers, Munson-Williams Proctor Institute):

> The finish of the interior, I would wish to be as plain as possible; all the wood work perfectly so. . . . A simple cornice for the best rooms would please me. . . .

Fountain Elms was truly endowed with the kind of restraint advocated by Downing who condemned "the indulgence of one's taste and pride in the erection of a country-seat of great size and cost." He considered such indulgence "contrary to the spirit of republican institutions." On the other hand he commended,

> . . . the beautiful, rural, unostentatious, moderate home of a country gentleman, large enough to minister to all the wants, necessities, and luxuries of a republican, and not too large or too luxurious to warp the lives or manners of his children.

The library's purple-striped walls make a fitting background for the quiet contemplation of those "objects that touch the heart and awaken the understanding."

Twenty years after Downing's death, a *Harper's Magazine* author wrote that "no American has built himself a more permanent monument than Downing the landscape gardener." He was wrong. Although Victorian furniture is generally prized, too often it has been considered a mark of progress to tear down as many Victorian buildings as possible. Every generation, no doubt, has its own insights and blindnesses. For too long we overlooked the originality of America's mid-19th century while admiring the more academic ideas of the 18th and completely neglecting the fact that they are two different chapters in the same book.

Although Palmiter had previously worked on several 18th-century restorations, Fountain Elms was his first experience with the mid-19th century and he found it an exciting challenge. The two centuries, he thought, were totally different particularly in the philosophy of the people. He didn't believe the furniture makers of the mid-19th century understood what they were doing as well as those of the 18th. "They were striving for something quite different from anything they had known and there were no exacting formulae to be followed."

They were innovators, in other words, heady with confidence in their country and their own creativity. Such a climate can produce monstrosities as well as masterpieces, and so it did. In any case they were our ancestors and without necessarily admiring them we owe them a chance to speak for themselves. And it is difficult to walk through Fountain Elms' richly patterned and exuberantly colorful rooms without developing a secret affection for, if not a little jealousy of, those superbly starry-eyed and vigorous Victorians who although pompous must have had fun.

The last word, however, belongs to Downing who had so much to do with it all. He, we can assume, would appreciate the value of such a restoration as Fountain Elms when he speaks of the

natural conservatives whom Providence has wisely distributed, even in the most democratic governments, to steady the otherwise too impetuous and unsteady onward movements of those who, in their love of progress, would obliterate the past, even in its hold on the feelings and imaginations of our race.

"The most powerful source of pleasure in all interiors, next to style, is colour. . . ." the master bedroom boasts both.

*Davis' drawing of the west elevation and
plans for Paulding.*

Lyndhurst

Near Tarrytown, New York

Romanticism may be said to consist in a high development of poetic sensibility towards the remote, as such. It idealizes the distant, both of time and place; it identifies beauty with strangeness.　Geoffrey Scott

To the modern eye Lyndhurst is more like something out of an Edgar Allan Poe fantasy than a house in which real people lived. It arouses curiosity and interest but it does not involve the heart as some houses do. It has, as Edmund Wilson says of Poe, "a dash of the actor who delights in elaborating a part."

Lyndhurst was designed in 1838 by Alexander Jackson Davis, one of the most enthusiastic exponents of Gothic Revival architecture in America, and enlarged by the same architect in 1865. It stands on a bank of the Hudson River below Tarrytown, a dramatic country seat in the Pointed Style and a perfect monument to an era in which the romantic gesture was the fashion in everything from landscapes and literature to stage sets and living rooms.

Gothic Revival architecture in the United States has been called everything from "a confusion between rationalism and materialism," "as foreign to our language as the dialects of Boccaccio and Chaucer," and "undemocratically eccentric," to "the only native type of architectural design that this country has ever witnessed." But more than anything else it was part of the theatricality of its time—one facet of the romantic outpourings of a period that included Bryant's "cool shades and dews," and Poe's "ghoul-haunted woodland of Weir," along with the romantic landscapes of Durand, Cole, and Doughty. "One scarcely distinguished between the literary and pictorial in the Hudson River enchantment," writes Oliver Larkin in *Art and Life in America*, "as poet and painter exchanged imagery."

Evolution of an American Gothic Castle

The romantic taste may well have been an escape from the realities of industrialism which began to beset the young republic early in the 19th century. By 1838, when Davis designed the Gothic country retreat for William Paulding, a former New York congressman and New York City mayor, industries were growing, wealth was accumulating, cities and railroads were multiplying. No wonder Gothic architecture, with its aura of romance and mystery and ennoblement, enjoyed a brief but intense popularity in the 1830s and 1840s.

On seeing the house Davis designed for Paulding, Andrew Jackson Downing, another devotee of Gothic, was enthusiastic. On October 18, 1840, he wrote Davis:

> Mr. Paulding's mansion I was exceedingly pleased with. I think it does you great credit—indeed I have never seen anything to equal it, as I conceive it will be when finished. I passed a couple of days very pleasantly in the Tarrytown vicinity; we visited the Irvings, the Constants, Sheldons, Mrs. Jones, etc. and I came away with a highly favorable opinion of the neighborhood.

In 1864, wealthy New York merchant George Merritt purchased Paulding's country retreat, or Paulding's Folly as it was sometimes called, and commissioned Davis to enlarge it in the same Gothic style. It was, incidentally, Merritt who named it Lyndhurst. The original plan was almost doubled in size in 1865 with a new wing to the north, a new porte-cochere to the east, and a tower to the west—all in the original Gothic style. "By virtue of its consistent additions," writes R.H. Newton in his *Town & Davis Architects* (1942), "the Paulding manor at Tarrytown far exceeded any similar structure in point of elegance and harmony of scheme." It is, moreover, a splendid example of the unbalanced individualistic plan that distinguishes the work of Gothic Revival architects from their predecessors and makes them the unexpected godfathers of such 20th-century architects as Frank Lloyd Wright. The main significance of the style, in fact, is its break with the classic symmetry of earlier house plans. For the first time asymmetric plans were developed that might best serve the conditions of the site or the needs of the owner. Wayne Andrews has, not unreasonably, compared the irregularity and infor-

(Top) East or entrance facade of Lyndhurst as it appears today. (Above) The porte-cochère on the left and tower on the right were added in 1865.

mality of a Gothic Revival house with Wright's Falling Water.

After enlarging the mansion, Merritt turned his attention to the grounds and had much to do with creating the romantically landscaped setting in which Lyndhurst stands today. He also had a great greenhouse constructed in the style of the Royal Pavilion at Brighton. It later burned and was replaced by a less fanciful but still impressive one. In an account of Lyndhurst appearing in a sale catalog after Merritt's death in 1873, the greenhouse was described as "the largest in the United States," and costing "nearly as much as the mansion." The same account informs us that after Merritt retired as a prosperous New York merchant he:

> received a large income from a Patent Car Spring, which he devoted to art, and in liberal donations to worthy objects.
> . . . [He was] a member of the Episcopal Church and a friend of Bishops Potter and Coxe."

In 1880 Jay Gould, "the very symbol of aggressive capitalism," purchased Lyndhurst and lived there with his family until his death in 1892. Although by the time Gould took over Davis's Gothic castle in the Pointed Style, the romantic spell had passed and millionaires were establishing themselves in medieval splendor for less spiritual and more materialistic reasons, Gould continued to preserve the integrity of Lyndhurst. So did his two daughters, the

successive owners. Helen Gould Shepard was her father's heir, and when she died in 1938 her sister Anna, Duchess of Talleyrand-Perigord, inherited Lyndhurst. She lived there off and on until she died in Paris in 1961 and bequeathed Lyndhurst with all its furnishings and art collections to the National Trust. Anna Gould made headline news with her famous transatlantic marriages—the first in 1895 to the French dandy, Count Boni de Castellane, who reputedly spent some $5,500,000 of her inheritance during the six years of their marriage; and the second in 1906 to his cousin, the Duc de Talleyrand-Perigord, Prince de Sagan, collateral descendant of the great Talleyrand, Napoleon's foreign minister.

Because the Goulds kept the Gothic decoration and furnishings of Lyndhurst largely intact—merely adding furniture and paintings to those that had been in the house since the Merritts, and in some cases the Pauldings, lived there—the National Trust decided not to restore the mansion to its earliest period but to present it as a reconciliation of the contributions of the three families who lived in it. Thus Lyndhurst today portrays within the shell of one architectural monument a reconciliation of three important eras in American life.

From the porte-cochere, which Davis added in the 1860s, one enters Lyndhurst through a tile-floored entrance lobby. The reception room with its stained-glass windows facing the Hudson and its richly painted ceiling is directly ahead. The par-

lor, to the left of the entrance lobby, runs across the entire south end of the mansion. A passage on the right of the entrance lobby leads to the dining room which was the most important room in the addition made by Davis for Merritt and appears today essentially as it did then. On the second floor are bedrooms and the lofty art gallery, with a ceiling that reaches up to the ridgepole and a large traceried window that looks down on the Hudson.

Era of Change

The Gothic, of course, was but one of many styles derived from history and archaeology that succeeded one another in rapid succession throughout the 19th century. It was a century of radical changes in everything from social mores to architectural concepts. It might be said to have opened with the Lewis and Clark Expedition in 1804 and closed with the publication of Veblen's *The Theory of the Leisure Class* in 1899; or to have opened with the exquisite symmetry of Jefferson's Monticello and closed with the wild abandon of George Vanderbilt's Biltmore in North Carolina. The century saw the end of the artisan and the beginning of architecture as a profession.

When James H. Dakin arrived in New York in 1832 he noted that the firm of Town and Davis (of which A.J. Davis was a partner from 1829 to 1835) was the only architect's office of the "modern" kind he had known in England. Davis, who had much to do with raising architecture to professional

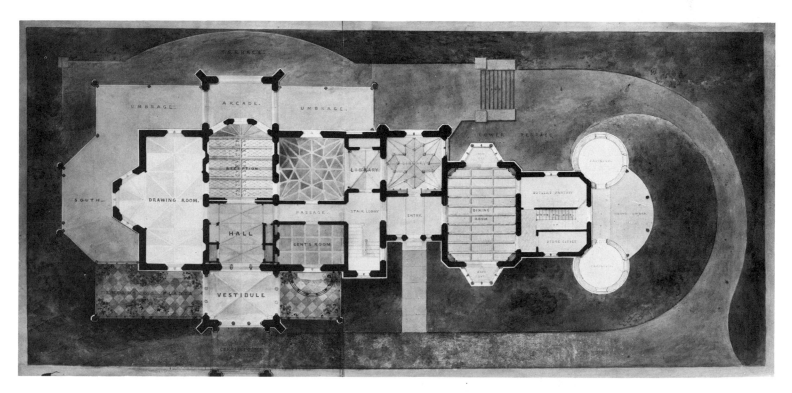

Davis' first floor plan for Merritt.

In the reception room, which the Pauldings called the "saloon," is the only mantelpiece still retaining its original Gothic overmantel mirror. The stained glass in the windows was replaced in the 1890s. The Renaissance Revival upholstered furniture was bought by Merritt in 1865. The ceiling is copied from Raphael's Hours and was painted in 1865 directly on the plaster.

The original carriage entrance was enclosed in 1865 and turned into this entrance lobby. The floor, as in most rooms of the house, was installed in 1865. (The floors in Paulding's villa were pine painted in places to resemble stone.) The plaster ceiling was painted to imitate blocks of stone and the wood door frame was painted with sand for a stonelike texture. The Gothic benches were probably designed for the house by Davis in 1840. The reception room is in the distance.

status, was a founder of the American Institute of Architects. He referred to himself as an "architectural composer," a description that not only fits the romanticism of the age but implies that he was also an artist. His drawings of villas, colleges, and other buildings were reproduced in a variety of publications between 1820 and 1850.

Davis more than any other architect, as his biographer Jane B. Davies points out, developed the Gothic style for country houses in America. She also compares him with Wright in his conviction that an interior and its furnishings should form a unity with the building. Davis not only designed all the interior architectural elements of his houses but much of the furniture including large bookcases, hall chairs, and other elaborately carved pieces which seem part of the architecture. Lyndhurst's great variety of interior details—vaulted and ribbed ceilings, windows, mantels—attest to Davis's skill and inventiveness.

Flamboyant Gothic Furniture

Davis's records show that he made at least 50 separate furniture designs for Lyndhurst between 1840 and 1847 including Gothic grates, Gothic chairs, Gothic bookcases, and other Gothic pieces, which must have given it an exceptionally Gothic appearance inside as well as out. The interior of just such a castellated villa is described by Mrs. Anne Sophie Winterbotham Stephens in her mid-19th-century romance *Fashion and Famine* as "fairylike" and "graceful" with:

> rich bronzes, antique carvings in wood, and the most sumptuous upholstery. . . . Grand, imposing and unsurpassed for magnificence, it was nevertheless filled with a sort of gorgeous gloom.

When Davis was employed by Merritt to enlarge the house in 1864 he again designed Gothic furniture for the addition, principally the dining room. Davis's "rich Flamboyant Gothic furniture" for Lyndhurst, as Newton says, achieved its "happiest treatment of all" in the dining room where "a beautifully carved suite of furniture echoed the elaborately trimmed mantelpiece."

The furniture in the restored house includes pieces from all three of its major periods ranging from four "wheelback" chairs and other Gothic pieces designed by Davis for Paulding and the dining-room furniture designed for Merritt, to Jay Gould's 1872 Wooton patent desk, a status symbol in the latter part of the century.

Both Davis's Lyndhurst clients—the Pauldings and the Merritts—apparently had complete trust in their architect's taste. There is a letter to Davis of November 10,

(Top) The parlor was Victorianized by Merritt in 1865 and went through further changes when Jay Gould bought Lyndhurst in 1880, but Davis' hand is still recognizable in such architectural elements as the vaulted ceiling and two marble fireplaces (not visible). (Above) The great art gallery, located above the entrance hall running in the same axis, looks down the Hudson through its great traceried window. The corbels of cast heads which receive the exposed roof beams along both sides of the room represent Washington, Franklin, Shakespeare, Milton, Dante. Originally Paulding's library, it became a gallery and billiard room when Merritt added the new wing and turned the original dining room into a library. The great ring chandeliers have been in the room since 1865. The Gothic table in the center was designed by Davis as were the two types of Gothic chairs on the right and in the background. Two upholstered armchairs are from Jay Gould's yacht, the "Atlanta."

The dining room with its Gothic furniture and mantelpiece was the most important addition made by Davis for Merritt. The walls of painted plaster with a raised stencil design in gold have been carefully restored by mixing sand in paint to create the raised pattern and then washing the entire wall with red glaze. The graining imitates oak. Marbleized woodwork imitates the three kinds of marble used in the mantelpiece.

(Opposite page) The "state bedroom," as the Pauldings called this room over the front entrance, was the principal guest room from 1840 to 1940. It has been refurnished according to the 1894 inventory and a photograph taken in the 1870s. The Gothic bed was made for the house and may have been designed by Davis. The ceiling with its meticulous red, blue, and gold design was probably painted in 1865. A painted border around the base of the room was not known to exist until it appeared in the 1870s photograph. Cleaning revealed a section of it which was then reproduced around the room.

1841, from Philip R. Paulding (William's son who built the original house with his father) in which he asks the architect to oblige him

> by calling at Underhill and Ferris as soon as possible . . . and inspecting the mantels before they are sent up. If you see any thing offensive to your gothick eye (you dont *squint* so no offence) put your veto upon it. They are extremely elegant and I wish them to be correct specimens of the style How the ladies will dote on them—
>
> I will thank you also as soon as you can possibly do it, to make designs for all the windows of the library $250 must be the highest mark for these windows: Two hundred must do it if possible—The side windows may be quite plain; a little patch or two of colour and the outside tracery followed in lead and colours will be all sufficient. Rich colours will tell well in the small windows above the big one, having regard to its western aspect and the defect of light thereby. Here expense may be encreased. The big window should be a nonpareil. I should like also to have a flat coloured light to put at the bottom of the lantern but if it cannot be included in the $250 let it go—I leave this thing entirely to your taste and Mr. Gibsons; you can consult with him and get his ideas as to colours and prices. When you have made the drawings, I will have them put into the hands of Mr. Wells to make the best bargain with him that he can—
>
> I received your letter and am delighted to hear you have had such an able committee on taste to aid you in your labours. I hope you will favour me with a visit soon. . . .

Everyone who has ever lived at Lyndhurst, says John Pearce, former curator of the National Trust's department of properties, "would recognize it today and part, at least, of its furnishings." Although no inventory or other documentation has yet been found to verify exactly what was in the house or how the rooms were furnished when the Pauldings lived there, the basic interior architectural elements are of that period. The Merritt period is better documented, with photographs of certain rooms taken around 1870. These provided important information for the restoration as did Davis's careful notes on architectural details. When Jay Gould died in 1892, painstaking inventories were made of every item in the house down to "a mouse trap valued at eight cents" in one room and "an ear of corn hanging on a gas jet" in another. Inventories were also made when Helen Gould Shepard died in

1938, so that from Merritt's time on there was little doubt about the furnishings or the appearance of the rooms.

Gothic Rebels

The Gothic Revival style was largely an expression of the intellectual class and the avant-garde. Alan Gowans compares its advocates in the 1830s and 40s with the advocates of abstract expressionism in painting a century or so later. "Their rank included so many assorted crackpots, fanatics, and social climbers," he contends, "that the average person . . . tended to assume anybody connected with it was some kind of dissembler or fool." And while William Paulding has been called "a very 18th-century

type" and not a person you would expect to build a house of such avant-garde design, Davis—"a sensitive barometer in the intellectual climate of his time"—was something of an eccentric. And among the decidedly offbeat admirers of the style were the actor Edwin Forrest who celebrated the Fourth of July every year at his Gothic Fonthill Castle on the Hudson reciting the Declaration of Independence "under waving flags and amidst booming guns" and a certain New Jersey Bishop, who had an elaborate Gothic library built into his villa and then had himself boxed and shipped to New York to fulfill a speaking engagement. Even the famous English Gothicist Augustus Welby Pugin, whose Gothic furniture designs influenced Davis, was convinced there was

(Left) Wheelback chair designed by Davis for the Paulding "saloon" is one of four now in the hall. (Right) One of a pair of Gothic chairs probably designed by Davis.

Dining table designed by Davis is similar to the design of an "Octagon table" by English Gothic Revivalist A.W. Pugin.

(Opposite page) Jay Gould's Wooton paten desk in office on the first floor.

nothing worth living for but Gothic architecture and boats and he kept disappearing into the North Sea.

Not all Gothic enthusiasts, however, were quite so eccentric although they may have been counted among the avant-garde such as James Fenimore Cooper, who remodeled his Otsego Hall in Gothic and convinced telegraph inventor Samuel F.B. Morse to do the same. Perhaps the landscape gardener Andrew Jackson Downing who shared the responsibility with Davis for making Gothic castles a symbol of the avant-garde, had the answer:

> There is something wonderfully captivating in the idea of a battlemented castle, even to an apparently modest man, who thus shows to the world his unsuspected vein of personal ambition. But unless there be something of the castle in the man, it is very likely . . . to dwarf him to the stature of a mouse.

There can be little doubt that Davis who saw no reason why anyone should be "foolishly frightened by a few crockets and finials" was the main architectural inspiration for America's Gothic interlude. As a member of the firm of Town & Davis he worked on many of the fine Greek Revival designs which came out of that office, including the New York Custom's House and the State Houses of North Carolina and Indiana. But he always leaned toward the romanticists and away from the purists. "The Greek Temple form, perfect in itself, and well adapted as it is to public edifices, and even town mansions," he wrote in 1837, "is inappropriate for country residences." The Gothic style, he added, "is for many reasons to be preferred. It admits of greater variety both of plan and outline . . . its bay windows, oriels, turrets, and chimney shafts give a pictorial effect."

In the final analysis perhaps it is as that earlier Gothicist Horace Walpole suggested: one must have taste to be sensible to the beauties of Grecian architecture, whereas one only wants passion to feel the Gothic.

In any case, while the Duchess of Talleyrand bequeathed Lyndhurst to the National Trust as a memorial to her parents, it will certainly be far more important historically as the definitive domestic monument to the Gothic Revival style in America—"by far and away the most celebrated and grandiose manorial pile to be designed by any one until after the Civil War," as Roger Hale Newton put it. It stands today in its picturesque setting of sweeping vistas, curving drives, and great trees, a haunting reminder of a romantic age.

Lucy the Margate Elephant as she appeared about 1895. In the background is Fishers Turkish Pavilion, built for the Philadelphia Centennial Exposition of 1876 and later moved here.

Lucy, the Margate Elephant

Near Atlantic City, New Jersey

So geographers in Afric maps,
With savage pictures fill their gaps,
And o'er unhabitable downs
Place elephants for want of towns.
                              Jonathan Swift

Just five years after the Philadelphia Centennial Exhibition of 1876 had proclaimed the wonders of architecture in all its multifarious forms, one of the most amazing of all architectural follies appeared on the southern New Jersey coast—a colossal elephant-shaped "house" solidly constructed of wood and tin. So solidly, in fact, that the six-story-high pachyderm is still a strange and familiar landmark almost a century after its construction.

Architectural follies, which Kenneth Clark aptly describes as "monuments to a mood," are a picturesque feature of the English countryside. But eccentricity is notably an English trait, as well as a form of romanticism, and during the 18th century, the eccentricity of England's aristocratic landowners often took the shape of exotic follies to adorn their parklands and to contrast with the purity of their Palladian villas. America, however, had to wait for the more confident years of the late 19th century to indulge in such architectural eccentricities. And then they were more often inspired by the romance of commerce than by the undiluted romanticism that gave 18th-century England its bevy of charming follies.

But every romantic style, as Lord Clark says, "reflects the daydream of its creator," and although he was referring to the architectural curiosities of 18th-century England, his theory applies to the elephant "house" that appeared on the Atlantic coast in 1881. Philadelphia real estate promoter James V. Lafferty conceived of the 90-ton elephant (later to be known as Lucy) as a means of luring potential land buyers to an almost uninhabited ocean-front area below Atlantic City. Since the area could only be reached by carriage or horseback some kind of attraction was necessary, and what could be more logical than an elephant. To enhance the natural magnetism of a 65-foot, or 19.5m, high elephant standing on the New Jersey shore, Lafferty decided it should sport a *howdah* on its back and a restaurant inside. The *howdah*, of course, was to serve as an observation platform from which prospective buyers could view the beauties of the sea-skirted landscape.

William Free of Clifton Heights, Pennsylvania, designed the unusual creature for Lafferty who then commissioned J. Mason Kirby, a Philadelphia Quaker, to build her. Construction started in the spring of 1881 and on July 9 Lafferty inserted his first advertisement in the *Philadelphia Public Ledger*:

> The Novel Restaurant in the shape of an Elephant, is in course of Construction. For further particulars apply to J.V. Lafferty, 432 Liberty St., Phila.

Lafferty, who was obviously a showman as well as a dreamer, knew how to keep his audience with him. On August 20 he inserted another advertisement:

> South Atlantic City . . . Public Sale of Choice Building Lots. . . . A novel feature in architecture is the erection of a restaurant in the form, shape and anatomy of an elephant, which is the only building of the kind in the world. It will be completed in a few weeks. . . . James V. Lafferty, 432 Liberty St., Phila.

And in his advertisement of October 29 Lafferty revealed more of Lucy's remarkable characteristics to the readers of the *Public Ledger*:

> South Atantic City. Lots for Sale. Improvements are progressing rapidly. Magnificent view can be had from the "howdah observatory" of the Elephant Hotel of South Atlantic City, Somers Point, Ocean City, Atlantic City and the surrounding country, being the only hotel in the world in that novel shape, 86 feet long, 29 feet wide and 65 feet high, 10 feet diameter of legs, 22 feet from platform to floor of hall, 15 feet depth of foundation. Personal attendance will be given to parties who wish to view premises, going and returning same day. For plans or information, etc. Apply to James V. Lafferty 432 Liberty St., Phila.

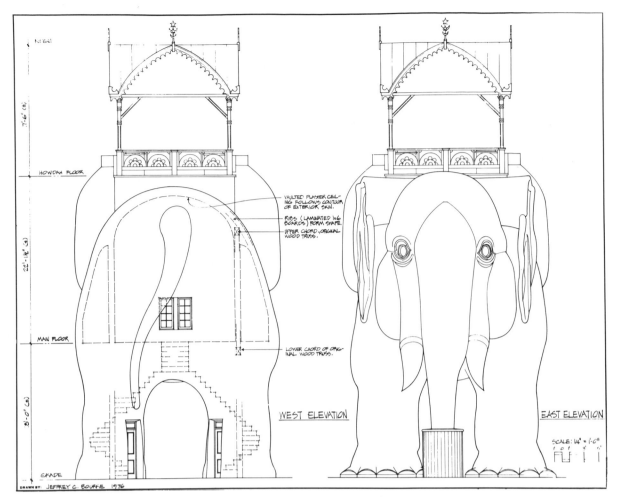

Scale drawing from the front and rear.

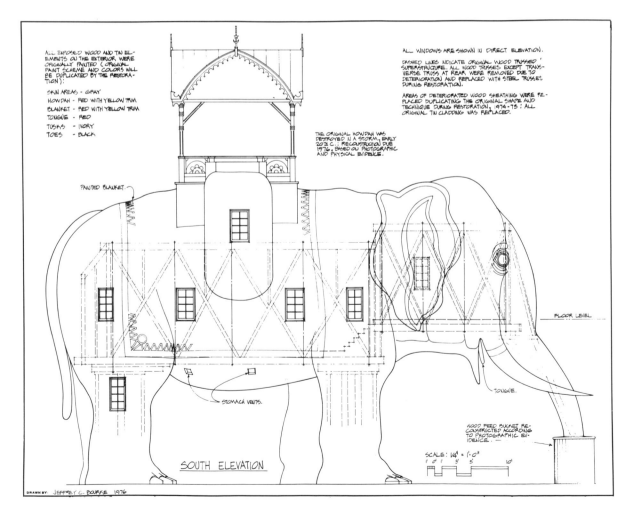

South elevation.

U.S. Patent No. 268,503

Lafferty was so convinced that he had something unique he decided to have his elephant patented. In his application of May 19, 1882, addressed to the United States Patent Office, he states:

My invention consists of a building in the form of an animal body of which is floored and divided into rooms, closets, etc. and the legs contain the stairs which lead to the body, said legs being hollow so as to be of increased strength for properly supporting the body . . . the entire device presenting a unique appearance. . . .

His description concludes: "The building may be of the form of any other animal than an elephant, as that of a fish, fowl, etc."

Familiar as they must be with the oddities of American inventors, nevertheless one can't help wondering how the officials of the U.S. Patent Office looked at Lafferty's petition. One would like to think that they decided favorably on its merit with a slight twinkle of the collective Patent Office eye. But the truth is that the worthy gentlemen of the Patent Office studied Lafferty's application with great solemnity. The record shows, as historical consultant Jack E. Boucher tells us, that they even compared the plans for Lucy with those of the Statute of Liberty, which is not too unreasonable when you think about it. In any case United States Patent No. 268,503 was granted to Lafferty on December 5, 1882, for his invention of an improvement in buildings.

By 1887 Lafferty's dream apparently had not produced the desired results and he sold his elephant to John Gertzon, a resident of the area. Gertzon used the pachyderm as a tourist attraction along with the Turkish exhibition that had been brought to South Atlantic City from the 1876 Philadelphia Centennial. In 1902 he rented Lucy to an English physician as a summer beach cottage. The Englishman partitioned the interior into four rooms but there is no record of what went on in those rooms. In 1904 Lucy became a tavern and later a bathhouse. After John Gertzon's death in 1916, his widow carried on until she died in 1963 and left

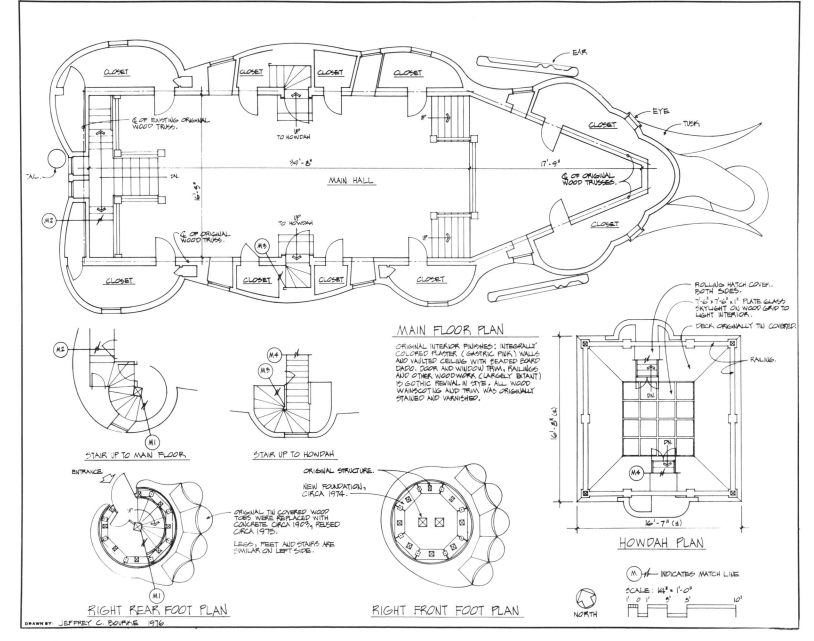

Scale drawings of Lucy's parts. The main floor plan (top) is accompanied by the following description: "Original interior finishes: integrally colored plaster (gastric pink) walls and vaulted ceiling with beaded board dado. Door and window trim, railings, and other woodwork (largely extant) is Gothic Revival in style. All wood wainscoting and trim was originally stained and varnished." Lucy's right rear foot plan and stairway is below left; right front foot plan, center, and howdah plan lower right.

Lucy to her children Joseph F. Gertzon and Caroline M. Bonelli.

By this time it wasn't only the gentlemen of the Patent Office who took Lucy seriously. In 1966 she was recognized by the state of New Jersey as a designated historic site and was included as part of the Historic American Building Survey, the National Register of Historic Landmarks, and the New Jersey Register of Historic Landmarks. Lucy may have started life in lowly commerce, but now she was a highly respected lady of landmark status. After all, as Jack Boucher puts it, she was

> familiar to literally millions upon millions of visitors to a resort area just a bit older than Lucy herself. Indeed, she was almost thirty years old before South Atlantic City became Margate! Without Lucy, the City of Margate would soon fade into that aura of obscurity that the lack of distinctive landmarks inflicts upon all cities and nations that destroy their heritage and landmarks.

The people of Margate understandably admire the pluck of the oversized lady in their midst as well as her powers of seduction which no city with any self-respect could ignore. Lucy had been buffeted by hurricane winds, swamped to her knees in sand and tide, but although her original *howdah* succumbed to the winter gales of the Atlantic, she stood firm. Nevertheless time and the elements were taking their toll and when she was condemned by a building inspector, the citizens of Margate lost no time in forming a "Save Lucy Committee." In 1970 John Gertzon's children donated the revered elephant to the committee provided she was moved to a new site. At the committee's request restoration-architect John B. Milner inspected Lucy and found her in "structurally sound condition" and "eminently worth preservation" because of her "unique historic architectural merit." Thus Lucy was moved to an available beachfront site just two blocks south of her original stomping ground and plans were made for her preservation and restoration by Milner's firm, National Heritage Corporation.

An Oversize Lady in Gothic Revival Style

Lucy's basic structure, explains Milner, consists of

> two sets of longitudinal wood trusses supported on wood columns in the legs and connected with transverse truss. The building's shape was achieved by attaching curved built-up wood ribs to the truss frame, and covering those ribs with wood sheathing and a heavy tin skin. The interior is composed of one large domed space within the body and an elevated platform within the head. Small closets located in the sides and jowls surround the main space. Access from the ground is by means of two sets of winder shafts, one in each rear leg. A wood and cast-iron howdah with a tin roof was constructed on Lucy's back with access from the main floor by two more sets of winder stairs. The floor of the howdah contained a large glass panel which provided natural light for the interior. Windows were placed in the sides, eyes, behind the ears and in the "derriere."

> The exterior color scheme was gray, accented by a red and yellow howdah and blanket, red tongue, ivory tusks and black toes. The interior walls and ceilings were plastered with a beaded board wainscot. The woodwork for doors, windows, and railings was in the Gothic Revival style.

The only major alterations that had been made in the original fabric were the addition of an intermediate floor and several partitions added by the English physician in 1902 and replacement of the original *howdah* around 1928.

In recognition of Lucy's "significant place in the evolution of American architecture," says Milner, "and in consideration of her importance in the history of the New Jersey shore, the building has been restored as a museum and community center with special emphasis on activities for children." Lucy's exterior and interior have been returned to their original configuration and a park has been developed on the site.

And so a spruced-up Lucy looking much as she did when Lafferty applied for his patent is about to begin her second century as an honorable member of what Professor Nikolaus Pevsner has called that "delightful and crazy tribe of the Follies."

There is a lot to be said for preserving some of our light-hearted architecture along with the great monuments. And no matter how heavy-handed one might think the U.S. government sometimes is, it was first the U.S. Government Patent Office that protected Lucy's extraordinary design, and then it was the U.S. Department of Housing and Urban Development that made her restoration possible by granting the sum of $61,750, under its special program to preserve and restore historic structures, to the Margate Elephant Project in 1972. This sum, matched by a public subscription plan through the efforts of the "Save Lucy Committee," provided the funds for the restoration.

Even as recently as 1970 Jack Boucher wrote in *Preservation News* that this "unique and rather incredible architectural folly of the Victorian era, may be headed for the last round-up." But if he really thought so he was underestimating Lucy herself, to whom the ravages of old age were as nothing. She is, after all, part of that sturdy American tradition that produced jazz, P.T. Barnum, and *Huckleberry Finn*.

It should be mentioned, however, that Lucy is not without an ancestry. Clay Lancaster, in his book *Architectural Follies in America*, has traced the history of elephant architecture from the 13th century. He even tells of an 18th-century elephant described (but never built) by its French inventor in a publication called *Architecture Singulière: L'Eléphant Triomphe, Grand Kiosque, à la Gloire du Roi*, as having a bath in its hind parts, an amphitheatre in front, a *Grand Escalier*, as well as a throne for the King in its head.

"What is bigger than an elephant?" asked Plutarch. "But this also is become man's plaything, and a spectacle of solemn ceremonies...."

Lucy in the 1930s.

Illustration Credits

18, 20–28 (top) Photos by Edwin Smith

29, 30 Photos by Marian Page

32 Photos by Frances B. Johnston, Library of Congress

34 Plans measured by Albert Simons and drawn by Frank E. Seel and Lewis B. Middleton

35–36, 38–39 (top) Photos by Frances B. Johnston, Library of Congress

39 (bottom) Photo by Louis Schwartz

41 Photo by Frances B. Johnston, Library of Congress

42, 44, 46–49 Courtesy The Preservation Society of Newport County, Newport, R.I.

44 Plans drawn by William Wong

50, 52–56 (top), 57–58 Photos Courtesy Sleepy Hollow Restorations, Inc.

52 Plans drawn by William Wong

56 (top) Photo Helga Photo Studio, courtesy Museum of the City of New York

60 Photo by Cortlandt Hubbard for Historic American Buildings Survey

64, 66 Photos by Jack E. Boucher for HABS

67 Photo by Cortlandt Hubbard for HABS

68 (bottom), 69 Photos by Jack E. Boucher for HABS

76–85 Photos courtesy Britain's Department of the Environment

86–97 Photos by Bord Failte

86, 96 Collection The Honorable Desmond Guinness

98 Photo by Ed Roseberry

100 (top) Photo by Ralph Thompson (bottom) Courtesy Massachusetts Historical Society

102, 103 Photos by Ralph Thompson

104 (top) Photo by Frances B. Johnston (middle and bottom) Photo by Milton L. Grigg

110, 111 Photos by Mel Chamowitz

112 (top) Portrait on loan from the Pennsylvania Academy of Fine Arts. Photo by Mel Chamowitz (bottom) Photo by Marian Page

113 On loan from the American Colonization Society. Photo by Mel Chamowitz

114, 115, 117 Photos by Wm. Edmund Barrett

122, 124, 126 Courtesy The Trustees of Sir John Soane's Museum

127 Country Life Photos

129 Courtesy The Trustees of Sir John Soane's Museum

132 HABS photo

133 Library of Congress

134 (top) Photo by Marian Page (bottom) Photo by Marler

135 (top) Bed on loan from Mr. and Mrs. William F. Machold. Photo by Marler

136 Collection of Mr. and Mrs. William F. Machold

137 The I.N. Phelps Stokes Collection of American Historical Prints, The New York Public Library

138 HABS phots

144–157 Courtesy Historic Columbia Foundation

158–167 The Royal Pavilion, Art Gallery and Museums, Brighton

162 (bottom) Collection of the Cooper-Hewitt Museum of Decorative Arts and Design, Smithsonian Institution

168, 170, 172 Photos by James K. Mellow

173 (top) Photo by Gleason (bottom) Photo by James K. Mellow

174, 175 National Trust for Historic Preservation

176–183 Munson-Williams-Proctor Institute

178–179 Plans drawn by William Wong

184 Collection Metropolitan Museum of Art

186 Photos by Louis Reens

187 Collection Metropolitan Museum of Art

188–191, 193 Photos by Jack E. Boucher

196–198 HABS photos

Bibliography

Architectural History

Ackerman, James S. *Palladio.* New York: Penguin Books, 1966.

Andrews, Wayne. *Architecture, Ambition and Americans.* London: Collier-Macmillan Ltd., 1964.

Architects Emergency Committee. *Great Georgian Houses in America.* New York: Scribner's, 1937.

Bailey, Rosalie Fellows. *Pre-Revolutionary Dutch Houses and Families in Northern New Jersey and Southern New York.* New York: W. Morrow & Co., 1936.

Brown, Glenn. *History of the United States Capitol.* Washington, D.C.: Gov. Printing Office, 1900.

Bryan, Wilhelmus Bogart. *A History of the National Capital.* Vol. 1, 1790–1814 (1914).

Clark, Kenneth. *The Gothic Revival.* New York: Penguin Books, 1964.

Downing, Andrew Jackson. *The Architecture of Country.* New York: Dover Publications, Inc., 1969.

Downing, Antoinette F., and Scully, Vincent, Jr. *The Architectural Heritage of Newport, Rhode Island.* Cambridge: Harvard University Press, 1952.

Eberlein, Harold Donaldson, and Hubbard, Cortlandt Van Dyke. *Historic Houses of George-Town & Washington City.* Richmond, Va.: The Dietz Press, Inc., 1958.

Fitch, James Marston. *American Building, The Historical Forces That Shaped It.* 2nd ed., rev. Boston: Houghton Mifflin, 1966.

Fleming, John. *Robert Adam and His Circle.* Cambridge: Harvard University Press, 1962.

Frary, I.T. *They Built the Capitol.* Richmond, Va.: Garrett & Massie, 1940.

Gifford, Don, ed. *The Literature of Architecture, The Evolution of Architectural Theory and Practice in Nineteenth Century America.* New York: E.P. Dutton & Company, Inc., 1966.

Girouard, Mark. *Robert Smythson and the Architecture of the Elizabethan Era.* New York: A.S. Barnes & Co.

Guinness, Desmond, and Ryan, William. *Irish Houses & Castles.* New York: Viking, 1971.

Hamlin, Talbot. *Greek Revival Architecture in America.* New York: Oxford University Press, 1944.

Hitchcock, Henry-R. *Architecture, Nineteenth and Twentieth Centuries.* New York: Penguin Books, 1958.

Jordan, Robert Furneaux. *Victorian Architecture.* New York: Penguin Books, 1966.

Kaufmann, Edgar, Jr., ed. *The Rise of an American Architecture.* New York: Praeger and The Metropolitan Museum of Art, 1970.

Kidson, Peter; Murray, Peter; and Thompson, Paul. *A History of English Architecture.* New York: Penguin Books, 1965.

Kimball, Fiske. *Domestic Architecture of the American Colonies and of the Early Republic.* New York: Dover Publications, Inc., 1966.

Lancaster, Clay. *Architectural Follies in America.* Rutland, Vt.: Charles E. Tuttle Co., 1960.

Lethaby, W.R. *Form in Civilization.* London: Oxford University Press, 1957.

Maas, John. *The Gingerbread Age, a View of Victorian America.* New York: Holt, Rinehart & Winston, 1957.

Morrison, Hugh Sinclair. *Early American Architecture.* New York: Oxford University Press, 1952.

Mumford, Lewis. *The South in Architecture.* The Dancy Lectures, Alabama College, 1941. New York: Harcourt, Brace and Company, 1941.

Mumford, Lewis. *Sticks & Stones, a Study of American Architecture and Civilization.* 2nd rev. ed. New York: Dover, 1955.

Nichols, Frederick Doveton. *The Early Architecture of Georgia.* Chapel Hill: The University of North Carolina Press, 1957.

Pevsner, Nikolaus. *An Outline of European Architecture.* New York: Penguin Books, 1963.

———. *The Buildings of England: Derbyshire.* New York: Penguin Books, 1953.

Pierson, William H., Jr. *American Buildings and their Architects, the Colonial and Neoclassical Styles.* New York: Garden City, Doubleday, 1970.

Ruskin, John. *The Seven Lamps of Architecture.* New York: Farrar, Straus and Giroux, 1969.

Scott, Geoffrey. *The Architecture of Humanism.* New York: Doubleday, Anchor Books, 1954.

Sitwell, Sacheverell. *British Architects and Craftsmen.* London, 1945.

Smith, Robert. *Two Centuries of Philadelphia Architecture, 1700–1900.* Included in *Historic Philadelphia from the Founding until the Early Nineteenth Century.* Philadelphia: Transactions of the American Philosophical Society, 1953.

Stoney, Samuel Gaillard. *Plantations of the Carolina Low Country.* Charleston, S.C.: The Carolina Art Association, 1955.

Summerson, John. *Architecture in Britain, 1530 to 1830.* New York: Penguin Books, 1954.

———. *Heavenly Mansions and other Essays on Architecture.* New York: W.W. Norton, 1963.

Tatum, George B. *Penn's Great Town.* Philadelphia: University of Pennsylvania Press, 1961.

Tinkcom, Henry M. and Margaret B., and Simon, Grant Miles FAIA. *Historic Germantown from the Founding to the Early Part of the Nineteenth Century.* Philadelphia: The American Philosophical Society, 1955.

Waterman, Thomas Tileston. *The Dwellings of Colonial America.* Chapel Hill: University of North Carolina Press, 1950.

Whiffen, Marcus. *American Architecture Since 1780: a Guide to Styles.* Cambridge: M.I.T. Press, 1969.

Architects

Clark, Allen C. *Doctor and Mrs. William Thornton.* Records of the Columbia Historical Society. Vol. 18, 1915.

Dumbauld, Edward. *Thomas Jefferson American Tourist.* Norman, Oklahoma: University of Oklahoma Press, 1946.

Frary, I.T. *Thomas Jefferson: Architect and Builder.* Richmond, Va.: Garrett & Massie, 1950.

Gallagher, H.M. Pierce. *Robert Mills, Architect of the Washington Monument.* New York: Columbia University Press, 1935.

———. "Robert Mills, 1781–1855, America's First Native Architect." The Architectural Record, April 1929.

Goodfellow, G.L.M. "William Jay and the Albion Chapel." *Journal of the Society of Architectural Historians,* December 1963.

Hamlin, Talbot. *Benjamin Henry Latrobe.* New York: Oxford University Press, 1955.

Jourdain, Margaret. *The Work of William Kent.* London: Country Life Ltd., 1948.

Kimball, Fiske. *Thomas Jefferson, Architect.* Printed for private distribution. Riverside Press, 1916.

Kimball, Marie. *Jefferson, the Scene of Europe 1784 to 1789.* New York: Coward-MaCann, Inc., 1950.

Lehmann, Karl. *Thomas Jefferson: American Humanist.* Chicago: The University of Chicago Press, 1965.

McDonough, James Vernon. *William Jay—Regency Architect in Georgia and South Carolina.* Unpublished doctoral dissertation presented to the faculty of Princeton University June 1950, reprinted by University Microfilm, Ann Arbor, Michigan.

Newton, Roger Hale. *Town and Davis: Architects.* New York: Columbia University Press, 1942.

Nichols, Frederick Doveton. *Thomas Jefferson's Architectural Drawings.* Boston, Mass. Historical Society, and Charlottesville, Thomas Jefferson Memorial Foundation of the University Press of Virginia, 1961.

Ravenel, Beatrice St. Julien. *The Architects of Charleston.* Charleston, S.C.: Carolina Art Association, 1945.

Reynolds, James. *Andrea Palladio and the Winged Device.* New York: Creative Press, 1948.

Stroud, Dorothy. *The Architecture of Sir John Soane.* Introduction by Henry-Russell Hitchcock. London: Studio, 1961.

Summerson, John. *Sir John Soane 1753–1837.* London: Art and Technics, 1952.
———. *John Nash, Architect to King George IV.* London: 1935.

Furnishings, Interiors

Bridenbaugh, Carl. *The Colonial Craftsmen.* Chicago: The University of Chicago Press, Phoenix Books, 1964.

Burton, E. Milby. *Charleston Furniture, 1700–1825.* Charleston, S.C.: The Charleston Museum, 1955.

Carpenter, Ralph E., Jr. *The Arts and Crafts of Newport, Rhode Island 1640–1820.* The Preservation Society of Newport County, 1954.

Fastnedge, Ralph. *English Furniture Styles, 1500–1830.* New York: Penguin Books, 1955.

Franco, Barbara. "New York City Furniture Bought for Fountain Elms by James Watson Williams." *Antiques,* September 1973.

Metropolitan Museum of Art. *19th-Century America, Furniture, and Other Decorative Arts.* Boston: New York Graphic Society, 1970.

Montgomery, Charles F. *American Furniture, the Federal Period.* New York: Viking Press, 1966.

Rogers, Meyric. *American Interior Design.* New York: W.W. Norton, 1947.

Wainwright, Nicholas B. *Cliveden and Its Furniture.* Philadelphia: The University Hospital Antiques Show Catalogue, 1970.

Social and Historical Background

Birket, James. *Some Cursory Remarks made by James Birket in his voyage to North America, 1750–51.* New Haven, 1916.

Bremer, Fredrika. *Homes of the New World*. New York: Harper & Brothers, 1854.

Bridenbaugh, Carl. *Cities in Revolt, Urban Life in America, 1743–1776*. New York: Capricorn Books, 1964.

———. *Myths & Realities, Societies of the Colonial South*. New York: Atheneum, 1965.

Bridenbaugh, Carl and Jessica. *Rebels and Gentlemen*. New York: Oxford University Press, 1965.

Buckingham, J.S. *The Slave States of America*. London: Fisher Son & Company, 1842.

Buxton, John. *Elizabethan Taste*. London: Macmillan, 1963.

Caruthers, William Alexander. *The Kentuckian in New-York*. New York: Harper & Brothers, 1834.

Crèvecoeur, J. Hector St. John. *Letters from an American Farmer*. New York: The New American Library of World Literature, Inc., 1963.

Drayton, John. *A View of South Carolina; as Respects her National and Civil Concerns*. Charleston, 1802.

Fithian, Philip Vickers. *Journal and Letters*. Princeton, N.J.: Princeton University, 1900.

Foster, Sir Augustus John. *Jeffersonian America—Notes on the United States of America Collected in the Years 1805–06–07 and 1811–12*. San Marino, Calif.: The Huntington Library, 1954.

Gowans, Alan. *Images of American Living*. New York and Philadelphia: J.B. Lippincott, 1964.

Granville, Mrs. Mary. *The Autobiography and Correspondence of Mary Granville, Mrs. Delany*, edited by Lady Llanover, 3 vols. London, 1861.

Grund, Francis J. *Aristocracy in America—from the Sketch-Book of a German Nobleman*. New York: Harper, 1959.

Guinness, Desmond. *Portrait of Dublin*. London and New York, 1967.

Hamilton, Dr. Alexander. *Gentleman's Progress: The Itinerarium of Dr. Alexander Hamilton 1744*. Edited by Carl Bridenbaugh. Chapel Hill, N.C.: University of North Carolina Press, 1948.

Historic Savannah. Historic Savannah Foundation, Inc., 1968.

James, Henry. *The American Scene*. New York: Horizon Press, 1967.

Jones, Katharine M. *The Plantation South*. New York: Bobbs-Merrill, 1957.

Kalm, Peter. *Travels into North America by Peter Kalm*. Barre, Mass.: The Imprint Society.

Kane, Harnett T. *The Bayous of Louisiana*. New York: William Morrow, 1944.

Konkle, Burton Alva. *Benjamin Chew 1722–1810*. Philadelphia: University of Pennsylvania Press, 1932.

Kouwenhoven, John A. *Made in America: the Arts in Modern Civilization*. New York: Doubleday, Anchor Books, 1962.

Larkin, Oliver W. *Art and Life in America*. New York: Rinehart & Co., 1949.

Laughlin, Clarence John. *Ghosts Along the Mississippi, an essay in the poetic interpretation of Louisiana's plantation architecture*. New York: Scribner's, 1951.

Lees-Milne, James. *Tudor Renaissance*. London: B.T. Batsford, Ltd., 1951.

———. *Earls of Creation, Five Great Patrons of Eighteenth-Century Art*. London: House of Maxwell, 1963.

Lynes, Russell. *The Tastemakers*. New York: Grosset & Dunlap, 1954.

Martineau, Harriet. *Retrospect of Western Travel*, 2 vols. New York: Harper & Brothers, 1838.

Maxwell, Constantia. *Dublin under the Georges 1714–1830*. London: Faber & Faber, Ltd.

Miller, Henry. *The Air-Conditioned Nightmare*. New York: New Directions, 1945.

Nairn, Ian. *Nairn's London*. New York: Penguin Books, 1966.

O'Faolain, Sean. *The Irish*. New York: Penguin Books, 1969.

Parrington, Vernon Louis. *Main Currents in American Thought: an Interpretation of American Literature from the Beginning to 1920* 3 vols. New York: Harcourt, Brace & World, Inc., 1930.

Peden, William, ed. *Notes on the State of Virginia by Thomas Jefferson*. Chapel Hill, N.C.: University of North Carolina Press, 1955.

Pevsner, Nikolaus. *The Englishness of English Art*. New York: Penguin Books, 1956.

———. *Studies in Art, Architecture and Design: From Mannerism to Romanticism*. Vol. 1. New York: Walker and Company, 1968.

Pierson, George Wilson. *Tocqueville in America*. New York: Doubleday, Anchor Books, 1959.

Plumb, J.H. *England in the Eighteenth Century (1714–1815)*. New York: Penguin Books, 1966.

Power, Tyrone. *Impressions of America during the Years 1833, 1834, 1835*. London, 1836.

Quennell, Peter. *Alexander Pope, the Education of Genius 1688–1728*. New York: Stein and Day, 1968.

Redford, George, and James; and Angell, John. *The Autobiography of the Reverend William Jay*. New York: Robert Carter & Brothers, 1855.

Roberts, Kenneth and Anna M., eds. *Moreau de Saint-Mery's American Journey*. New York: Doubleday, 1947.

Rothery, Agnes. *Houses Virginians Have Loved*. New York: Rinehart & Co., Inc., 1954.

Sackville-West, V. *English Country Houses*. London: Collins, 1947.

Saxon, Lyle. *Old Louisiana*. New York: D. Appleton-Century, 1929.

Scharf, John T., and Westcott, Thompson. *History of Philadelphia*, 3 vols. Philadelphia, 1884.

Smalley, Donald, ed. *Domestic Manners of the Americans* by Frances Trollope. New York, 1949.

Trevelyan, G.M. *Illustrated English Social History: 2*. New York: Penguin books, 1968.

Ussher, Arland. *The Face & Mind of Ireland*. New York: The Devin-Adair Company, 1950.

Walpole, Horace. *Journal of Visits to Country Seats, Chiswick 1760.* Walpole Society. Vol. XVI, 1927–28.

Wharton, Anne Hollingsworth. *Social Life in the Early Republic.* New York: Benjamin Blom, 1902.

Williams, E. Carleton. *Bess of Hardwick.* London: Longmans, Green and Co., Ltd., 1962.

Woolson, Constance Fenimore. "Up the Ashley and Cooper." *Harper's New Monthly Magazine,* December 1875.

Young, Stark. *River House.* New York: Scribner's, 1930.

Individual Houses

Binney, Marcus. "An Extension to the Soane Museum." *Country Life,* May 23, 1972.

Boucher, Jack E. *Lucy the Margate Elephant.* Margate, N.J.: The Save Lucy Committee, Inc.

Boylan, Lena. "The Conollys of Castletown, a Family History." *Quarterly Bulletin of the Irish Georgian Society,* Oct.–Dec. 1968.

Butler, Joseph T. *The Family Collections at Van Cortlandt Manor.* Tarrytown, N.Y.: Sleepy Hollow Restorations, 1967.

Charlton, John. *A History and Description of Chiswick House and Gardens.* London: Her Majesty's Stationery Office, 1958.

Cooper, Nicholas. "Cliveden, Philadelphia." *Country Life,* January 2, 1975.

Cornforth, John. "The Future of Drayton Hall." *Country Life,* August 1, 1974.

Craig, Maurice, and Cornforth, John. "Castletown, Co. Kildare." *Country Life,* March 27, April 3, April 10, 1969.

Dreher, Jennie C. "A Mansion in the Classical Manner." [The Robert Mills House] *Sandlapper, the Magazine of South Carolina,* January 1970.

Fauber, J. Everette, Jr. "The Octagon." *AIA Journal,* January 1970.

Guinness, Desmond, and Lines, Charles. *Castletown, Co. Kildare.* Irish Georgian Society.

Massay, James C. "Robert Mills Documents, 1823: a House for Ainsley Hall in Columbia, South Carolina." *Journal of the Society of Architectural Historians,* December 1963.

Musgrave, Clifford. *Royal Pavilion: a Study in the Romantic.* Brighton, Bradon & Heginbothom Ltd., 1951.

———. *The Royal Pavilion, a Brief History and Guide.* The Royal Pavilion Committee, Country Borough of Brighton, 1965.

National Trust for Historic Preservation. *Decatur House.* Washington, D.C.: Preservation Press, 1967.

———. *Lyndhurst.* Washington, D.C.: Preservation Press, 1970.

Pearce, John N. "A.J. Davis' Greatest Gothic." [Lyndhurst] *Antiques,* June 1965.

Shepherd, Raymond V., Jr. "Cliveden." *Historic Preservation* July–September 1972.

Southall, James P.C. "Malvern Hills, Henrico County, and Edgemont, Albermarle County, Houses of James Powell Cocke." *Virginia History Magazine,* Jan. 1935.

Summerson, John. *A New Description of Sir John Soane's Museum.* London: Pub. by Trustees, 3rd ed., 1972.

Winchester, Alice. "Cliveden, the Germantown house of Mr. and Mrs. Samuel Chew." *Antiques,* December 1959.

Restoration and Preservation (a brief list)

Abel, Betts, researcher and compiler. *A Guide to State Historic Preservation Programs.* Washington, D.C.: Preservation Press, 1976.

Batcheler, Penelope Hartshorne. *Paint Color Research and Restoration.* Nashville, Tenn.: American Association for State and Local History, 1968.

Braun, Hugh. *The Restoration of Old Houses.* London: Faber and Faber, 1954.

Bullock, Orin M., Jr. *The Restoration Manual.* Norwalk, Conn.: Silvermine Publishers, 1966.

Frangiamore, Catherine L. *Rescuing Historic Wallpaper: Identification, Preservation, Restoration.* Nashville, Tenn.: American Association for State and Local History, 1974.

Hosmer, Charles B., Jr. *Presence of the Past.* New York: G.P. Putnam's Sons, 1965.

Insall, Donald. *The Care of Old Buildings Today: A Practical Guide. New York: Watson-Guptill, 1974.*

Judd, Henry A. Before Restoration Begins: Keeping Your Historic House Intact. Nashville, Tenn.: American Association for State and Local History, 1973.

Little, Nina Fletcher. *Historic Houses: an Approach to Funishing.* Nashville, Tenn.: American Association for State and Local History, 1970.

McKee, Harley J., FAIA. *Introduction to Early American Masonry: Stone, Brick, Mortar and Plaster.* New York: Columbia University, and Washington, D.C., Preservation Press, 1973.

Merrill, William. *Wood Deterioration: Causes & Prevention.* Nashville, Tenn.: American Association for State and Local History, 1974.

Morrison, Jacob H. *Historic Preservation Law.* Washington, D.C.: Preservation Press, 1974.

National Endowment for the Arts—Guide to Programs: 1975–1976. Washington, D.C: National Endowment for the Arts, 1975.

National Trust for Historic Preservation. *A Guide to Federal Programs.* Washington, D.C.: Preservation Press, 1974.

———. *New Approaches to the Historic House Museum: Papers from the 1974 Annual Meeting of the National Trust.* Washington, D.C.: Preservation Press, 1976.

———. *Preservation Bookshop Catalogue.* Washington, D.C.: Preservation Press, 1976.

———. *Preservation & Building Codes: Papers from the May 1974 Preservation and Building Codes Conference Sponsored by the National Trust.* Washington, D.C.: Preservation Press, 1975.

National Trust for Historic Preservation and the Colonial Williamsburg Foundation. *Historic Preservation Today: Essays Presented to the Seminar on Preservation and Restoration.* Charlottesville, Va.: University Press of Virginia, 1966.

Historic Preservation Tomorrow: Revised Principles and Guidelines for Historic Preservation in the United States, Second Workshop. Washington, D.C.: National Trust for Historic Preservation, and Williamsburg, Va.: Colonial Williamsburg, 1967.

Nelson, Lee H. *Nail Chronology as an Aid to Dating Old Buildings.* Nashville, Tenn.: American Association for State and Local History, 1968.

Nylander, Jane C. *Fabrics for Historic Buildings.* [Information on fabrics for curtains, bed hangings, and upholstery.] Washington, D.C.: Preservation Press, 1976.

Phillips, Morgan, and Whitney, Christopher. "The Restoration of Original Paints at Otis House. *Old-Time New England,* July–Sept. 1971.

Rains, Albert, chairman, and Henderson, Laurance G., director. *With Heritage So Rich: A Report of a Special Committee on Historic Preservation under the Auspices of the United States Conference of Mayors with a Grant from the Ford Foundation.* New York: Random House, 1966.

Rath, Frederick L., Jr., and O'Connell, Merrilyn Rogers. *Volume One: Historic Preservation, a Bibliography on Historical Organization Practices.* Nashville, Tenn.: American Association for State and Local History, 1976.

Stewart, John J. *Historic Landscapes & Gardens.* Nashville, Tenn.: American Association for State and Local History, 1974.

Timmons, Sharon, ed. *Preservation and Conservation: Principles and Practices.* [Papers presented by leading professionals in the field of preservation and conservation at a five-day conference in Williamsburg and Philadelphia in 1972 sponsored by the International Centre for Conservation and the American Committee of the International Centre.] Washington, D.C: Preservation Press and Smithsonian Institution Press, 1976.

Tubesing, Richard L. *Architectural Preservation in the United States, 1965–1974.* [A bibliography of federal, state and local government publications dealing with architectural preservation.] Monticello, Ill.: Council of Planning Librarians, 1975.

United States Department of Housing and Urban Development. *Rehabilitation Guide for Residential Properties.* Washington, D.C.: 1968.

United States Department of the Interior, National Park Service, Historic American Buildings Survey. *Historic American Buildings Survey: Catalog of the Measured Drawings and Photographs of the Survey in the Library of Congress, March 1, 1941. Washington, D.C.: U.S. Government Printing Office, 1941.*

———. *Historic American Buildings Survey: Catalog of the Survey in the Library of Congress, Comprising Additions Since March 1, 1941.* Washington, D.C.: U.S. Government Printing Office, 1959.

United States Department of the Interior, National Park Service. *National Register of Historic Places, 1972.* Washington, D.C.: U.S. Government Printing Office, 1973.

———. *The National Register of Historic Places: Supplement, 1974.* Washington, D.C.: U.S. Gov. Printing Ofc., 1975.

United States Department of the Interior, National Park Service, Office of Archeology and Historic Preservation, *A Technical Handbook for Historic Preservation.*

Waite, Diana S. "19th Century Tin Roofing and Its Use at Hyde Hall." *Home and Garden Bulletin No. 73.* Washington, D.C.: Government Printing Office, 1960.

Ziegler, Arthur P., Jr.; Adler, Leopold II; and Kidney, Walter C. *Revolving Funds for Historic Preservation: a Manual of Practice.* Pittsburgh: Ober Park Associates, Inc., 1975.

Some Major Organizations Actively Interested in Historic Preservation in the United States

Advisory Council on Historic Preservation, Suite 430, 1522 K Street, N.W., Washington, D.C. 20005

American Association of Conservators and Restorers, 1250 E. Ridgewood Avenue, Ridgewood, New Jersey 07481

American Institute of Architects, Committee on Historic Resources, 1735 New York Avenue, N.W., Washington, D.C., 20006

Association of Preservation Technology, Box 2682, Ottawa 4, Ontario, Canada

Don't Tear It Down, Box 14043, Ben Franklin Station, Washington, D.C. 20004

General Services Administration, Historic Preservation Program, Room 6304, 18th and F Streets, N.W., Washington, D.C. 20405

National Endowment for the Arts, Architecture and Environment Arts, 806 15th Street, N.W., Washington, D.C. 20506

National Park Service, Office of Archeology and Historic Preservation, Interagency Services Division, Washington, D.C. 20240

National Trust for Historic Preservation, 740 Jackson Place, N.W., Washington, D.C. 20006

Society for Architectural Historians, Room 716, 1700 Walnut Street, Philadelphia, Pa. 19103

Victorian Society for America, The Athenaeum, East Washington Square, Philadelphia, Pa. 19106.

Index

Edited by Susan Braybrooke, Susan Davis, and Sarah Bodine
Designed by James Craig
Set in 10 point Laurel by Publisher's Graphics, Inc.
Printed and bound by Interstate Book Manufacturers, Inc.

Marian Page joined *Interiors* in the late 1950s to plan and write articles on design and architecture. This led to a series of articles called "Historic Restorations" on which this book is based. She also started a series called "Masters of Tradition U.S.A." which focused on colonial and early American designers. The author has attended many lecture courses on architecture and design in the United States and in 1967 enrolled in the National Trust Summer School in England to study English architecture with emphasis on country houses.

Marian Page is a member of the National Trust for Historic Preservation, The Society of Architectural Historians, and the Victorian Society in America. She is currently a freelance writer living in New York City.